RENEWALS 458-4574

DATE DUE

| | | | |
|---|---|---|---|
| | | | |
| | | | |
| | | | |
| | | | |
| | | | |
| | | | |
| | | | |
| | | | |
| | | | |
| | | | |
| | | | |
| | | | |
| | | | |
| | | | |
| | | | |
| | | | |
| | | | |
| | | | |
| | | | |
| | | | |
| | | | |
| | | | |
| | | | |
| GAYLORD | | | PRINTED IN U.S.A. |

# BABY AND CHILD HEROES
## IN ANCIENT GREECE

TRADITIONS

# Baby and
# Child Heroes
# in Ancient Greece

CORINNE ONDINE PACHE

UNIVERSITY OF ILLINOIS PRESS

URBANA AND CHICAGO

Publication of this book was supported by a grant from
the Frederick W. Hilles Publication Fund of Yale University

Library of Congress Cataloging-in-Publication Data

Pache, Corinne Ondine, 1963–
Baby and child heroes in ancient Greece /
Corinne Ondine Pache.
p.   cm.—(Traditions)
Includes bibliographical references and index.
ISBN 0-252-02929-1
1. Hero worship—Greece.   2. Heroes—Mythology—Greece.
3. Children—Greece.   4. Infants—Greece.   5. Greece—Religion.
I. Title.   II. Traditions (Urbana, Ill.)
BL795.H46P33      2004
292.2'13—dc22      2003023248

ΕΠΙΘΥΜΙΕς

Σάν σώματα ὡραῖα νεκρῶν πού δέν ἐγέρασαν
καί τἄκλεισαν, μέ δάκρυα, σέ μαυσωλεῖο λαμπρό,
μέ ρόδα στό κεφάλι καὶ στά πόδια γιασεμιά—
ἔτσ' οἱ ἐπιθυμίες μοιάζουν πού ἐπέρασαν
χωρὶς νὰ ἐκπληρωθούν· χωρὶς ν' ἀξιωθῆ καμιὰ
τῆς ἡδονῆς μιὰ νύχτα ἤ ἕνα πρωί της φεγγερό.


DESIRES

Like the beautiful bodies of the dead who never grew old
and are enclosed, with tears, in a splendid tomb,
with roses around their heads, and jasmine at their feet—
thus appear desires that passed
without fulfillment, without one being granted
one night's pleasure, or one of its light-filled mornings.
—C. P. Cavafy

# CONTENTS

## ACKNOWLEDGMENTS

   This book grew out of a dissertation, and I am grateful to my dissertation committee, Albert Henrichs, Gloria Ferrari Pinney, and Gregory Nagy, for their support and advice at all stages of this project. I am also grateful to the Whiting Foundation for a dissertation-completion fellowship. I have profited greatly by comments from the participants at the 1998 Corhali conference at Lille University, at the Seventh International Seminar on Ancient Greek Cult at Göteborg in 1999, and at the University of Chicago conference entitled "Hero Cult in the Greek East" in 2002, where parts of this study were given as talks. Many other people have helped along the way and commented on parts or all of the manuscript: Ellen Aitken, Margaret Alexiou, Justin Isenhart, Sara Iles Johnston, Christopher Jones, Charles Segal, Sari Takacs and the Between Magic and Religion group, and John Watrous. Judy Barringer deserves very special thanks for her generosity, enthusiasm, and encouragement. I also wish to thank the press's referees for their valuable advice, and David Aiken for his thoughtful copyediting. I am grateful to Betsy Gebhard for help with the archaeology at Isthmia and for plans and reconstructions. I also thank Stephen Miller and Jorge Bravo for help with the archaeology at Nemea, as well as providing me with photographs and drawings. I have been able to include many photographs of ancient art thanks to the generosity of the Hilles Fund. Bill Metcalf and Celia Schultz have been generous in helping me with locating coins and with scanning images. I also thank Hubert Lanz, at Numismatik Lanz, for letting me use photographs of ancient coins from his catalogue. I am deeply grateful to Zoie Lafis for her line drawings. And finally, I also wish to thank Hans Goette, at the Deutsches Archäologisches Institut in Berlin, who has been an invaluable help with finding images.

   I have had the good fortune of pursuing this project in two environments as stimulating as they are friendly, and I have very many more students, colleagues, and friends, too many to name here, to thank at both Harvard University and Yale University. They have been supportive in countless ways, small and great.

Most of all, I thank Adele Haft at Hunter College. She has been an extraordinary teacher and friend, and to her I dedicate this book.

A note on transliteration: I have adopted Greek forms for most names (Linos, Melikertes) but have stopped short of changing well-established ones (Oedipus, Plutarch).

Little children are vulnerable to many dangers, and potentially dangerous situations that are lesser threats to grown-ups—such as being asleep or left alone—can be fatal to infants and a source of great anxiety for parents. While individual parents' feelings in ancient Greece are of course not directly accessible, these subjective emotions do find their expression in Greek literature and culture as channeled through myth and ritual in a way that makes it possible for us to reconstruct them. Parental anxieties are expressed in literary and visual narratives, as well as through ritual in honor of heroized children. This study examines both the poetics and the ritual dimension of these narratives of heroization.

Besides worshiping gods and goddesses, the ancient Greeks also worshiped deceased human beings. The bare historical facts of hero cult are not controversial: some human beings were assigned the status of hero after their death and became objects of worship and recipients of sacrifices.[1] Over a hundred years of research on Greek hero cults have advanced our understanding of this fundamental aspect of ancient Greek religion, but there are still important gaps in our knowledge. It is difficult for modern researchers to recover the ancient thinking concerning cult heroes, and there is much disagreement on what exactly a hero is in Greek cultural terms. The criteria for inclusion among heroes are not easy to establish, and some categories of heroes—such as babies and children—present us with a complex problem of their own. Although child heroes play a significant part in Greek religion as objects of worship and as focal points of some of the most important Panhellenic religious festivals, they have never been systematically studied.

Heroes and heroines are traditionally defined in terms of the roles they performed as living beings (whether they are construed as purely mythic or historical characters), and their status as recipients of worship after death is explained in terms of functions: whether they be city founders, warriors, prophets, healers, lawgivers, discoverers, inventors, or ancestors, heroes provide a focal point for polis ritual. Some heroes can also be defined in terms of their deaths—violent, unjust, or miraculous—rather than in terms of their behavior when alive, so that their personalities and lives do not always conform to our modern definition of heroism.[2] Heroes typically supply an

1

explanation for the existence and cohesion of particular sociopolitical groups: polis, *genē*, phratries, or *orgeōnes*.[3] These themes have engaged historians and sociologists alike for a long time, and hero cult—as is made clear again and again by literary, archaeological, and epigraphical evidence—is indeed central to any explanation of these ancient institutions.

Unlike their grown-up counterparts, child heroes do not found cities or establish new laws, protect or heal, invent or discover, much less give birth to long lines of descendants. It would be vain, indeed, to try to explain child heroes in terms of their actions, since their diminutive lifetimes hardly give them opportunity to perform any of the deeds typically associated with heroes. While they do not as a rule perform any significant deeds before their premature deaths, baby and child heroes do play an essential role in Greek religion. Shrines for child heroes are found all over mainland Greece: the child heroes at Kaphyai in Arcadia, the children at Khalkis in Euboea, the children of Medea at Corinth, the children of Herakles at Thebes. Two of the four Panhellenic Games are closely associated with baby heroes: the Isthmian Games on the Isthmus were founded as a funerary ritual in honor of the drowned child Melikertes, just as the neighboring Nemean festival was established in honor of the serpent-smothered Opheltes.

What, then, are we to make of child heroes? How are we to recover their meaning for the ancient Greeks? And why have they been so neglected in modern scholarship?

One reason for the neglect of child heroes is methodological. Because of the nature of the evidence, it is impossible to apprehend the phenomenon of child heroes fully without using a great variety of methodological approaches. While the pieces of evidence are scattered across place and time, they all point to a complex system: the worship of baby and child heroes is not an isolated phenomenon, but an essential component of Greek religion and culture. In order to document and account for the role that child heroes play in Greek society, I rely on different kinds of sources: literary (including poetry and prose) and archaeological (including vase-paintings, which provide visual narratives parallel to the literary sources). Both are necessary in order to reconstruct ancient attitudes toward child heroes and the rituals themselves, and both come with their separate sets of methodological tools. Only by putting all these elements together is it possible to provide as complete a picture of child-hero cult as possible, as well as to put this phenomenon in its proper historical context. The following pages examine the extant textual and archaeological sources, provide an interpretative study of the different myths and rituals associated with child heroes, and consider them in the larger context of ancient Greek culture.

From archaic lyric poetry to tragedy and comedy, from the fifth century B.C. on to the Second Sophistic, ancient literature abounds with references to child heroes and their stories. Important literary sources include Pindar's commemorative poems and Euripides' aetiological tragedies (both fifth century B.C.). Later works also provide valuable information about Greek religious practices and beliefs. Both Pausanias's *Periēgēsis* (second century A.D.), his description of his own "pilgrimage" across Greece, and Plutarch's scholarly writings (first century A.D.) focus on the religious beliefs of their contemporaries and ancestors. Their numerous descriptions of heroic shrines and the stories associated with them are especially valuable because of the particulars they provide about local practices. Literary works, such as Statius's *Thebaid* (first century A.D.), Apollodoros's *Library* (first or second century A.D.), Philostratos's *Heroikos* (third century A.D.), and Hyginus's *Fabulae* (second century A.D.), also abound with narratives of child heroes. Here we encounter reflexes from the same mythical complex that we find in the archaic and classical periods. The works of a Roman author such as Statius are steeped in the Greek classical tradition and preserve the same motifs (and concerns) we find in earlier narratives. Iconographical representations, chiefly from the fifth and fourth centuries B.C., offer their own versions of the myths and provide important visual clues to the meaning of these myths. Such visual representations are not mere illustrations of versions of myths found in poetry, but narratives in their own right.[4] Archaeology, finally, provides (or confirms) evidence about the physical layout of hero shrines and the rituals performed there in the archaic and classical periods.

Another reason for the neglect of child heroes is historical. Historians of Greek religion have been interested in hero cult for a long time, but their focus has typically been on function. In the nineteenth century, hero worship was principally understood in two ways: as an outgrowth of ancestor worship or as a form of ritual performed for demoted divine beings. Rohde, for example, sees the origins of hero cult in ancestor worship.[5] Usener, by contrast, argues that heroes derive from ancient *Sondergötter,* gods whose single function is often reflected in their names: "Healer" (*Iatros*), "Leader" (*Stratēgos*), etc.[6] Rohde and Usener approach the problem of hero worship from very different perspectives, and although hero cult was not a central focus for either of them, they later came to be perceived as the representatives of two opposite points of view: Rohde as the champion of heroes' human origin, and Usener as the chief advocate of their divine origin.

Pfister's 1912 landmark study *Der Reliquienkult im Altertum,* in which he considers hero worship as a type of relic cult (siding with Usener on the question of the divine origin of hero cult), shows the importance of the hero's physical remains and grave, thereby linking hero worship with Christian relic cult and establishing a close parallel between pagan heroes and Christian saints. Foucart follows in the tracks of Rohde and argues that "the Greeks never doubted that their heroes had been men."[7] Meanwhile Farnell adopts a combination of these two views and develops a compromise approach to the problem: he argues that all heroes need not necessarily be explained by one single origin, and he divides them into seven categories.[8]

The debate on hero cult, then, was centered on this dichotomy between understanding heroes as powerful dead human beings or minor, local, highly specialized demoted gods—until Brelich offered a radically new approach in his 1958 study *Gli eroi greci*. By examining ritual and myth together in their historical context, Brelich undertook the study of hero cult as a whole (relying on *realia*) and sought to understand heroes in terms of wider patterns rather than by focusing on the differences between them. Brelich's "morphological" approach brought forth a new openness and new rigor to the study of the phenomenon that have greatly enriched our understanding of hero cult.

Although Rohde already noticed the connection between heroes and the Panhellenic Games, he did not expand on the role played by child heroes, who do not quite fit the model of heroes as ancestors.[9] Farnell devotes a few pages to the child heroes Kharila and Melikertes, noting the parallels between the latter's story and that of Opheltes, another child hero worshiped in the context of a Panhellenic athletic festival.[10] However, he places all these heroes in the category of vegetation *daimones* linked to fertility rituals. While the link between Greek ritual and nature remains strong, this equation between heroes and vegetation divinities is reductionist and ignores other fundamental aspects of their cults. Pfister draws parallels between children worshiped in groups and the Christian Feast of Innocents. He also mentions Opheltes and Melikertes in his discussion of ancient games, but the wide scope of his study prevents him from devoting much space to child heroes.[11] Brelich notices a number of child heroes and argues that the prevalence of *eroi-fanciulli* in mystery cults (children of Medea, Melikertes) must be significant. Brelich also examines the important role played by some of the child heroes (Kharila and the children of Medea) in initiation rituals.[12] Despite the attention that scholars give to hero cult, no studies focus specifically on child heroes.

A number of pioneering works focus on particular subsets of heroes or specific aspects of hero cult that had never been examined before. Some examine the political significance of heroes in Attica, and a great deal of attention is given to female heroes.[13] Larson notes the "various heroic cults of dead children," but she focuses on heroines.[14] Similarly, Lyons mentions some baby heroes (Opheltes, Melikertes) in connection with their mothers, but again her focus is on female heroines, and she does not concern herself with age distinctions. The archaeological and historical record demonstrates the prevalence of child heroes, yet none of the scholarly literature gives more than cursory attention to baby and child heroes—a gap that results in skewed interpretations of the phenomenon.

Before being able to answer the main question at hand—"what are we to make of child heroes?"—it will be essential to answer a series of simpler and more obvious questions: Who are the child heroes? What are the myths associated with them? Which rituals are performed in their honor? What did they mean to the ancient Greeks?

How do I define baby and child heroes? I mean children who have not yet reached puberty, died, and become recipients of heroic offerings. The Greek language uses a wide variety of terms to describe children, though unfortunately it is often difficult to pinpoint what those words express in terms of specific age. The Pythagorean philosophers divide human life into four different stages that correspond to the four seasons, and thus they equate childhood with spring (Diodorus Siculus 10.9.5):

| | |
|---|---|
| *pais* (child) | spring |
| *neos* (youth) | summer |
| *anēr* (man) | autumn |
| *gerōn* (elder) | winter |

Hippocratic writings recognize seven stages (*hēlikiai*):[15]

| | |
|---|---|
| *paidion* (little child) | 1–7 |
| *pais* (child) | 7–14 |
| *meirakion* (boy) | 14–21 |
| *neaniskos* (young man) | 21–28 |
| *anēr* (man) | 28–35 |
| *presbytēs* (old man) | 35–42 |
| *gerontikē* (old man) | 42 to death |

Aristophanes of Byzantium's translations entitled *Peri Onomasias Hēlikiōn* give yet a longer list of terms applied to children (fr. 37–90 Slater 1986):

*brephos* (infant)
*paidion* (little child)
*paidarion* (little child)
*paidiskos* (young boy)
*pais* (child)

Other terms to designate children not included in these ancient lists are *nēpios*[16] and *teknon* (lit., who is born).[17]

In some cases, child heroes are clearly identified as infants. The child sacrificed by Lykaon in Arcadian myth, for example, is described as an infant (*brephos;* Pausanias 8.2.3), while Opheltes is a baby child (*nēpion pais;* Apollodoros 3.6.4). Sometimes young children are described with a diminutive form of the word *pais* or with the word *pais* qualified with an adjective to indicate smallness: thus Plutarch describes the children of Khalkis as *paidaria* (*Greek Questions* 296d–e), while Kharila is a *pais mikra* (293c–f). In most cases, we find unmarked *pais,* which makes it difficult to establish a specific age since the word is used (a) of both children and adolescents up to their inclusion in a deme for boys or marriage for girls and can also describe (b) adults who are the younger partners in homoerotic relations or (c) slaves.[18] To complicate matters further, the word is also ambiguous since it can denote "child of"— without any reference to age—rather than "child" per se. Details of particular stories, however, often help determine heroes' ages: Opheltes is too small to walk on his own, and the children of Khalkis are seduced with toys.

As we can see in the above examples, the division into different age groups is more important than age per se. My focus in this study will be on baby and child heroes who die as prepubescent children, which include the first two categories of the Hippocratic writers and Solon (*paidion* and *pais*). Just as important as this division into different groups is the moment of transition between different categories. As Brelich and others show, age classes in ancient Greece are also defined through cult: in the context of ritual, preadolescent children form a distinct age class whose eventual change of status is very much linked to the performance of appropriate rites.[19] Narratives of child and baby heroes often offer their own mythical narratives of transition or initiation.

Narratives of child heroes thus stress the dangers inherent in childhood and making the transition to adulthood. Cults of child heroes fulfill obvious religious functions in ancient Greece, but they also were sources of inspiration for poets and artists who made them the focus of their work. Narratives of death and heroization then become sources of aesthetic pleasure, and mourning the hero is given aesthetic and ritual meaning through both storytelling and cult.

This study starts with the well-known story of the death of the children of Medea. It is difficult to imagine anything more dreadful than a parent causing her children's own death, and as we shall see, this primal parental anxiety, which is stressed in the accounts of the death of Medea's children, is an integral part of all the narratives surrounding child and baby heroes. The story of Medea's children continues after their deaths, as the Corinthians celebrate them in an annual festival involving the segregation of seven girls and seven boys. The myth emphasizes the horror of the children's deaths, but also the possibility for atonement.

The deaths of the children of Herakles examined in chapter 2 echo many themes present in the narrative of Medea's children: violation of sacred space, parental violence, and the need to atone for the children's brutal deaths. The myth of Herakles' killing his children also stresses a new element: parental loss of control and madness. In one version of the myth, Herakles kills his children by throwing them on a burning pyre. In another, he kills each of his three children in a different way, and each killing is ritualized in terms of hunting, war, and sacrifice. The children's violent death is atoned for by a cult in Thebes that includes a nocturnal fire festival and local athletic games.

The myths and rituals explored in chapter 3 make explicit the link between failed immortalization and heroization and the connection between mourning, lament, and poetry. The figure of Linos is the personification of lament (*thrēnos*), while similarly, the story of the children of Astarte functions, according to the Greeks, as an *aition* for the Egyptian lament. While Hera was indirectly involved with the narratives of Medea's and Herakles' children, goddesses become directly involved in children's heroization in the case of Demophon and the children of Astarte. Mourning songs and *thrēnoi* are sung not only at the children's death, but become part of the regularly held rituals established in their honor. The failed process of immortalization and subsequent heroization that are at the heart of these narratives can be understood as a metaphorical expression of the ordeal that worshipers endure in the rituals—and most particularly athletic competitions—performed in honor of the children.

Not strictly a baby hero because he survives his childhood death, Pelops nevertheless is a key figure for this study. Chapter 4 examines the myth of his death at his father's hand. Pelops ultimately grows up to participate in the very games that were established in compensation for his death as a baby, yet the myth of his childhood dismemberment remains part of the myths and rituals celebrated at the Olympic Games. Many elements of the myth and ritual in his honor at Olympia echo themes found in other narrative of child heroes. Pelops also provides the crucial link between local cults in honor of children and the Panhellenic festivals in honor of baby heroes examined in the last two chapters.

In chapter 5, we turn to Opheltes-Arkhemoros, the hero honored at the Nemean Games. Motifs associated with childhood and often expressed in popular songs and lullabies, such as flower-picking and falling asleep, emerge as important themes in the narrative of the death of Opheltes. The baby tragically enters the bucolic and sacred domain of a snake when he is left alone by his nurse and suffers the kind of horrible death that lullabies traditionally attempt to ward off. Here again, maternal fears come to their most dreadful fulfillment, but eventually converge with the sacred and become ritualized. Similar to the visual clues to the ritual dimension of the story of the children of Medea in the depiction of altars, the emotion of fear is symbolized by a fallen hydria consistently shown at the foot of Hypsipyle on visual representations of the death of Opheltes.

In chapter 6, we see Melikertes-Palaimon at Isthmia, a child who falls victim to his parents, like Medea's and Herakles' children. His mother Ino leaps into the sea with her small son in a doomed attempt to save him from his father's murderous rage. Elements familiar from other narratives of child heroes are all present in the narratives of the death of Melikertes: god-induced madness like that of Herakles and a cauldron used to boil a child, reminiscent of Tantalos boiling Pelops. The mother plays a unique role in this narrative, however, as Ino is welcomed by the Nereids and made into a goddess or a heroine according to different local traditions. The child's body is rescued by a dolphin and brought ashore at the Isthmus, where Sisyphos establishes funeral games in honor of the dead baby, renamed Palaimon. Melikertes provides the fullest example of a child hero, and both the literary and the visual sources consistently emphasize the boy's loveliness as death undergoes metamorphosis into ritual and myth.

From parental fears and sense of guilt arise the stories, songs, and sanctuaries honoring child heroes. Both myth and ritual articulate these very basic human anxieties, yet the emphasis is ultimately on the beauty that transcends the gruesomeness of these narratives and transforms dread into poetry.

# The Children
# of Medea

I start with a myth well known from tragedy, the death of the children of Medea. There are many different versions of this story besides Euripides' play. In his *Medea,* the children are killed by their own mother, while in other versions they are murdered by the citizens of Corinth in response to Medea's actions. No matter who the murderers are, the children's slaughter is a mythical representation of a parent's darkest fears: whether directly or indirectly, a mother is the ultimate cause of her children's death. While Greek myth often represents maternal murder and guilt, this phenomenon is not restricted to mothers (or nurses), and we will see in the following chapter that fathers too are represented as their children's killers.[1] In the case of Medea's children, however, the focus is squarely on the mother as threat, and we find this primal parental fear expressed both in the myth of the death of the children and in the rituals in their honor. The Corinthian cult in honor of the dead children contains elements typical of both initiation and mourning rites. Systematic examination of the ancient sources reveals that the story of the children of Medea is not simply a literary or iconographical topos, but that the narrative of their deaths derives from a complex religious system that can be uncovered by a close analysis of the myth variants.[2]

First, let us look at how the story of the death of Medea's children is told in the extant sources, both literary and visual. Then we will turn to the archaeological evidence for cult and finally to the relationship between the myth and the ritual in honor of the children.

For the earliest literary sources, we have to turn to a later author, Pausanias. The second-century A.D. writer relates the account of the Corinthian poet Eumelos (eighth–seventh century B.C.), whose *Korinthiaka* contains the oldest version of the events we have. The *Korinthiaka* is an epic poem devoted to the history of the kings of Corinth, starting with the god Helios. There follows a long genealogical account of the subsequent rulers of Corinth, which makes Medea both a direct descendant of the god Helios and the rightful ruler of Corinth. When Korinthos dies childless, the Corinthians send for Medea from Iolcus and hand over the kingdom to her (2.3.10), so that Jason becomes king by virtue of being her husband. Later on, whenever Medea gives birth, Eumelos's chronicle continues, she brings each of her children to the temple of Hera in order to "conceal" them:

> Μηδείᾳ δὲ παῖδας μὲν γίνεσθαι, τὸ δὲ ἀεὶ τικτόμενον κατακρύπτειν, αὐτὸ ἐς τὸ ἱερὸν φέρουσαν τῆς Ἥρας, κατακρύπτειν δὲ ἀθανάτους ἔσεσθαι νομίζουσαν· τέλος δὲ αὐτήν τε μαθεῖν ὡς ἡμαρτήκοι τῆς ἐλπίδος καὶ ἅμα ὑπὸ τοῦ Ἰάσονος φωραθεῖσαν—οὐ γὰρ αὐτὸν ἔχειν δεομένῃ συγγνώμην, ἀποπλέοντα δὲ ἐς Ἰωλκὸν οἴχεσθαι—,τούτων δὲ ἕνεκα ἀπελθεῖν καὶ Μήδειαν παραδοῦσαν Σισύφῳ τὴν ἀρχήν.

> [They say that] when children were born by Medea, she always <u>concealed</u> the newborn, bringing him <u>to the sanctuary</u> of Hera, thinking that the <u>concealing</u> would make them immortal. Finally she learned that her hope was in vain, and at the same time she was detected by Jason. And he refused to forgive her when she begged, and he sailed away to Iolcus, and because of these events, Medea too went away and handed over the rule to Sisyphos.
> —Eumelos fr. 5 (Bernabé) = Pausanias 2.3.11

Eumelos's account focuses on Medea herself and on her actions. Eumelos gives no details about the children's number or their ages, but his account implies that Medea brings them to the sanctuary of Hera as newborns.[3] Medea eventually realizes that her hopes of immortality for her children were futile—presumably because they die while they are "concealed"—at the very same time as Jason discovers what she is doing.[4] While her intentions are unambiguously benevolent, Jason refuses to forgive her and leaves Corinth. The language that Eumelos uses makes it clear that Medea did not know that her hopes were in vain, until she finally—too late—"learns" it (*mathein;* Pausanias 2.3.11). Yet the word used to describe how Medea was "detected" (*phōraein*) evokes discovery of a theft or a crime. Unable to reconcile with Jason, Medea decides to leave Corinth and hands over the kingdom to

Sisyphos. In Pausanias's retelling, Eumelos's poem does not mention the cult (which Pausanias does mention a little earlier in book 2; see below). Since Eumelos's *Korinthiaka* is an epic poem, a reason for this omission may be the gradual Panhellenization of the genre, which avoids overt local religious references in the narrative.[5]

Why does Medea conceal her children in the sanctuary of Hera? A scholion to Pindar's *Olympian* 13 fills some of the gaps and provides an explanation for Medea's strange behavior:

Μηδείας μέμνηται ὅτι ἐν Κορίνθῳ κατῴκει καὶ <u>ἔπαυσε</u> Κορινθίους <u>λιμῷ</u> κατεχομένους θύσασα Δήμητρι καὶ νύμφαις Λημνίαις. ἐκεῖ δὲ αὐτῆς ὁ Ζεὺς ἠράσθη, οὐκ ἐπείθετο δὲ ἡ Μήδεια τὸν τῆς Ἥρας ἐκκλίνουσα <u>χόλον</u>. διὸ καὶ Ἥρα ὑπέσχετο αὐτῇ <u>ἀθανάτους ποιῆσαι</u> <u>τοὺς παῖδας</u>. ἀποθανόντας δὲ τούτους <u>τιμῶσι</u> Κορίνθιοι καλοῦντες <u>μιξοβαρβάρους</u>.

He remembers Medea when she lived in Corinth and <u>brought an end to the famine</u> overcoming the Corinthians by sacrificing to Demeter and the Lemnian nymphs. Then, Zeus fell in love with her, but he did not win Medea over since she wanted to avoid the <u>anger</u> of Hera. Because of this, Hera promised her that <u>she would make her children immortal</u>. The Corinthians <u>honor them after their deaths</u>, calling them <u>semibarbarians</u>.
—schol. Pindar, *Olympian* 13.74 (Drachmann 1.373–74)

Both versions—Eumelos's and the scholia—agree that Medea wants and hopes to make her children immortal. The attempt to immortalize implicitly becomes the cause of the children's death. The scholia also elucidate the link between Medea and Hera and the reason for the latter's goodwill toward the former. Hera, however, does not keep her promise to make the children immortal (*athanatoi*). Yet, as we will see below, the children will, in fact, be *immortalized* with the establishment of the cult and the awarding of *timē* (honor) in compensation for their death. Is Medea victim to a misunderstanding? The "key to immortality" for recipients of hero cult, as Nagy shows, is the permanence of the cultural institution of which they become part through their death, a requirement that the cult for the children of Medea fulfills.[6] And paradoxically, it is only through death that the children can become immortal.

Euripides' *Medea* won third prize at the Greater Dionysia festival in 431 B.C. Whether we trust the scholion claiming that the Corinthians paid Euripides five talents to put the responsibility of the murder on Medea (schol. Euripides, *Medea* 10), Euripides' play is our first extant source to make Medea's implicit guilt explicit and literal by presenting her as the willful killer of her offspring and making her the paradigmatic murderous mother. In the play, Medea murders her children as an act of revenge against her husband. Although Euripides' depiction of Medea as a murderer is often presented as an innovative variation on a traditional myth, Medea was already known as a killer (albeit not of her own children) well before Euripides' version of the events: Pherekydes ("the genealogist") already reports that she killed her brother Apsyrtos (*FGrH* 3), and Pindar calls her "the killer of Pelias" (4.250).[7]

Euripides gives no details about the children's ages or their names, but we know that there are two children (*Medea* 1136). Euripides alternates between two words to describe them, *tekna* and *paides*, both of which connote the relationship between parents and children without conveying any specific information about the children's age (Kreon, for example, also uses the same words to address his dead grown daughter; *Medea* 1207–10).

The chorus compares Medea to an Erinys (*Medea* 1260), likening her crime to that of an avenging spirit. The killing takes place out of sight of the audience, but the children can be heard inside the house. They are given only a few words to say (starting with *iō moi*) as they cry for help. The women of the chorus answer them and speak of entering the house to prevent their murder, but instead of doing so—and at the very moment when the children are being killed by their mother inside—the chorus alludes to another mother who killed her children, Ino (*Medea* 1284–92). In the chorus's account, Ino is maddened by Hera, murders her two children, and leaps into the sea. The two mothers have much in common: both are associated with Hera, both are ultimately responsible for their own children's death, and in both cases their children become immortalized as heroes and recipients of cult.[8]

After the murder, Jason comes onto the scene. We see in Euripides the first appearance of Medea's magical chariot, given to her by Helios (*Medea* 1321), an element that will become important in later sources and especially in the visual representations of the myth. Jason tells Medea that the children, even though they are dead, still exist as avenging spirits (*miastōres;* 1371). The word Jason uses is derived from the verb *miainein* (to stain, defile). The children's violent death is in itself a transgression and a defilement of a kind that implies the need for revenge (Erinys) and subsequent atonement. By using the word *miastōres*, Jason makes it clear that the victims of such a transgression, the children's spirits, will seek revenge against their murderer through violence. Jason then asks Medea permission to give a funeral and mourn for the children, but she denies him this comfort:

οὐ δῆτ', ἐπεί σφας τῆδ' ἐγὼ θάψω χερί
φέρουσ' ἐς Ἥρας τέμενος Ἀκραίας θεοῦ,

ὡς μή τις αὐτοὺς πολεμίων καθυβρίσῃ
τύμβους ἀνασπῶν. γῇ δὲ τῇδε Σισύφου
σεμνὴν ἑορτὴν καὶ τέλη προσάψομεν
τὸ λοιπὸν ἀντὶ τοῦδε δυσσεβοῦς φόνου.

Indeed no, <u>I shall honor them with funeral rites</u> with my own hand,
taking them to the <u>sanctuary</u> of Hera the goddess of Akraia,
so that none of my enemies may outrage them,
tearing up their graves. And on this land of Sisyphos
I shall enjoin a <u>solemn festival and rituals</u>
for the rest of time <u>as a compensation</u> for this impious murder.
—Euripides, *Medea* 1377

Euripides' version makes Medea both the murderer and the agent of the sacralization and ritualization of the dreadful event. Along with the reference to the location of the cult, Medea's speech is replete with ritual words and syntax: *thaptein, temenos, semnē heortē, telē, anti*. When she speaks of the children's funeral, Medea uses the verb *thaptein*, a word sometimes translated "to bury," but which technically means "to honor with funeral rites." One of the reasons why Medea herself wants to give a funeral to the children is to ensure that her enemies will not defile or harm their bodies or their tomb. This implies a certain degree of hiding (and perhaps distance) from the Corinthians.

While the exact location of the children's grave must remain undisclosed, Medea makes it clear that it will be within the sanctuary (*temenos*) of Hera Akraia. The secret location is not unusual in itself: heroes' bodies are precious relics that need to be protected against enemies. The exact location of the grave of Oedipus according to Sophocles' account in *Oedipus at Colonus*, for example, is also kept secret from everyone except Theseus (1640–44).[9] By bringing the children to the *temenos* of Hera, Medea places their tomb within sacred space, which will ensure that the children's tomb is given the honor it deserves even if the exact location of their bodies within the sanctuary remains secret.

Medea declares that she will order the land of Sisyphos to hold a holy festival (*semnē heortē*) and perform sacred rites (*telē*) for all time. The word *telē* can refer to sacred rites in general and, as we shall see later, more specifically to rites of initiation. Medea establishes the rites in compensation for the impious murder of the children. The Greek word *anti*, like *temenos, heortē,* and *telē*, belongs to the vocabulary of ritual and is used specifically to mean "in compensation for" something (cf. Euripides, *Hippolytos* 1423). While Euripides makes Medea the killer of the children, her words here imply that the Corinthians, in fact, bear responsibility both for the sacrilegious death of her children and for its atonement.

To try to explain the cult from the evidence of the play would be futile. The passage makes more sense, however, if we accept that the cult in fact precedes Euripides' version and that the play needs to be interpreted in light of the cult. Euripides has woven an account of the events in which Medea is responsible for the death of her children. Medea bears the blame for their death and therefore institutes a cult for the dead children to atone for her guilt. Yet, as the character makes clear, there also is a need (unexplained in the play) for the Corinthians to atone for the death by participating in the festival and in the rituals to honor the young victims, just as if they shared responsibility for the murders.

The scholia to Euripides provide the oldest details extant about the cult. Parmeniskos, an Alexandrian grammarian of the second–first century B.C., reports a tradition in which the women of Corinth refuse to be ruled by a foreign witch and plot to kill her children, seven boys and seven girls:

καὶ τὰ τέκνα αὐτῆς ἀνελεῖν, ἑπτὰ μὲν ἄρσενα ἑπτὰ δὲ θήλεα· ταῦτα δὲ διωκόμενα καταφυγεῖν εἰς τὸ τῆς Ἀκραίας Ἥρας ἱερὸν καὶ ἐπὶ τὸ ἱερὸν καθίσαι· Κορινθίους δὲ αὐτῶν οὐδὲ οὕτως ἀπέχεσθαι, ἀλλ᾽ ἐπὶ τοῦ βωμοῦ πάντα ταῦτα ἀποσφάξαι. λοιμοῦ δὲ γενομένου εἰς τὴν πόλιν, πολλὰ σώματα ὑπὸ τῆς νόσου διαφθείρεσθαι. μαντευομένοις δὲ αὐτοῖς χρησμῳδῆσαι τὸν θεὸν ἱλάσκεσθαι τὸ τῶν Μηδείας τέκνων ἄγος. ὅθεν Κορινθίοις μέχρι τῶν καιρῶν τῶν καθ᾽ ἡμᾶς καθ᾽ ἕκαστον ἐνιαυτὸν ἑπτὰ κούρους καὶ ἑπτὰ κούρας τῶν ἐπισημοτάτων ἀνδρῶν ἐναπενιαυτίζειν ἐν τῷ τῆς θεᾶς τεμένει καὶ μετὰ θυσιῶν ἱλάσκεσθαι τὴν ἐκείνων μῆνιν καὶ τὴν δι᾽ ἐκείνους γενομένην τῆς θεᾶς ὀργήν.

And they were planning to kill the children, seven boys and seven girls. When the children were being pursued, they fled to the sanctuary of Hera Akraia and sat there. But this did not hold the Corinthians back from them in any way, and they killed all of them on the altar. A bane started in the city, and many bodies were destroyed by the illness. When they consulted the oracle, the god told them to expiate the pollution of the children of Medea, and from then until our own time, each year the Corinthians choose seven boys and seven girls from the most distinguished families to spend a year in the precinct of the goddess and to appease with sacrifices the wrath of the children and the rage of the goddess on their account.
—schol. Euripides, *Medea* 264 = Kreophylos *FGrH* 417 F 3

The nature of the bane striking the Corinthians remains vague, but the word used, *loimos,* could indicate that it mostly struck young children. While the word is commonly translated "plague," it can also refer more specifically to sterility. In her study of sterility and magic in the ancient world, Delcourt argues that the word *loimos* refers to infertility in a wide sense, be it of mothers or of the earth, rather than to an illness striking grown-ups.[10] It is also common belief that the spirits of the angry dead choose victims who are similar to them.[11] The link between the children and Hera, and the cause of her anger, is here made clear: the children are killed not only in Hera's sanctuary, but after they have taken refuge at the altar, a place where they should have been safe. It is also significant that the killers are women and implicitly mothers. Because they are guilty of having killed Medea's children, if I am right about the nature of the *loimos,* the Corinthian women become responsible for their own children's deaths and can expiate the original crime only by "sacrificing" seven boys and seven girls annually in honor of Hera.[12]

Parmeniskos also adds that another Alexandrian scholar, Didymos (first century B.C.), disagrees with this account and provides yet another version of the children's death, based on Kreophylos.[13] In this tradition, Medea poisons King Kreon of Corinth and flees to Athens:

τοὺς δὲ υἱοὺς, ἐπεὶ νεώτεροι ὄντες οὐκ ἠδύναντο ἀκολουθεῖν, ἐπὶ τὸν βωμὸν τῆς Ἀκραίας Ἥρας καθίσαι, νομίσασαν τὸν πατέρα αὐτῶν φροντιεῖν τῆς σωτηρίας αὐτῶν. τοὺς δὲ Κρέοντος οἰκείους ἀποκτείναντας αὐτοὺς διαδοῦναι λόγον ὅτι Μήδεια οὐ μόνον τὸν Κρέοντα ἀλλὰ καὶ τοὺς ἑαυτῆς παῖδας ἀπέκτεινε.

Her sons, since they were too young to be able to accompany her, she put on the altar of Hera Akraia, thinking that their father would care for their safety. But Kreon's relatives killed them and spread the story that Medea had not only killed Kreon, but her own children as well.
—schol. Euripides, *Medea* 264

This version clearly indicates that Medea is innocent of the crime, yet at the same time it shows both that she bears a certain responsibility for the deaths and also that the story of her murdering the children may in fact have been well known by the time of Euripides, even if only as a false rumor started by the true murderers. The new element introduced by the tragedian is the explicit guilt of Medea. I use the word *new* from the perspective of the extant sources we have at our disposal, since it is likely that Euripides, in fact, did not invent this tradition.[14] Here relatives of Kreon kill the children, but Medea's desertion of her children is the action that makes the murder possible. Regardless of the exact circumstances in which the children die, Medea's actions are always instrumental to their deaths in the extant sources, and she is—in Eumelos's version, for example—responsible for the catastrophe, even if she does not herself put the knife to their throats. Regardless of what she actually does in any one version of the myth, Medea's actions (or her status, as in Parmeniskos's first account) always lead to her children's death.

Eumelos and Parmeniskos (quoting Didymos and Kreophylos) agree that the deaths take place within the sanctuary of Hera, and both Parmeniskos and Didymos stress that the murders occur at the very altar where the children seek protection. The Corinthians therefore have to appease both the anger of the dead children and the wrath of Hera herself, against whom they transgressed by committing a crime inside her sacred precinct.

The scholia to Euripides' *Medea* include two more references to the cult. At line 1379, Hera Akraia is said to have been worshiped in Acrocorinth, a piece of information that has been discredited, as we shall see below. In the same passage, we learn that the festival for Hera Akraia is a mourning festival (*penthimos heortē*). Commenting on the rites instituted by Medea in Euripides' play, the scholia give more information about the festival:

ἐγὼ, φησίν, περιποιήσω αὐτοῖς πάνδημον ἑορτὴν ἐν ᾗ πανηγυρίσουσιν οἱ Κορίνθιοι. θύουσι δὲ αὐτοῖς καὶ Ἀργεῖοι κατὰ χρησμόν.

λιμωξάντων Κορινθίων ἔχρησεν ὁ θεὸς τιμῆσαι τοὺς τῆς Μηδείας παῖδας. ἐγὼ οὖν, φησί, περιποιήσω αὐτοῖς πάνδημον ἑορτήν.

I, she says, shall establish a city festival in their honor in which the Corinthians will celebrate them. And the Argives too sacrifice to them in accordance with the oracle.

Since the Corinthians were suffering from a famine, the god ordained them to honor the children of Medea. I, therefore, she says, shall establish a city festival in their honor.
—schol. Euripides, *Medea* 1382

The festival is described as public (*pandēmos*), and both the Corinthians and the Argives perform sacrifices in honor of the children, in accordance with the oracle. These lines purport to explain Medea's establishment of the cult, yet the emphasis is very much on the famine and the oracle. The famine that leads to consultation of the oracle is of course not mentioned in Euripides' play, since Medea establishes the cult immediately after she kills the children. In the scholia, however, the cult is always presented as an oracle-ordained remedy against the disaster (be it a plague or famine) brought along by the deaths of the children.

The tragic poet Karkinos (fourth century B.C.) composed a *Medea,* which we know through only a brief mention in Aristotle's *Rhetoric*. In Karkinos's play, Medea is accused of having killed her children because they are nowhere to be seen:

ἄλλος τόπος τὸ ἐκ τῶν ἁμαρτηθέντων κατηγορεῖν ἢ ἀπολογεῖσθαι, οἷον ἐν τῇ Καρκίνου Μηδείᾳ οἱ μὲν κατηγοροῦσιν ὅτι τοὺς παῖδας ἀπέκτεινεν, οὐ φαίνεσθαι γοῦν αὐτούς. ἥμαρτε γὰρ ἡ Μήδεια <u>περὶ τὴν ἀποστολὴν τῶν παίδων</u>. ἡ δ᾽ ἀπολογεῖται ὅτι οὐκ ἂν τοὺς παῖδας ἀλλὰ τὸν Ἰάσονα ἂν ἀπέκτεινεν· τοῦτο γὰρ ἥμαρτεν ἂν μὴ ποιήσασα, εἴπερ καὶ θάτερον ἐποίησεν.

Another topic consists of accusing or defending on the basis of mistakes, such as when, in Karkinos's *Medea,* some accuse Medea of having killed her children, since at any rate they have disappeared. For Medea made a mistake <u>by sending the children away</u>. She defends herself by saying that she would not have killed her children, but rather her husband Jason. For she would have made a mistake not doing this, if she had done the other.
—Karkinos II (Snell and Kannicht 70 F 1 e = Aristotle, *Rhetoric* 1400b)

Karkinos's *Medea* does not follow in the footsteps of Euripides' model. Although she appears to be guilty, Medea is innocent and clearly rejects the murder of her children as an inappropriate way of taking revenge against her husband. While Aristotle does not elaborate on the sending away (*apostolē*) of the children, it is tempting to see in it an allusion to Medea's concealing (*katakryptein*) her children in some secret place, as she does in the epic version of Eumelos.[15]

The poet Lykophron (second century B.C.) alludes to Medea twice, very succinctly, in his *Alexandra.* He mentions her once in connection with Achilles, who—in some traditions—marries her in the Elysian Fields (Ibykos, *PMG* 291). Achilles is described as the future husband of *"Kytaikē,* the strange bacchante [*xeinobakkhē*]" (175). Later, near the end of his poem, Lykophron refers to Medea as "the brother-killer [*gnōtophontis*] and children's murderer [*alastōr*]" (1318). The word *alastōr* can refer to the avenging spirit of the dead (cf. *miastōr* in Euripides, *Medea* 1371, discussed above), but also, by extension, to the victim's killer. While "unforgetting" is central to the concept of *alastōr,* there is a certain conflation of meaning in the word: *alastōr* can denote both the crime (and the criminal) that is unforgettable and the victim's dead spirit that cannot forget and haunts its killer.[16] Plutarch, in fact, defines *alastōr* as the criminal who has "committed unforgettable acts [*alēsta*], things that will be remembered for a long time" (*Greek Questions* 25 [*Moralia* 297a]). While Lykophron does not expand on the story of Medea, the words he uses to describe her encapsulate the earlier tradition represented by Pindar's and Euripides' murderous Medea: she is foreign, dangerous, and a killer.

The scholia to Lykophron comment at length upon Medea and describe the circumstances of the Argo trip and how Jason and Medea take refuge in Corinth after killing Pelias. There they live peacefully for ten years. Jason then decides to marry Glauke, the daughter of the king, which provokes Medea's wrath. She kills Glauke and Kreon with drugs (*pharmaka*) and slays her own children, Mermeros and Pheres, with a sword and flees to Athens (schol. Lykophron 175). The only details about the children are their names, Anxiety (*Mermeros*) and Bringer (*Pheres*), which clearly evoke important aspects of the myth. There is nothing about their age, but since Jason and Medea have been living in Corinth for ten years and the children were born during that time, they must be under ten. The scholion to line 1318 describes how Medea killed her own brother long before she kills her own children in Corinth because of her wrath against Jason. Here the children are described as *ta tekna,* a word that can be used of small children, and named, again, Mermeros and Pheres.

Medea also appears in Diodorus Siculus's *Library of History* (first century B.C.). In his account, Medea starts out as a compassionate character who recoils at her father's crime in Colchis (4.46.1–3); she is innocent of murder until she slays Pelias to help the Argonauts and avenge the death of Jason's parents (4.50.6–7). After the murder, Jason and Medea settle in Corinth. There Jason lives with Medea as his wife for ten years and fathers her children: the two oldest, Thessalos and Alkimenes, are twins, while the third one, Tisandros, is much younger.

During those ten years, Jason approves of his wife, since she is both beautiful and virtuous, but as time passes, she starts to age, and Jason falls in love with Glauke, Kreon's daughter. He decides to marry her and tries to persuade Medea to let him go of her own free will, but Medea becomes enraged and calls on the gods who witnessed their wedding vows. Jason disregards both his wife and his vows and marries Glauke. Kreon banishes Medea from the city, giving her one day to make her preparations. Medea takes advantage of the night to enter the palace and set fire to it with the help of a root that, once kindled, is impossible to put out. Jason escapes the fire, but Glauke and her father die in the blaze. Diodorus Siculus also acknowledges that other historians give a different version of the story, in which Medea's children bring poisoned gifts to Glauke that cause both her death and that of her father (4.54.1–6).

The death of Glauke and Kreon is not revenge enough for Diodorus's Medea, and, in an account that seems to be inspired by Euripides', she sets her heart on destroying Jason by killing their children. Although up to this point Diodorus Siculus has presented Medea as a benevolent figure who used violence against Pelias only because she considered it to be rightful retribution, he now describes her as reaching a state of rage so intense that it brings out pure savage cruelty (*ōmotēs*) in her (4.54.7). One of the twins, Thessalos, escapes (4.55.2), but she kills (*aposphaxai*) her other two sons, Alkimenes and Tisandros. After she kills the children, Medea flees Corinth with her most faithful servants and takes refuge with Herakles in Thebes (4.54.7). By an odd coincidence, she arrives right after Herakles has slain his own children, and she cures his madness with drugs (4.55.4) (cf. chap. 2).

Meanwhile in Corinth, everyone agrees that Jason got what he deserved when he lost his children and wife. Unable to endure his misfortunes, he commits suicide. The Corinthians are perplexed by all these violent deaths and do not know what to do with the children's bodies. They send to Delphi to ask the god for advice, and the Pythia orders them to give a funeral for the children in the precinct of Hera and to consider them worthy of heroic honors:

προστάξαι τὴν Πυθίαν ἐν τῷ τεμένει τῆς Ἥρας αὐτοὺς θάψαι καὶ τιμῶν ἡρωικῶν αὐτοὺς ἀξιοῦν.

[They say] that the Pythia enjoined them to give them a funeral in the sanctuary of Hera and to consider them worthy of heroic honors.
—Diodorus Siculus 4.55.1–2

While Diodorus Siculus follows Euripides' version in its outline, the connection between the children and the *temenos* of Hera is left unexplained. The Corinthians themselves are not responsible for the children's death, yet they need to expiate Medea's crime. Although revenge is often aimed at the killer, the angry spirits of those who have died a violent death can also turn against the community as a whole, and it is not uncommon, in fact, for innocent inhabitants of a city to have to pay for crimes committed by one of their fellow citizens.[17]

Medea clearly is a central character in Greek myth, and she also remains a popular figure in Latin literature. Many Roman authors allude to the story of Medea's children, but their focus is on Medea herself rather than on the deaths of her children or the consequences thereof. Ovid (43 B.C.–A.D. 17) gives an extremely concise version of the events at Corinth in his epic poem, the *Metamorphoses*. In his account, Medea comes to Corinth on winged dragons. There she spends some years until Jason's new marriage:

sed postquam Colchis arsit nova nupta venenis
flagrantemque domum regis mare vidit utrumque,
sanguine natorum perfunditur impius ensis
ultaque se male mater Iasonis effugit arma.

But after the new wife had been burned by Colchian poisons
and the two seas had seen the king's house blazing,
the impious sword was drenched with the blood of her children
and, once avenged, hardly a mother, she escaped the sword of Jason.
—*Metamorphoses* 7.394–97

Except for the graphic description of their blood drenching Medea's impious sword, Ovid omits details concerning the children. Here again, we find the same elements we know from Euripides' tragedy: Jason's new wife, Medea's revenge and infanticide, and her escape. Carried off by dragons, Medea flees to Athens, where she marries Aegeus. Ovid's Medea, like Euripides' and Pindar's Medea, is a vengeful foreign witch who kills through both witchcraft and pure savagery. Ovid emphasizes Medea's magic powers and her cunning in evading punishment for her actions, as well as the religious transgression she commits by killing her children. Yet there is no mention of atonement or ritual; the stress is on the gruesome violence, and Ovid transforms the burning of the poisoned gifts into a blaze so spectacular that it becomes almost cosmic as it is observed by "the two seas."

One Roman tragedian also focuses on the story of Medea. By the end of Seneca's eponymous tragedy, Medea is a woman driven insane by jealousy and torn between her love for her two sons and her hate for Jason. She starts by killing one of the children and then brings his dead body and the surviving child to the top of the house. There she kills her other son in the sight of Jason. Right after she kills the second child, Medea throws both corpses down at Jason's feet and flees on her winged chariot. Seneca, like Ovid, ignores the cultic dimension of Euripides' tragedy. There is no reference to any rites or cult established after the children's deaths. In a striking departure from the Greek versions, Medea in fact tells Jason he should be the one to prepare a funeral pyre for his dead children (997–98). No ritual is instituted for the children, and Medea shows no concern for the treatment of their bodies or the care of their dead spirits. The play ends with her escape and Jason's bitter last words: "Bear witness that there are no gods!"

We find a similar lack of interest in the ritual dimension of the myth of Medea's children in later authors such as Hyginus (second century A.D.) and Apollodoros (first or second century A.D.). Both of these writers are concerned with recording Greek myths, and they often report different versions of the same story. Hyginus tells the story of the Argonauts and of Medea in his *Fabulae* 22–27. *Fabula* 25 deals specifically with the events at Corinth. In his account, Jason and Medea have two sons named, as in the scholia to Lykophron, Mermeros and Pheres. The family lives in harmony until Jason realizes that a man as strong, handsome, and noble as he is deserves a better wife than Medea, a foreigner and a witch (*advenam atque veneficam*). Kreon gives him his daughter Glauke in marriage, and Medea is so outraged at being mistreated in this way that she prepares a poisonous garland and orders her sons to bring it to their future stepmother. Creusa (Hyginus's name for Glauke) accepts the gift that kills her alongside Kreon and Jason. Medea, after she sees the palace in flames, kills her two sons by Jason and flees Corinth. Hyginus's account reflects many elements familiar from Euripides' play. Medea is also included in Hyginus's list of "those who killed their children," and here again he gives the names of her sons as Mermeros and Pheres (*Fabula* 239).

Apollodoros gives two different versions of the death of Medea's children in book 1 of his *Library* (1.9.28). In the first, Medea kills her two children (*paides*) by Jason after she has killed Glauke and her father. The two children are named, again, Mermeros and Pheres, and although their ages are not mentioned, Apollodoros does specify that Jason and Medea had been living happily in Corinth for ten years before Jason decided to divorce Medea and marry Glauke. The second version has Medea fleeing Corinth and leaving behind her children, who are still infants (*nēpioi*), as suppliants at the altar of Hera of Akraia. In this version, the Corinthians take the babies away from the altar and kill them. Apollodoros then goes on to tell how Medea flees Corinth and marries Aegeus in Athens, but nothing about what happens in Corinth after the children's death.

The first version corresponds closely to Euripides' tragedy and the scholia to Lykophron (which also preserves the names Mermeros and Pheres), while the second repeats the pattern we find in Eumelos, Parmeniskos, and Didymos: we could describe the first as the Athenian narrative, which attributes responsibility for the murders to Medea herself, while we might call the second, which ascribes the murder to the Corinthians, the Corinthian account. What sources did Apollodoros use for the second version? A tragedy, perhaps, but certainly not Euripides' play. The focus on the altar is important, since this element is absent from the Athenian version, but persistent in all the other accounts of the death of the children of Medea, as well as a recurring motif in visual representations, as we shall see.

While the authors discussed above show little interest in the ritual dimension of the story, one writer from the second century A.D. turns his attention to the cult of the children. By the time Pausanias visited the Isthmus, the Romans had colonized Corinth and eradicated the earlier Corinthian population (2.1.1). Although the new Roman inhabitants put a stop to the ancient customs, Pausanias gives a detailed account of the place where Medea's children died and of the rituals in their honor, in which the ancient Corinthians used to participate (2.3.6–9). On the road from the agora to Sikyon is the fountain of Glauke, into which the princess threw herself, seeking a remedy to the drugs of Medea. Right above the well is a music hall (*ōdeion*), and next to it is the memorial (*mnēma*) for the children of Medea.

In his first version of the events, Pausanias gives the children the same names (Mermeros and Pheres) we know from Lykophron, Hyginus, and Apollodoros.

As in Pausanias's account, Medea bears no direct responsibility for the death of the children. The Corinthians themselves, angry because the children brought the gifts that eventually killed Glauke, avenge their princess's death by stoning them to death (2.3.6). There is no indication of the children's ages at the time of their death. Following the death of Medea's children, however, Corinthian babies start to die:

ἅτε δὲ τοῦ θανάτου βιαίου καὶ οὐ σὺν τῷ δικαίῳ γενομένου, τὰ τέκνα Κορινθίων τὰ νήπια ὑπ᾽ αὐτῶν ἐφθείρετο.

Since their deaths had been violent and unjust, the Corinthians' babies were being destroyed by them.
—Pausanias 2.3.7

The Corinthian infants ( *ta tekna . . . ta nēpia*) die by the agency of Medea's children, more specifically because their own deaths were violent ( *biaioi*) and unjust ( *ou syn tō dikaiō*). In ancient Greek accounts of violent death, the angry spirits of the deceased often wreak havoc on their killers. We have seen before how reprisals often take the form of a bane ( *loimos*) or a famine ( *limos*), and it is not uncommon for the vengeance to be very closely related to the injury done. Pausanias relates another story in which the unjust killing of children provokes the death of more children in the town of Kaphyai:

παιδία περὶ τὸ ἱερὸν παίζοντα—ἀριθμὸν δὲ αὐτῶν οὐ μνημονεύουσιν— ἐπέτυχε καλῳδίῳ, δήσαντα δὲ τὸ καλῴδιον τοῦ ἀγάλματος περὶ τὸν τράχηλον ἐπέλεγεν ὡς ἀπάγχοιτο ἡ Ἄρτεμις.

Children playing by the sanctuary—their number is not remembered— found a rope and tied it around the neck of the statue and said that Artemis was strangled.
—Pausanias 8.23.6

Both the word that describes them, *paidia,* and their playing indicate that the children are small. When the Kaphyaians discover what the children did, they stone them to death. Subsequent to the children's death, all the women in the city are afflicted by a sickness that causes their babies to die in their bellies before birth, until they obtain advice from the oracle:

ἐς ὃ ἡ Πυθία θάψαι τε τὰ παιδία ἀνεῖπε καὶ ἐναγίζειν αὐτοῖς κατὰ ἔτος. ἀποθανεῖν γὰρ αὐτὰ οὐ σὺν δίκῃ.

Until the Pythia proclaimed that they should give a funeral to the children and sacrifice to them as heroes each year because they were killed unjustly.
—Pausanias 8.23.7

The Kaphyaians not only kill the children, but also neglect to give them a funeral. Like the children of Medea, the children of Kaphyai are killed by angry adults who do not understand the consequences of their transgression. The Pythia orders the Kaphyaians to give the children a proper funeral and to perform in their honor sacrifices of the kind that is reserved for heroes (*enagizein*).[18] As in the case of the death of Medea's children, the city as a whole is punished, and an annual ritual needs to be established as a compensation for the unjust (and violent) deaths of the children. From that day on, the Kaphyaians call Artemis the Strangled One (*Apagkhomenēnone*), and, according to Pausanias, they still obey the oracle in his own day (8.23.6–7).

In both the Kaphyaian narrative and some versions of the death of the children of Medea, revenge is wrought upon victims belonging to a particular age class corresponding to that of the original victim. It is puzzling to see dead children seeking revenge on other children. Yet the myths of their revenge, very much like the ritual that will be instituted on their account, are, in fact, reenactments of the original transgression (as we will see when we turn to the analysis of the cult evidence below).[19]

Let us return to Pausanias's account of the Corinthian myth. The Corinthians are so puzzled by the death of the city's babies that they consult the oracle, who orders them to set up yearly sacred rites (*thysiai*) for the children of Medea and to set up a statue of Fear (*Deima;* Pausanias 2.3.7). Pausanias adds that this figure of Deima, in the likeness of a woman terrifying to look upon (*phoberōteron*), was still in Corinth in his own time. A *deima* usually designates a sign sent by the gods, often following some pollution that requires purification (there are other examples of *deimata* in Pausanias).[20] This image of a terrifying female in Corinth symbolizes both the mythical event that took place there and the feeling it cannot fail to evoke, terror. The figure of Deima, Fear Incarnate, functions as a marker of a fear that has been ritualized through myth, and the commemorative *deima* set up by the Corinthians can be understood as a memento of the notionally original *deima,* which must have happened at the time of the transgression.

Pausanias relates that the sacred rituals for the children were abandoned by the Roman settlers after the sack of Corinth, and so we learn of the ritual only in negative terms:

οὐκέτι ἐκεῖναι καθεστήκασιν αὐτοῖς αἱ θυσίαι παρὰ τῶν ἐποίκων οὐδὲ ἀποκείρονταί σφισιν οἱ παῖδες οὐδὲ μέλαιναν φοροῦσιν ἐσθῆτα.

Those sacrifices are no longer performed by the inhabitants, and their children no longer cut their hair or wear dark clothing [in honor of Medea's children].
—Pausanias 2.3.7

Both here and earlier in the same passage about the rituals performed by the original inhabitants of Corinth, Pausanias uses the unmarked term *thysiai* to describe the annual sacrifices for the children. The haircutting and special clothing are elements typical of initiation rituals.[21]

Aelian (c. A.D. 170–235) includes the story of Medea in his *Varia Historia* and partly agrees with Pausanias's account: the rumor concerning Medea is false: she did not kill her children (*tekna*), but the Corinthians did (5.21). He goes on to say that Euripides devised the story of Medea's killing her children at the command of the Athenians (cf. schol. Euripides, *Medea* 10) and that the lie overcame the truth because of his excellence as a poet. Then, Aelian turns to the ritual:

ὑπὲρ δὲ τοῦ τολμήματος, φασί, τῶν παίδων <u>μέχρι τοῦ νῦν ἐναγίζουσι τοῖς παισὶ</u> Κορίνθιοι, οἱονεὶ δασμὸν τούτοις ἀποδιδόντες.

On account of their recklessness against the children, they say that the Corinthians <u>still now perform heroic sacrifices for the children,</u> as if they were paying them tribute.
—Aelian, *Varia Historia* 5.21

Aelian uses good heroic terminology, *enagizousi,* but he also contradicts Pausanias's earlier claims that the rituals ended with the sack of Corinth by the Romans in 146 B.C. One possible reason for the discrepancy may be that Aelian used a Corinthian source dating from the time when the rituals were still performed (and predating Pausanias's visit to the Isthmus).

Philostratos, a near contemporary of Aelian, also alludes to the ritual at Corinth in his dialogue on hero cult, the *Heroikos* (early third century A.D.).[22] The *Heroikos* records a conversation between a vinegrower and a traveling Phoenician merchant that takes place at Elaious on the north shore of the Hellespont.[23] At the beginning of the dialogue, the merchant makes clear that he does not believe in heroes, and the vinegrower proceeds to persuade him of their existence. The rest of the dialogue is concerned with proofs of the existence of heroes and with the correction of Homer's account of the events at Troy. Near the end of the *Heroikos,* the vinegrower and his interlocutor agree that digressions make for worthwhile conversations as they start discussing the rituals in honor of Achilles:

καὶ μὴν καὶ ὕμνων ἐκ Θετταλίας ὁ Ἀχιλλεὺς ἔτυχεν, οὓς ἀνὰ πᾶν ἔτος ἐπὶ τὸ σῆμα φοιτῶντες ᾖδον ἐν νυκτί, <u>τελετῆς τι ἐγκαταμιγνύντες τοῖς ἐναγίσμασιν,</u> ὡς Λήμνιοί τε νομίζουσι καὶ Πελοποννησίων οἱ ἀπὸ Σισύφου.

From Thessaly, Achilles also received <u>hymns,</u> which they sang at night when they visited his tomb every year, <u>mixing something of an initiatory rite</u> with their <u>heroic offerings,</u> just as the Lemnians and the Peloponnesians descended from Sisyphos practice.[24]

—Philostratos, *Heroikos* 52.3 (Lannoy)

The vinegrower describes the rites in honor of Achilles as a mixture of heroic and initiatory rites. He then compares the mixture of rituals in honor of Achilles to that offered to the hero Melikertes and the children of Medea:

τὰ μὲν γὰρ Κορινθίων <u>ἐπὶ Μελικέρτῃ</u> (τούτους γὰρ δὴ τοὺς ἀπὸ Σισύφου εἶπον), καὶ ὁπόσα οἱ αὐτοὶ δρῶσιν ἐπὶ τοῖς τῆς Μηδείας παισίν, οὓς ὑπὲρ τῆς Γλαύκης ἀπέκτειναν, <u>θρήνῳ</u> εἴκασται <u>τελεστικῷ</u> τε καὶ <u>ἐνθέῳ</u>. τοὺς μὲν γὰρ <u>μειλίσσονται</u>, τὸν δὲ <u>ὑμνοῦσιν</u>.

The rites of the Corinthians <u>for Melikertes</u> (for these are the ones I called the descendants of Sisyphos), and what the same people do in honor of Medea's children, whom they killed for the sake of Glauke, resemble a <u>lament</u> that is both <u>initiatory</u> and <u>inspired,</u> for they <u>propitiate</u> the children and <u>sing hymns</u> to Melikertes.

—Philostratos, *Heroikos* 53.4 (Lannoy)

The rites for the children of Medea (who were killed on account of Glauke's death) and those for Melikertes (which were established by Sisyphos) are similar in nature. They include lament (*thrēnos*), initiatory rites (*telestikos*), and divine possession (*entheos*). This passage agrees with the earlier sources' descriptions of the ritual: we see here again a combination of different kinds of rituals—mourning and initiation.[25]

◻

The elements of the myth that are emphasized in the literary sources—violence, sacred space, transgression, and mourning—are also found in the visual sources. When we turn to iconography, we find that Medea killing her children is indeed a popular subject for vase-painters and sculptors. Extant representations of the death of her children, however, are all late (after 400 B.C.) and South Italian, and all seem to be influenced by drama. No representations illustrate the variants of the story in which the children are killed by the Corinthians or where the alternate numbers of children, three or seven, are mentioned. Yet, the altar, an element absent from Euripides but pervasive in the other sources, is a constant presence. The children are occasionally shown without their mother, at the moment when they bring the fatal gift to Glauke. Medea is shown either as she meditates her crime, while she is committing it, or escaping in her magical chariot just after the deed.[26]

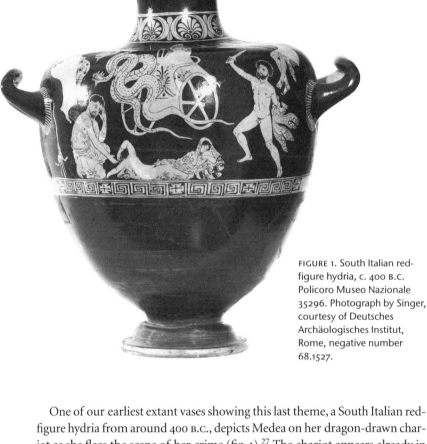

FIGURE 1. South Italian red-figure hydria, c. 400 B.C. Policoro Museo Nazionale 35296. Photograph by Singer, courtesy of Deutsches Archäologisches Institut, Rome, negative number 68.1527.

One of our earliest extant vases showing this last theme, a South Italian red-figure hydria from around 400 B.C., depicts Medea on her dragon-drawn chariot as she flees the scene of her crime (fig. 1).[27] The chariot appears already in Euripides, and it becomes a common motif on vases from the same period. Here Medea—her name is inscribed below her left arm—stands in the middle on her chariot; she wears a Phrygian hat and oriental-type sleeves and holds a whip in her right hand, while her left arm holds up her veil. The scene is full of motion: the wind lifts both her hat and her veil. The chariot goes toward the left, but Medea turns her head back toward the right, where Jason runs to try to reach her as she rises into the air. Two dragons draw the chariot. A female figure—probably Aphrodite—stands in the upper-left corner, looking at herself in a mirror. In the upper-right corner is a winged Eros. The dead bodies of the children lie on the ground below the chariot: one is wrapped in a veil, the

FIGURE 2. Lucanian red-figure calyx-krater, attributed to
the Policoro Painter, Southern Italy, c. 400 B.C. Red-figure
earthenware with added white, red, yellow, and brown
wash, height 50.5 cm. © The Cleveland Museum of Art,
2003. Leonard C. Hanna Jr. Fund, 1991.

other is naked. A man, probably their *paidagōgos*, kneels to the left, with his left
hand raised to his head in a gesture of mourning and his right arm extended
as if to touch the children.

A variation on the same theme is found on a Lucanian red-figure calyx-
krater from the same era (fig. 2). Here Medea and her chariot are shown inside
a spiked-crown frame at the center of the scene. The chariot is drawn by two
stocky serpents, and Medea again wears a Phrygian hat and oriental garb.
Below the crown-shaped frame, we find a scene very similar to the one on the

FIGURE 3. Apulian red-figure amphora by the Dareios
Painter, c. 340 B.C. Naples, Museo Nazionale 81954
(H 3221). Photograph courtesy of Soprintendenza
Archeologica della Provincia di Napoli e Caserta,
Naples.

Policoro hydria (see fig. 1), but with two new elements: the altar and the fallen
hydria. The altar, as we will see, is a recurrent motif in depictions of the death
of the children of Medea, as well as in many representations of other child
heroes. Next to the altar lies the fallen hydria, as if it had just been dropped
by the servant upon discovery of the children—a visual mise-en-abîme.
Plants and an animal indicate that the scene takes place outside. As
Sourvinou-Inwood argues, the altar acts "as a kind of iconographic equivalent to the boys' cries."[28] I would add that it also signals the enormity of the
transgression and sacralizes the event by placing it within sacred space.

On an Apulian red-figure amphora by the Dareios Painter from around
340 B.C., Medea is also depicted just after the murder of her children (fig. 3).
Medea stands on a chariot drawn by two serpents arranged in a double-eight
pattern. She holds her veil with her right hand and guides the chariot with
her left. At her feet, barely visible, is part of the body of one of her children;

the other child's body lies on the ground behind the chariot, next to Medea's sword. The actions of Medea's killing her children and her fleeing are conflated in this one scene: she must have just let her sword drop after killing the second child, and now she rushes to escape (see figs. 1–2, where the same actions are depicted). On the left, two warriors (only one is visible here) and a man on a horse, perhaps Jason,[29] pursue Medea. On the right, a female figure stands in front of the chariot, holding a torch in her left hand and a sword in the right. To her right, a female figure, Selene—traditionally the protector of magicians—sits on a horse, with both the horse and the woman turning their heads back toward Medea. The standing figure next to the serpents is identified as an Erinys or a personification such as Ate, Lyssa, Mania, or Oistros, which were popular on vases from that era and of which we will see another example shortly.[30]

A Faliscan red-figure bell krater from the second half of the fourth century B.C. shows another escape scene with Medea in her chariot (fig. 4). On

FIGURE 4. Faliscan red-figure bell krater, second half of fourth century B.C. The State Hermitage Museum, St. Petersburg, B.2083. Photograph courtesy of The State Hermitage Museum.

FIGURE 5. Apulian red-figure krater, c. 360–350 B.C. Naples, Museo Nazionale SA 526. Photograph courtesy of the Deutsches Archäologisches Institut, Rome, negative number 898.

the right, Medea is standing on the dragon-drawn chariot, which is turned toward the left side. In this version, she holds a dead child in each hand, perhaps getting ready to bring the children to a safe sanctuary for burial.

The children of Medea are usually depicted as dead or as they are being killed. One exception is a scene showing the children with Glauke on a krater at the Naples Museum (fig. 5).[31] At the center of the picture is a throne, from which a young woman has just fallen: she half-kneels down, trying to take off the poisoned crown and veil. On her left, a man holding a scepter runs to her help, while behind him a woman runs away from the scene, looking back toward the young woman in the center. On the right, a *paidagōgos* leads two small children (wearing oriental garb) away and tries to prevent them from looking back. A winged Erinys sits above the *paidagōgos* and children, as if she were floating in the air, apparently taking delight in the scene. Although the children do not witness the death of Glauke in Euripides, Séchan notes

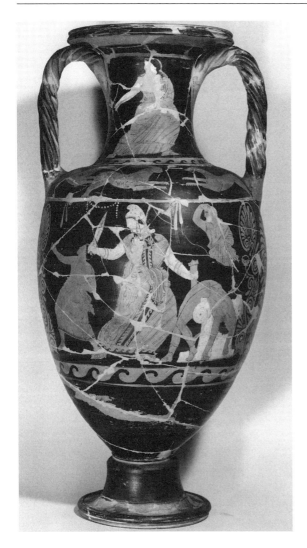

FIGURE 6. Campanian red-figure amphora, c. 330 B.C. Paris, Cabinet des Médailles 876. Photograph courtesy of Bibliothèque nationale de France.

how their presence on the picture provides both the cause and the explanation for Glauke's death.[32]

A Campanian red-figure amphora from around 330 B.C. shows Medea in the process of killing her two sons (fig. 6).[33] Medea stands in the middle. Her left hand still holds the sheath from which she drew the sword that she just used to kill the first child, on the right, whose corpse is lying across an altar. The second child, on the left, tries to run away, but she holds him back with her right hand (in which she also holds the sword), clutching his hair. Medea wears a Phrygian hat and a richly decorated Greek dress. Her mantle is wrapped around her waist and tied in front of her in the same manner that aprons are worn by someone performing a sacrifice.[34] This gesture, as Burkert notes, echoes the sacrificial language of Medea in Euripides' play.[35] In the background at the top of the scene is a straight line on which hang fillets or ribbons. The *paidagōgos* can be seen on the upper-right corner, holding his right hand to his head in a gesture of mourning. The scene is extremely dramatic, and the child trying to escape on the left makes a heartbreaking figure, with his head held backward by the strength of Medea's hold on his hair. Medea is portrayed as completely in control of the situation, cool, and emotionless. She is killing her children methodically, efficiently, and (one is tempted to say) professionally.

A Campanian red-figure amphora from the same period depicts a very similar scene, with only one child shown (fig. 7). Both Medea and the child are shown in profile. Medea is again wearing her mantle tied around her waist as if it were an apron, though this time she does not wear the Phrygian hat. While she is wearing a Greek chiton and himation, the sleeves are of oriental type. Medea stands in the middle, while the child, on the right, is trying to escape her. She holds the child's hair with her left hand while she pulls the sword out of his bleeding body right below the arm with her right hand; she is presumably getting ready to finish the job. A pillar rises on the right of the child, with a statue of a winged divinity standing on top. The scene focuses on Medea's slaughtering the helpless child, and again she is very much in control of both the situation and her own emotions. The background showing two columns is reminiscent, as Trendall and Webster note, of a stage background,[36] but also of a temple, where Medea kills her children in a distorted sacrifice.

Another vase by the Dareios Painter portrays Medea in a setting that has no parallel in the extant literary sources. A volute krater from the late fourth century b.c. shows Medea at Eleusis in the company of another parent who kills his children, Herakles.[37] Although tradition depicts Herakles as an initiate in the Mysteries, no such tradition connects Medea with Eleusis. Medea is shown in the center of the krater, and her name is inscribed at her feet. She is not wearing the usual oriental costume seen on other images, but is dressed in a long garment with a cloak. She is standing in a *naiskos,* inscribed ELEUSIS TO IERON, with a *paidagōgos* at her side. Two children are sitting on an altar below the *naiskos.* To the right, Demeter and Kore appear in the upper register. Herakles, dressed in his lion skin and holding branches and his club, stands below them with Iris. On the upper left are Nike and Athena, with two youths below them, identified as the Dioskouroi.[38] Are the children sitting on

FIGURE 7. Campanian red-figure amphora, 340–330 B.C., Ixion Painter. Louvre K 300. Musée du Louvre, Paris. Photograph by Chuzeville, © Réunion des Musées Nationaux / Art Resource, NY.

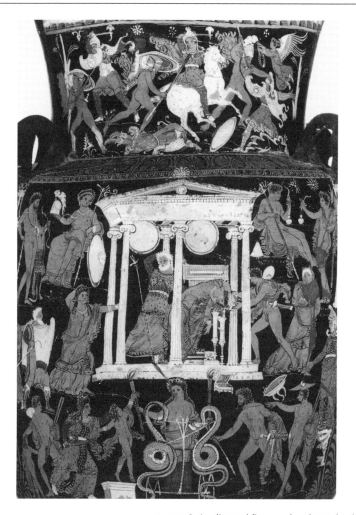

FIGURE 8. Apulian red-figure volute krater by the Underworld Painter from 330 B.C. Munich, Staatliche Antikensammlungen 3296 (J 810). Photograph by Koppermann, courtesy of Staatliche Antikensammlungen und Glyptothek München.

the altar Medea's or Herakles'? This image opens up more questions than it answers, and the link between Eleusis and Medea remains puzzling.

One remarkable Apulian red-figure volute krater by the Underworld Painter from 330 B.C. shows several major episodes of the myth at once (fig. 8). Both the death of Glauke and Medea killing her children are depicted on the vase, while the escape of Medea is hinted at with the presence of the chariot. There are three different levels, with a *naiskos* in the center. Inside the temple, a young woman has just collapsed on a throne with her right hand raised to her crown, while an old man holds on to her and calls for help. The inscription on the *naiskos* reads KREONTEIA, and on the left, KREON is proposed as a restoration (only the first two letters are legible). A young warrior—identified as Hippotes by an inscription above his head (IPPOTES)—reaches for the woman's head to help her take the crown off as he straddles the exterior of the middle register and the inside of the *naiskos* on our right side.[39] Immediately below is an open jewel case, probably another poisoned present from Medea, which also links the scene on the middle register with the one below it. To the left of the *naiskos,* a woman rushes to Kreon's help. To her left, a little below, a *paidagōgos* also rushes in the direction of the temple, with another woman at his side.

The lower register shows Medea in the process of killing her children. On the extreme left, a young man carrying a spear leads one of the children away, presumably to protect him.[40] Next to him, Medea (EMEDIA) stands, turned toward the right, with a sword in her right hand. She wears a Phrygian hat and an elaborate oriental costume. The pattern on her sleeves—white dots on dark background—matches the pattern on Kreon's garment. Medea holds her son by the hair with her left hand, ready to strike. The child stands on an altar and reaches for help with his left hand. To the child's right, in the center, is the dragon-drawn chariot, apparently waiting for Medea. A male figure stands inside the chariot, holding torches with both hands and with serpents rising out of his head. Simon describes the figure as "similar to a male Erinys."[41] The figure is in fact identified by an inscription above its head, OISTROS, the personification of madness or frenzy.[42] To the right of Oistros, Jason rushes to stop Medea. He has a spear in his right hand and a sword in the other. Halfway between the lower and the middle register, an old man stands with an ornate costume and Asian hat. An inscription identifies him as the ghost of Medea's father, Aetes (EIDOLON AETOU). The ghost of Aetes is also wearing an oriental costume with a lozenge pattern. He is drawn in a different manner, and his position halfway between the lower and middle zone also identifies him as a unique character.

Although some of the episodes depicted on the vase do not correspond to any events described in Euripides' play, the vase no doubt represents a tragic scene—or rather several such scenes. The topmost register showing the gods belongs to the traditional decoration scheme used by South Italian vase-painters.[43] Some of the details shown, such as Hippotes rushing to help his sister and the ghost of Aetes, are not in Euripides' play but must be part of a different tradition, written or oral.

FIGURE 9. Wall-painting from Pompeii XI 5, 18. Naples, Museo Nazionale 114 321. Photograph courtesy of the Deutsches Archäologisches Institut, Rome, negative number 56.443.

Although many of the details depicted on this vase do not reflect any episode found in Euripides, it is nevertheless often interpreted as an illustration of his play. Sourvinou-Inwood, for example, understands the variations not as a sign that the painter was not following Euripides, but as a sign that the painter was adding his own touch to the play by Euripides and was creating his own "particular articulation of the myth." She argues that the image of the three gods in the upper register "shows that the vase painter was indeed creating his own version and was not simply reproducing tragic incidents."[44] If the painter is creating his own version of the events, there is no need to attempt linking it with Euripides' or any other specific play for that matter. Yet the vase obviously depicts scenes from a tragedy. The presence of Hippotes makes it very hard indeed to reconcile this version with Euripides'. Whether the painter is creating his own version of the myth or illustrating a contemporary tragic version of the story, the scenes depicted here follow a different tradition—perhaps Corinthian—than the one we find in Euripides.

Medea killing her children is also a popular subject for wall-paintings and reliefs. Although all the extant paintings come from the Roman world, they probably reflect Greek iconography and offer a different perspective on the narrative of the children of Medea than the one we find on vase-paintings. We have literary descriptions of some Greek paintings, but the extant paintings are all from Pompeii and Herculaneum. They often show a very stern Medea, holding a sword and contemplating murder, with her children at her side or behind her.

One such depiction from Pompeii shows Medea deep in thought (fig. 9). Medea sits pensively, with her right hand supporting her chin. Her sword is still in its sheath. A *paidagōgos* approaches in the center through a door. The children, unaware of their fate, play a game of knuckle bones.

Another example from Pompeii shows Medea standing up as she conceals her sword (fig. 10). To her left and a little behind her, Medea's two sons are playing on an altar, with their *paidagōgos* standing watchfully behind them. This is an interesting variation on the motif of the altar. The children are here depicted playing peacefully, whereas Greek or South Italian vases (see figs. 2, 6, 8) often show the children in the process of being killed or their corpses spread on an altar.

Another painting from Herculaneum shows a contemplative Medea (fig. 11). There might have been a companion painting showing the children playing, but it is not extant.[45] Medea occupies most of the space of the picture. She is standing with her hands crossed in front of her, still holding the sword in its sheath. Her body is facing the front, but her head is turned slightly to the left, and her stern gaze is directed toward something there. While Medea is depicted on vases after the fact as cool, determined, and efficient, on wall-paintings she seems sterner, sadder, and alone as she premeditates her crime.

The *Greek Anthology* preserves ancient writers' descriptions of a painting of Medea by the Greek painter Timomakhos. These accounts emphasize the combination of opposite emotions in Medea: the painting evokes a mixture of love and jealousy, according to one of the authors, or pity and wrath, according to another. As on the extant wall-paintings, Medea, holding her sword, is just about to kill her children, but the actual murder is not depicted: poised between action and inaction, Medea half-acquiesces and half-denies, wishing both to save and to kill her children (*Greek Anthology* 16.135–41).[46]

Many later sculptures depict Medea and her children. Reliefs show more action and movement and more figures. The children become smaller and

FIGURE 10. Wall-painting from Pompeii VI 9.6–7. Naples, Museo Nazionale 8977. Photograph courtesy of the Deutsches Archäologisches Institut, Rome, negative number 54.67.

FIGURE 11. Wall-painting from Herculaneum. Naples, Museo Nazionale 8976. Photograph courtesy of Soprintendenza Archeologica della Provincia di Napoli e Caserta, Naples.

chubbier, more realistic.[47] In his *Descriptions,* Kallistratos (third or fourth century A.D.) mentions one such sculpture that he saw in Macedonia. The statue shows Medea—without her children—as she prepares to commit her crime. According to Kallistratos, this work of art reflected all the conflicting emotions at work in Medea's mind (*psykhē*) or provided, in short, an "explanation" (*exēgēsis*) of her entire story (14.1). The statue, which resembles the Roman paintings, looks as if it were reflecting Euripides' *Medea,* combining both rational intelligence and wrath (14.3). Medea is depicted as wearing mourning garb and holding a sword in her hands (14.4).

Since statues of Medea often seem to have been inspired by the way in which she is depicted on sarcophagi, I confine myself here to the Roman sarcophagi showing Medea and her children. They usually depict the same four episodes of the tragedy: Glauke receiving the poisoned gifts, Glauke's death, Medea killing her children, and Medea escaping on her chariot.

Three sarcophagi from the middle of the second century A.D. show essentially the same sequence of events (figs. 12–14). On the extreme left, Glauke accepts the gifts brought to her by the children of Medea; in the center, Glauke has put on the poisoned dress and is trying to escape, while Medea stands next to her children right before she kills them; and finally, on the extreme right, Medea flees the murder scene in her dragon-drawn chariot.[48]

All the images of the murder depict Medea as the killer of her children, and the tradition of the Corinthians killing the children is nonexistent. All the representations showing Medea and the death of her children also happen to be either South Italian, Etruscan (Faliscan), or Roman. Yet, the wall-paintings from Pompeii and Herculaneum are the only representations that may readily be linked to the tragic Medea we know from Euripides' play. The location, action, and mood are in tune with the monologue of Medea just before the murders. The vases that show Medea killing her children at the altar, by contrast, cannot refer to Euripides' play. In this visual version of the myth, Medea kills the children at the altar, which is placed outside the house (see especially fig. 2). This Medea belongs to a different tradition, a tradition that places the murder within sacred space and has room for Medea's chariot and for Hippotes as well as the ghost of Aietes, both of whom appear on the volute krater by the Underworld Painter (see fig. 8).[49]

On vases, Medea wears either a Greek dress (see figs. 3 and 6), an oriental costume (see fig. 2), or a combination thereof (see figs. 7–8). Whether there is a pattern to the Greek or oriental emphasis of the costume remains elusive. Sourvinou-Inwood argues for an increasing tendency to show Medea wearing oriental costumes and that oriental-type sleeves are used either to depict oriental figures or to denote figures "who can be seen metaphorically as oriental,"

FIGURE 12. Roman sarcophagus, c. A.D. 140–50. Berlin, Staatliche Museum SK 843 b. Photograph courtesy of Antikensammlung, Staatliche Museen zu Berlin—Preussischer Kulturbesitz, Berlin.

FIGURE 13. Roman sarcophagus, c. A.D. 170. Rome, Museo Nazionale 222. Photograph by Singer, courtesy of Deutsches Archäologisches Institut, Rome, negative number 69.2502.

FIGURE 14. Roman sarcophagus, c. A.D. 150. Vatican Casino di Pio IV = *LIMC* Medeia 55. Photograph courtesy of Deutsches Archäologisches Institut, Rome, reproduced with permission of Monumenti Musei e Gallerie Pontificie, Vatican.

that is to say, negatively.[50] By contrast, a figure like Andromeda, who is an oriental princess rescued by Perseus and whose representations might also have been influenced by tragedy, is often shown in Greek dress on fourth-century images, perhaps because Greek equals "good."[51]

The degree of the orientalism of Medea's costumes seems to vary according to the type of scene depicted (although vase-painters are hardly perfectly consistent). Sourvinou-Inwood distinguishes two main categories: scenes in which Medea is seen killing the children and scenes of her escape after the killing. According to Sourvinou-Inwood, scenes showing the murder depict Medea at the Greek end of the spectrum, while scenes that combine the murder with the magical chariot present her as more oriental. This could simply reflect Medea's costumes in the play, or, as Sourvinou-Inwood argues, it could indicate that by committing the murder she shows herself to be non-Greek.[52]

Sourvinou-Inwood herself, however, agrees that the dichotomy between murder and escape scenes is not completely clear-cut. Both the small number of extant vases and the imperfect correlation between the costumes and the scenes depicted undermine Sourvinou-Inwood's argument. The Underworld Painter's krater provides a problematic example (see fig. 8). According to Sourvinou-Inwood's equation, Kreon's sleeves, which match Medea's, show the Greek king's guilt through the metaphor of orientalism.[53] The ghost of Medea's father, Aetes, also wears an oriental costume, which in his case simply denotes his actual foreignness. How can the oriental features of Medea's costumes then be understood as metaphorical? Is she wearing oriental dress because she is guilty of a "barbarian" act? Or is she wearing oriental dress because she is foreign?[54] How can we detect the "metaphor of orientalism" in the visual depictions of a character who is defined as alien? In many ways, it is Medea in Greek dress that remains to be explained.

Does the wearing of costumes similar to theater costumes by some characters on South Italian paintings necessarily mean that they depict scenes directly derived *from* tragedy? While it is likely that theater costumes influenced such depictions, we should be careful to distinguish between the origins of a practice and its later function.[55] Regardless of the controversy about the link between drama and these representations, we should also note that most of the vases depict scenes that could not have been staged: the killing of the children and the escape of Medea in a magical chariot drawn by serpents, for obvious reasons, would not have been part of the staged story.

The link between vase-painting and tragedy, then, cannot be taken for granted. Vases are not photographic records or illustrations of performances, but narratives in themselves. Vase-painters, like poets, are interested in telling a story. There is no need to assume that a particular tragedy could be the only

source for the iconography on a particular vase. Tragedy is one way of expressing myth, vase-painting another; both artists—playwright and painter—draw
on a common stock of stories that were part of traditional narratives handed
down through poetry—be it epic, tragic, or lyric—and iconography (sculpture,
painting, and even architecture).[56]

The vases, statues, and sarcophagi offer their own telling of the myth. Like
the poetic versions, the visual representations use a common stock of motifs.
Whereas the written sources emphasize ritual and sacred vocabulary, the
visual sources offer visual clues. The altar is a recurrent motif that recalls the
religious dimensions of the myth (a motif that we will encounter again in
depictions of another child hero, Opheltes; see chap. 3).[57] Often the children
are shown playing on an altar or taking refuge on an altar right before Medea
catches them, or, finally, Medea is shown slaughtering them on an altar, almost
as if she had deliberately chosen the location of the murder. The killing of the
children at the altar both intensifies the transgression and sacralizes the act
of murder. The element of fear symbolized by the figure of Deima in the literary source is expressed by the fallen hydria in the visual sources. The other
element emphasized in many of the representations is grief: figures are shown
with their arms lifted in a gesture characteristic of mourning. This is perhaps
not surprising considering the function of South Italian vases, which, after
being displayed prominently during a funeral, would be placed in graves.
Mourning—in the case of both vases and sarcophagi—is appropriate both
to the function of the object and to the story it depicts. Thus we find in the
visual sources the same elements we found in the written sources: violence,
transgression, sacred space, fear, and mourning ritual.

❑

Let us turn to the archaeological evidence for the cult in honor of the dead
children. There is some disagreement about the location of the temple of
Hera Akraia, where the cult took place according to the literary sources. Some,
following the description of Pausanias, assume that the temple had to be
within the city limits of Corinth, near the *mnēma* for the children. Others,
however, locate it elsewhere, in Acrocorinth or at Perachora.[58]

The scholiast's hypothesis *ad Medea* 9 that the temple of Hera Akraia must
be located at Acrocorinth can be discarded at the outset. Although the epi-
thet for Hera Akraia, "dwelling on the heights," leads some to believe that the
temple was built on the heights of Acrocorinth,[59] archaeology refutes this
assumption: the only temple for Hera at Acrocorinth is dedicated to Hera
Bounaia. Literary sources concur, since Pausanias also describes the temple
of Hera Bounaia and makes no reference to Medea or her children. Instead

he tells how the temple at Acrocorinth was set up by Bounos son of Hermes, which makes it unlikely that this temple could have been associated with the cult of Hera Akraia (2.4.7). The epiclesis Akraia, in fact, has nothing to do with the location of the temple, but was brought to Corinth when the cult was imported from Hera's sanctuary in Argos.[60]

As we saw above, Pausanias locates monuments commemorating the death of the children of Medea within the city of Corinth. On the road from the agora to Sikyon, not far from a temple of Apollo, is the well of Glauke, in which the princess is supposed to have thrown herself to alleviate the pain caused by Medea's poisons; above the well is the Odeion, next to which is the *mnēma* for the children of Medea (2.3.6).

The *mnēma* for the children has not been excavated, but some make a case for a sanctuary in Corinth. Scranton, for example, argues for an archaic sanctuary built by the fountain of Glauke where mimetic dances and a reenactment of the death of Glauke would have taken place.[61] The other, more likely, candidate for the location for the ritual in honor of the children of Medea is the temple of Hera Akraia at Perachora, across the Corinthian bay. Whether the cult in honor of the children was divided between Perachora and Corinth or whether it all took place at Perachora, the sanctuary of Hera at Perachora was probably the focus of the ritual of segregation of the fourteen Corinthian children chosen annually to spend a year propitiating the goddess, while some of the rites were located in Corinth, where the *mnēma* of the children is.[62]

How do the different elements of the myths fit with what we know about the rituals? We know, in fact, very little about the cult itself. The literary sources give different aetiologies for the ritual, and the role of Hera is on the surface confusing. The ancient sources—both literary and visual—emphasize the violent and transgressive nature of the deaths. The emphasis of the written sources seems to be on the expiatory and mourning aspects, while the descriptions of the rites stress initiatory elements: as we have seen, the haircutting, the special clothing, and the yearlong segregation of the fourteen children are all elements that are typical of initiation rites.[63]

Parmeniskos mentions the rite of the annual segregation of seven boys and seven girls, while Pausanias—silent about the yearly rite of choosing fourteen children in the sanctuary of Hera Akraia—provides the details about the children cutting their hair and wearing dark clothes. Diodorus Siculus and Aelian speak of heroic sacrifices (*timē hērōikē, enagizein*). Philostratos and the scholiast to the *Medea* talk of the initiatory and mourning character of the rituals, but without giving details. All this amounts to too little for us to reconstruct the cult with any certainty, and scholars interpret the evidence in different ways. As Brelich notes, the lack of evidence makes it impossible to understand the cult in isolation, and a comparative approach is necessary to achieve a fuller understanding of its nature.[64] Brelich concludes that although the cult for the children of Medea shows some initiatory aspects, it is not in itself an initiatory ritual, but part of the public cult of Hera and the child heroes who are purportedly buried in her sanctuary.[65] The cult of the children of Medea is also interpreted by others as both an initiation rite and an apotropaic ritual to protect children.[66]

One motif of the myth indeed has strong links with initiation rituals. Both Eumelos and the scholiast to Pindar's *Olympian* 13 report that Medea tries to make her children immortal: Eumelos specifies that Medea brings each of the children to the sanctuary of Hera and conceals (*katakryptein*) them there, while the scholiast tells of Hera's broken promise to make the children immortal. Interpretation of the story of the concealing of the children depends partly on what meaning we choose to give to *katakryptein*. While the verb basically means "to conceal," "to cover over," or "to hide," in some contexts, it can also mean "to bury."[67] This problem of the meaning of *katakryptein* is at the heart of many scholars' interpretation of the myth.

Like Brelich, I take *katakryptein* to refer to hiding and concealing in an initiatory context. Segregation of an initiatory nature is sometimes understood as concealment (as in the Spartan *krypteia*).[68] This motif of concealing is also reminiscent of myths of attempted immortalization of human children by "concealing" them in the fire.[69] Just like Demeter with Baby Demophon and Thetis with Baby Achilles, Medea attempts—and spectacularly fails—to make her children immortal.[70] In all these myths, the emphasis is on a failed attempt to change the status of mortal children. Yet the mythical failure can also be understood in terms of a successful change of status in ritual terms, and a mythical death can very well translate into a successful initiation.

One interesting element of the ritual in honor of the children is the number seven. There is a parallel in Pausanias's description of a Sikyonian ritual involving seven boys and seven girls.[71] Pausanias describes a sanctuary of Persuasion (*Peithō*) that stands in the agora of Sikyon. The cult of Persuasion started when Apollo and Artemis came to Aigialeia (the ancient name of Sikyon) to seek purification after they killed the Python in Delphi. They were struck with dread in a place now named Fear (*Phobon*) and turned aside toward Karmanor in Crete. A plague (*nosos*) came upon the people of Aigialeia. Seers ordered them to propitiate Apollo and Artemis, and they sent seven boys and seven girls as suppliants to the river Sythas. The two gods were persuaded by them and came to the place that is now the sanctuary of Persuasion. Pausanias says that the same ritual was still performed in his day and that children reenacted the story by going to the river Sythas during the festival of Apollo: the children say that they bring the gods back to the sanctuary of Persuasion and then on to the temple of Apollo (Pausanias 2.7.7–8). Pausanias adds that this temple of Apollo was supposedly built by Proitos because his daughters had recovered from their madness in this place. Meleager's spear and Marsyas's pipe were also dedicated there, though they were all destroyed by a fire prior to Pausanias's coming (2.7.9). While these details may seem irrelevant at first, as Brelich notes, they all have an initiatory backdrop.[72]

In both cities, at Corinth and at Sikyon, a terrible sickness seizes the inhabitants; in both cases, the oracle orders the citizens to choose seven boys and seven girls. The children are entrusted with representing their city and saving it from the plague, a plague that is closely associated with a violent death. Reenactment is central to both rituals. The Corinthian ritual reenacts in some ways the very incident it is supposed to atone for: the killing of the children of Medea is symbolically represented by the seclusion of the fourteen children. The Corinthians ritually reproduce the original crime, while the children undergo metaphorical death in the ritual that commemorates the actual death of the children of Medea.[73]

Many other myths deal with groups of children who are killed by close relatives (or through their parents' fault) or by citizens of a given town. The death of the children of Khalkis may function as a foil to myths of townspeople guilty of killing children.

"What is the children's tomb by Khalkis?" asks Plutarch in one of his *Greek Questions* (296d). In answer, Plutarch tells the story of Kothos and Aiklos, sons of Xouthos, and how they came to dwell (*oikēsontes*) in Euboea when the Aeolians owned the greater part of the island. A prophecy was made to Kothos that he would have much success and overcome his enemies if he bought the land. When he landed on the island with his men, he encountered children playing by the sea. The children are still small (*paidarioi*), and they are playing (*paizein*). Both the words used to describe the children and their behavior establish them as very young (296d–e). Just as Baby Dionysos, in another myth, is tricked by the Titans' charming toys, the children of Khalkis cannot resist the stranger's toys (*paignia polla;* see Clement of Alexandria, *Protreptikos* 2.15). When Kothos sees how eager the children are to obtain his gifts, he refuses to give them unless they give him some earth in exchange, and so the children pick up some earth from the ground and give it to him, thereby "selling" the land to him; the children then leave, taking the toys with them. When the Aeolians later discover what happened and as their enemies start sailing against them, they become enraged and kill the children (296e).

The manner in which the children die is similar to the way in which the children of Kaphyai and the children of Medea find their death: in both cases the children do something inappropriate (playing with a goddess's statue, accepting gifts from an ill-intentioned stranger), and in both cases the citizens of their town react in an even more inappropriate way, killing them. The Kaphyaians and the Corinthians indeed kill the children violently and "unjustly," but even less justly, they do not acknowledge the transgression inherent in their actions and deprive their young victims of proper burial. The citizens of Khalkis, however, immediately bury the children and thus avoid the kind of dreadful consequences that the citizens of Kaphyai (or of Corinth for that matter) have to face. The act of giving a funeral in itself includes an act of atonement.

Pausanias also records other traditions concerning Medea and her children, and one particularly interesting tradition is that of Kinaithon of Lakedaimon (sixth century B.C.), a composer of genealogies, who identified Medea's children by Jason as a son, Medeios, and a daughter, Eriopis, although he gives no further information about the children (2.3.9 = fr. 2 Bernabé). While the majority of the sources describe the children as male, it is significant that some traditions, such as Kinaithon and Parmeniskos, identify one or several of Medea's children as female.

The death of the children of Medea, whether killed by the citizens of Corinth or by their own mother, serves as an aetiological myth for a ritual that includes both mourning and initiatory rites. The story is an expression of a mother's darkest fears: children are left within sacred space (here at the altar or in the sanctuary of Hera Akraia) for their protection, only to be killed in the most violent fashion. What was supposed to protect the children is the cause of their death. Fear is symbolized by the figure of Deima, which is set up in Corinth to commemorate the death of the children. Both the statue of Deima in Corinth and the motif of the fallen hydria—conspicuously displayed on the foreground of the Cleveland krater (see fig. 2) as though the old nurse had dropped it on her way from the fountain—symbolize the primal parental fear expressed in the religious narrative of the death of the children.

The sources that describe the story of the death of the children of Medea stress different aspects of the story. In the early Greek sources (Euripides as well as the scholia to Pindar and to Euripides), we find an emphasis on the ritual and its aetiology. The scholia to Pindar give an explanation for the establishment of the ritual, and Kreophylos, via the scholia to Euripides, gives the details about the seven boys and seven girls chosen every year to live in the sanctuary of Hera. There is a sacralization of the myth and a focus on ritual vocabulary. *Hieron, temenos, katakryptein, thaptein, heortē,* and *telē* are the keywords in these accounts. This emphasis on sacred space, funeral and heroic honors is picked up by later authors such as Diodorus Siculus, who uses similar ritual vocabulary (*temenos, thaptein, timē herōikēnone*). There is an obvious difference between authors who tell the aetiological myth (Euripides) and those who give an account of the ritual itself and report what they describe as facts (Pausanias and Aelian). Pausanias, in fact, is the one who brings everything together—the story, the ritual, the sacred space dedicated to commemorating the mythical (yet historical from a Greek perspective) event and space.

When we come to the Roman writers, we see a noticeable lack of interest in the ritual. Ovid and Seneca are interested in Medea as a character and focus their poetry on her and her deeds. They are interested in the murder of the children only insofar as it says something about Medea, but the religious consequences of her transgression are not explored. With Philostratos, however, we find a renewed interest in cult. The *Heroikos* is devoted to the proper practice (and proper beliefs) of hero cult. Philostratos introduces the intriguing notion that the cult in honor of the children of Medea is a mixture of different kinds of rituals, at once heroic and initiatory. He also emphasizes the importance of singing laments and hymns in the context of hero cults in general and in the context of the cult of the children of Medea. Even more enticing is his comparison of the cult in honor of the children of Medea to that of another child hero, Baby Melikertes. We will come back to this passage in the course of our examination of child-hero cults.

From the archaic period on, the killing of the children of Medea is a popular subject for artists and writers. Despite the differences in details, the basic story remains constant and the same elements are highlighted throughout: violence, transgression, violation of sacred space, the inevitability of the victims' wish for vengeance, and the need to establish a ritual in compensation for the transgression, which all lead to mourning.

Whether Medea is explicitly guilty or whether her actions accidentally cause the children's deaths seems to reflect different local traditions. In the early versions (Eumelos's *Korinthiaka* and the traditions reported in the scholia to Euripides), Medea's children die because of her status as a foreign princess or because of her attempt to immortalize or protect them. In both cases, a mother attempting to shelter her children from death causes their demise. After Euripides, the focus is often on Medea as a killer. Yet in Corinth, where the cult takes place, the emphasis is on the children and on the shared guilt of the Corinthians, more specifically on the shared guilt of the Corinthian mothers who kill the children of Medea, only to see their own offspring die as a consequence. The myth, like other narratives of child heroes, evokes fear, especially a mother's fear, yet as we will see in the following chapters, these myths also always offer the possibility for atonement. The children of Corinth remember the children of Medea by performing annual rites in their honor, and the survivors mark their own survival by keeping alive the memory of the dead children.

# CHAPTER 2

# The Children
# of Herakles

The Theban myth of the madness of Herakles echoes many of the same themes we saw in the narrative of Medea killing her children: parental violence, violation of sacred space, and the need for compensating unjust deaths. The myth of the children of Herakles is also chronologically and thematically linked to the story of Medea's children: after Medea slays her offspring, she flees to Thebes; there she finds Herakles in a fit of madness just as he is killing his children and cures him (Diodorus Siculus 4.55.4). Some details, such as the number, age, and gender of children or the exact manner of their deaths, vary according to different sources.[1] Some authors describe Herakles' madness as the result of Hera's jealousy because he is the result of one of Zeus's illicit liaisons, thus Herakles' very existence is an affront to her. Herakles' children are either shot with arrows, have their skull smashed with a club, or are thrown on a burning pyre. Because different versions disagree, it is impossible to locate this event precisely in the chronology of Herakles' deeds, but regardless of the exact sequence of events, the essential facts remain: Herakles kills his children, and a cult devoted to them—including athletic games—is subsequently established in Thebes.

First let us look at the literary sources. Although the story of Herakles killing his children does not appear in Homeric epic, Herakles' wife, Megara, is mentioned in Odysseus's catalogue of heroines as the daughter of "proud

Kreon, whom the strong and unyielding son of Amphitryon [Herakles] had married" (*Odyssey* 11.269–70). Herakles himself, or rather his *eidōlon* (11.601), appears at the end of Odysseus's visit to the underworld in *Odyssey* 11, "lamenting" (*olophyromenos;* 11.615), as he compares his tragic destiny to that of Odysseus. Herakles does not say anything about his children, but he talks of his labors and describes his life as endless suffering (*oizys . . . apeiresiē;* 11.620–21). Although not explicitly acknowledged in Homeric epic, the myth of Herakles killing his children is compatible with the tradition described in the *Odyssey,* and Megara is consistently linked with the dead children in later sources. Eustathios, for example, specifies that Megara and Herakles had three children, all of whom Herakles killed because of the madness sent by Hera, just after he killed Lykos, who was tormenting Megara and the children during Herakles' absence (Eustathios 1683, 38).

The madness of Herakles appears in the epic cycle. According to Proklos's summary of the *Kypria,* Nestor mentions Herakles in a digression that tells of Epopeus killing the daughter of Lykourgos, the story of Oedipus, the madness of Herakles, and the story of Theseus and Ariadne.[2] Proklos offers no details about Herakles' madness or its consequences, but Nestor's digression forms a parallel to, or rather a mirror image of, Odysseus's catalogue of heroines in *Odyssey* 11: Antiope and Epopeus, Epikaste and Oedipus, Megara and Herakles, and Ariadne and Theseus and their stories are part of both passages, and thus we can deduce that the murder of the children was also included. In other words, the murder of the children is not explicitly mentioned, but the madness of Herakles doubtless refers to this episode. The story of Herakles killing his children by Megara, then, seems to be part of a tradition already included in catalogues such as the ones we find in the *Odyssey* and the epic cycle.

We know that the sixth-century B.C. lyric poet Stesikhoros composed a poem about the adventures of Herakles and that Panyassis (fifth century B.C.) wrote an epic in fourteen books about Herakles. Unfortunately, only very few fragments are left from these two poets, but Pausanias reports that their accounts of the death of the children are similar to what the Thebans still tell in his day when they show him the memorial in their honor (Pausanias 9.11.2 = Stesikhoros 230 *PMG;* Panyassis fr. 1 Bernabé).

One important early literary source for the myth of the children of Herakles as well as the ritual in their honor is Pindar's fourth *Isthmian,* dated to the 470s B.C.:

τῷ μὲν 'Αλεκτρᾶν ὕπερθεν δαῖτα πορσύνοντες ἀστοί
καὶ νεόδματα στεφανώματα βωμῶν αὔξομεν

ἔμπυρα χαλκοαρᾶν ὀκτὼ θανόντων,
τοὺς Μεγάρα τέκε οἱ Κρεοντὶς υἱούς.
τοῖσιν ἐν δυθμαῖσιν αὐγᾶν
   φλόξ ἀνατελλομένα συνεχὲς παννυχίζει,
αἰθέρα κνισάεντι λακτίζοισα καπνῷ,

Beyond the Elektran [Gate], we the citizens offer him a feast
and we honor him with a wreath of newly built altars
<u>and burnt sacrifices for the bronze-armed ones,</u>
<u>the eight dead sons,</u> whom Megara, daughter of Kreon, bore him.
The flame, mounting up for them at dusk,
shines continuously through the night,
grazing the sky with its steamy smoke.
—Pindar, *Isthmian* 4.61–67

This gives us the first—and, in fact, only—classical reference to the cult for the children of Herakles. Pindar does not describe the manner of the death of the children, and, in the absence of other sources, it would be easy to conclude—especially in light of the adjective *khalkoarēs* (bronze-armed)—that they "grew to manhood and were slain in battle," a conclusion reached by many commentators, both ancient and modern.[3] The scholia already observe that Pindar uses the adjective "because the children of Herakles died fighting" or "violently" (Drachmann 3.237). Be that as it may, even though Pindar does not specify that Herakles' sons die as children, this myth was already known to the poet Stesikhoros in the sixth century B.C. and the story was also implicit in the epic cycle.

Herakles, of course, fathers other children who do reach adulthood and who could be fittingly described as "bronze-armed." Yet his children by Megara traditionally do not survive childhood, and by specifying that the heroes honored in Thebes are her sons, Pindar cannot fail to evoke the myth of Herakles killing his own children. Does Pindar reject or modify the story to distance Herakles from the murder?[4] Or is his silence on the children's age the result of a certain reluctance to tell myths describing the death of children? This is indeed reminiscent of Pindar's reluctance to accept the myth of the boiling of Pelops and of his efforts to refute (yet simultaneously attesting) that tradition in *Olympian* 1 (see chap. 4). Yet nothing in *Isthmian* 4 points to Pindar's rejection of a traditional myth, in contrast with *Olympian* 1, where he explicitly disallows the tradition.

In any case, Pindar's *Isthmian* 4 focuses on the cult rather than the myth and describes a Theban fire ritual in honor of the sons of Herakles. Burkert argues that this ritual was a "nocturnal fire festival which was really in honour of the sons of the strong ones, the Alkeidai, but the association with Heracles was never contradicted."[5] The fourth-century B.C. writer Menekrates explains the link between the children of Herakles and the Alkeidai and records that the children of Herakles were not called the Herakleidai, since their father was no longer called Herakles, but the Alkeidai, the "children of the Strong One" (*FGrH* 3 F 14); this is a mirror image of Apollodoros's account, which, as we will see below, tells of the opposite name change, from Alkeides to Herakles.

Pindar does not explain why the children of Herakles are honored with sacrifices and a nocturnal fire ritual, but he describes what happens after the nocturnal fire festival:

καὶ δεύτερον ἆμαρ ἐτείων τέρμ᾽ ἀέθλων
γίνεται, ἰσχύος ἔργον.

And the second day is the time of the annual <u>athletic contests,</u>
a feat of might.
—Pindar, *Isthmian* 4.67–68

Pindar's description of the Theban Games, along with the mythic tradition of Herakles killing his children in a moment of madness known from other literary sources, all point to the existence of athletic funeral games established in honor of the dead children near the site of their deaths in Thebes. This is an important point, since we will see later that child heroes are the focus not only of local athletic competitions, but also of some of the most important Panhellenic athletic contests. The scholia to Pindar's *Isthmian* 4 further comment on the rituals, specifying that the Thebans both offer heroic honors (*enagizein*) to the children near the house of Amphitryon by the Elektran Gate—where Herakles brought the bodies after killing his children—and hold funeral games (*agōnes epitaphioi*) for them every year.[6]

The scholia also record several slightly different versions of the story, including various traditions regarding the names and number of the children. Among these is preserved a fragment from Pherekydes of Athens (fifth century B.C.) that describes Herakles throwing his five children in a fire:

λέγων αὐτοὺς <u>εἰς τὸ πῦρ</u> ὑπὸ τοῦ πατρὸς <u>ἐμβεβλῆσθαι</u>.

He says that they <u>were thrown into the fire</u> by their father.
—schol. Pindar, *Isthmian* 4.104g (Drachmann 3.238 = *FGrH* 3 F 14)

Destruction by fire is indeed an important theme in Greek myth. Fire can be used either to destroy or to strengthen, and fathers and mothers use it for very different purposes. As we saw in chapter 1 and shall explore in more detail in subsequent chapters, women—mothers, nurses—put children in fire as a means of making them immortal, while men use fire as a means of destruction.[7]

Herakles is clearly the sole murderer of his children in Pherekydes' account, yet, although Herakles is the usual perpetrator, a few other versions exist in which the children die by another's hand. According to Lysimakhos (schol. Pindar, Drachmann 3.237), the children are treacherously killed by strangers, while Socrates (schol. Pindar, Drachmann 3.237) points to Augeas as the murderer. Already in these early versions preserved by the scholia to Pindar, the murder of the children is the focus of the myth. Regardless of the killer's identity (as in the case of the death of Medea's children), the children die a violent death of the kind that requires atonement.

In his *Herakles Mainomenos* (dated to 414 B.C.), Euripides places the murders after the labors, perhaps "so that earlier triumphs can be followed by tragedy."[8] As the play begins, Herakles is still performing his last labor. Meanwhile, Megara, her three children by Herakles, and Amphitryon are besieged by the new king Lykos, who wants to kill them. By the middle of the play, the children have been prepared for their deaths, and everything seems lost. Herakles, however, appears at the last minute and saves his family, but not for long.

*Teknon,* the word most often used by Megara and Herakles to describe their children in the play, is the same one we saw used of Medea's children and the same one we will see used of other child heroes such as Opheltes and Melikertes. It often denotes young children, and although it is impossible to pinpoint with precision the ages of the children in the play, it is clear that they are little. Some of them are old enough to speak, and Megara describes them as "baffled in their youth" (75). Yet, they are small enough so that Megara can drag them after her all at the same time (445), and one child, at least, is light enough so that Megara can grab and carry him as she tries to escape her maddened husband.

In the last quarter of the play, Madness (*Lyssa*), urged on by Hera's messenger, Iris, comes upon the house of Herakles. Madness (somewhat reluctantly) incites him to attack his own children. The messenger describes the killings:

φαρέτραν δ' εὐτρεπῆ σκευάζεται
καὶ τόξ' ἑαυτοῦ παισί, τοὺς Εὐρυσθέως
δοκῶν φονεύειν. οἱ δὲ ταρβοῦντες φόβῳ
ὤρουον ἄλλος ἄλλοσ', ἐς πέπλους ὁ μὲν
μητρὸς ταλαίνης, ὁ δ' ὑπὸ κίονος σκιάν,
ἄλλος δὲ βωμὸν ὄρνις ὡς ἔπτηξ' ὕπο.

> And he readied his <u>quiver</u>
> <u>and arrows</u> against his own children,
> thinking that he was killing the children of Eurystheus.
> They, <u>in fear</u>, rushed in all directions,
> one to the robes of his wretched mother, the other in the shade of a
>     column,
> and the third to the foot of an <u>altar</u>, cowering like a bird.
> —Euripides, *Herakles* 969–74

The children try to hide, but Herakles in his deluded state is keen on destroying what he thinks are his enemy's children, and he slays his sons systematically, one by one. He first hunts for the child hiding behind the column and shoots him through the heart (979). He then goes on to the boy cowering by the altar. The child seizes his father's knees and begs him not to kill him, but Herakles, realizing that he is too close to shoot him with an arrow, smashes the boy's skull with his club (993). Megara snatches the third child and attempts to escape. Yet Megara does not flee outside, but instead seeks refuge inside a room, barring the door behind her (996). This hardly stops Herakles. He digs under the door, breaks it open, and slays both mother and child with a single arrow (1000). As he slays his first victim, Herakles cries *alala* (981), a war cry, and boasts that he killed his enemy's child. Clearly Euripides takes great care to depict each murder as a different transgression: hunting a child, killing a suppliant, and hunting (and metaphorically violating) a young woman holding a baby.[9] Herakles then prepares to murder his own father, but he is prevented from completely annihilating his family by Athena, who stops him by throwing a stone at him. At this point, Herakles falls into a deep, unnatural, sleep (1005).

The scholia to Homer preserve another fourth-century B.C. version recorded by Asklepiades of Tragilos, a mythographer especially interested in myths as they appear in tragedy (*FGrH* 12 F 27). His account resembles—indeed perhaps follows—Euripides' version of the events: while Herakles is in Hades, King Lykos of Thebes prepares to sacrifice the children of Herakles and Megara, thinking that Herakles will not be able to intervene. But Herakles unexpectedly comes back and does away with Lykos and his children. Later, Hera strikes Herakles with madness, and he slays his own children. Herakles would also have killed his twin brother, Iphikles, were it not for Athena's intervention.

The second-century B.C. poet Moskhos composed a dialogue, the *Megara*, between Herakles, his wife Megara, and her mother-in-law Alkmene. Although, in most other versions of the story, Megara does not survive, in this one she does and provides an eyewitness account of Herakles' madness and the deaths of their children. Megara does not offer any specific explanation for Herakles' madness beyond describing the arrows he shoots at his children as the missiles from one of the goddesses of Death or an Erinys:

σχέτλιος, ὃς <u>τόξοισιν</u>, ἅ οἱ πόρεν αὐτὸς Ἀπόλλων,
ἠέ τινος Κηρῶν ἢ Ἐρινύος <u>αἰνὰ βέλεμνα</u>,
<u>παῖδας ἑοὺς κατέπεφνε</u> καὶ ἐκ φίλον εἵλετο θυμὸν
<u>μαινόμενος</u> κατὰ οἶκον, ὃ δ' ἔμπλεος ἔσκε <u>φόνοιο</u>.

Wretched one, who shot and <u>killed his own children</u>
with the <u>arrows</u> which Apollo himself gave him, the <u>dread darts</u>
of one of the goddesses of Death or of an Erinys, and he deprived them
    of their life,
<u>raging</u> through the house and filling it with <u>murder</u>.
—Moskhos, *Megara* 13–16

Megara emphasizes Herakles' madness (*mainomenos*). Emotion also attaches itself to the weapons that Herakles uses: his arrows are "dread" (*aina belemna*) and, according to Megara, belong to one of the goddesses of Death or an Erinys. Herakles rages through the house and fills it with blood and death. Megara later also specifies that the children are buried in Thebes, an important detail for the ritual.

Lykophron (second century B.C.) calls Herakles the Child Destroyer (*Teknoraistēs*) (*Alexandra* 38), and the scholia explain the name with reference to Herakles killing his own children by Megara. The different versions recorded there resemble Euripides', and again we find Lykos seizing the city and attempting to kill Megara and her children, although there are more children (four) here than in Euripides' play. The scholia to Lykophron also add that Pindar says that Herakles slew his children by Megara, which seems to confirm that Pindar was aware of the story.

The scholia to Lykophron also report versions that have Herakles kill the children of his brother Iphikles alongside his own. We find an echo of this version in the first-century B.C. historian Nicolaus of Damascus, in which Herakles in his madness first kills two of Iphikles' sons. Another of Herakles' nephews, Iolaos, is saved by his father. Then, Herakles kills his sons by Megara, of whom the youngest is still nursing, and he would also have killed Megara herself had it not been for the intervention of Iphikles (*FGrH* 90.13).

Diodorus Siculus (first century B.C.) places the death of the children of Herakles between the latter's victory over the Minyans and the labors, but he ascribes Herakles' madness to a different cause. Right after overcoming the Minyans, Herakles is summoned by Eurystheus and later by Zeus as well. Herakles is upset by Zeus's command, and he seeks the advice of the oracle at

Delphi. The oracle tells him that the gods have decided he should perform twelve labors at the behest of Eurystheus and that this will bring him immortality.

After consulting the oracle, Herakles returns home and hesitates between two courses of action: should he obey Zeus's orders and enter the service of Eurystheus and perform the labors, or should he disobey his divine father? Hera chooses this moment to strike him with a raging madness (*lytta*). Herakles attacks Iolaos, but his nephew successfully escapes; Herakles' children, however, do not:

καὶ τῶν παίδων τῶν ἐκ Μεγάρας πλησίον διατριβόντων, <u>τούτους ὡς</u> <u>πολεμίους κατετόξευσε</u>.

But his children by Megara were nearby, and <u>he shot them with arrows as if</u> <u>they were enemies</u>.
—Diodorus Siculus 4.11.1

Herakles in his delusion mistakes his sons for enemies. This is a common pattern: other parents, similarly misguided, mistake their children for animal prey. Athamas (see chap. 6), for example, is deluded by Hera into hunting his own children as if they were prey (and another Theban, Agave, is tricked into mistaking her son Pentheus for a lion). Herakles eventually comes out of his mad frenzy and realizes what he has done. He becomes despondent over his deeds and isolates himself in his house, avoiding contact with others. With time, his grief lessens, and he decides to obey Zeus's order and present himself at the court of Eurystheus (4.11.2). Thus the labors, although they were enjoined on Herakles *before* he kills his children, become a way of atoning for his transgression.

Seneca (first century A.D.) reproduces, with some modifications, Euripides' triple murders in his version of the events: thinking that he is attacking Lykos's children, Herakles kills his first victim with an arrow; the two other children subsequently try to flee their crazed father, but Herakles catches one of them and, despite the child's supplication, kills him by smashing his head on the wall; Megara seizes the last survivor and runs away, but the third child dies of terror in her arms.[10] Herakles then kills his wife with his club. This variegated way of killing his family is reminiscent of Euripides' account.

In Apollodoros's account (first or second century A.D.), Herakles kills his children just after his battle against the Minyans:

μετὰ δὲ τὴν πρὸς Μινύας μάχην συνέβη αὐτῷ κατὰ ζῆλον Ἥρας μανῆναι καὶ τούς τε ἰδίους παῖδας, οὓς ἐκ Μεγάρας εἶχεν, <u>εἰς πῦρ</u> <u>ἐμβαλεῖν</u> καὶ τῶν Ἰφικλέους δύο.

After the battle against the Minyans, Herakles was driven mad because of Hera's jealousy, and he <u>threw</u> his own children from Megara <u>into the fire,</u> as well as two of Iphikles' children.
—Apollodoros, *Library* 2.4.12

Apollodoros's account agrees with Pherekydes': Herakles kills his children by throwing them in the fire. After he kills the children, Herakles condemns himself to exile, is purified by Thespios, and asks the oracle at Delphi where he should dwell. The Pythian priestess changes his name from Alkeides to Herakles and tells him to go to Tiryns in order to serve Eurystheus for twelve years and accomplish the ten labors that will allow him to become an immortal. Thus there seems to be two variants on the theme of Herakles killing his children: the "tragic" way in which he kills his children and wife with various weapons (arrows, skull smashing, club), which we find in Euripides and Seneca as well as in Moskhos and Diodorus (arrows only), and throwing the children in the fire, which we find in Pherekydes of Athens and Apollodoros's *Library.*

Although there are countless ancient representations of Herakles, especially of his labors, few of the extant images show his madness or the murder of his children. All such representations date from the late fourth century B.C. and, like the vase-paintings representing the death of the children of Medea, are from Southern Italy.

The most well-known representation of the madness of Herakles is a Paestan red-figure calyx krater signed by Asteas from the late fourth century B.C. (fig. 15).[11] Herakles, carrying a small child in his arm, stands in the center. He turns toward an improvised pyre—a burning pile of furniture—on the left. Megara, on the right, watches the scene in terror, holding her left hand to her chest and her right to her head, in a gesture that denotes both panic and mourning. His nephew, Iolaos, and his mother, white-haired Alkmene, watch Herakles from a balcony above. Mania, to the left of Iolaos, also watches the scene from the balcony. All the characters' names are inscribed except for the child's. Although South Italian vases often deal with tragic themes, we can see immediately that the Asteas vase resembles the fifth-century B.C. version of the story by Pherekydes of Athens in which Herakles throws his children into the fire and that it does not bear any resemblance to the Euripidean version.[12]

A hydria has fallen to the ground between Herakles' legs. This is a detail we also encountered in one depiction of the death of the children of Medea (see fig. 2) and that we will see again in representations of the death of child heroes.

FIGURE 15. Paestan red-figure calyx krater signed by
Asteas from the late fourth century B.C. Madrid 11094.
Photograph courtesy of Archivo Fotográfico, Museo
Arqueológico Nacional, Madrid.

The fallen vessel occupies a central place in the image and, whether it was
dropped by Megara in her panic or thrown by Herakles in his madness, functions as a symbol of both violence and fear.

We saw in chapter 1 that one Apulian volute krater by the Dareios Painter
from the fourth century B.C. depicts both Herakles and Medea at Eleusis (see

chap. 1, fig. 3). Herakles first appears in an Eleusinian setting on vases from the mid-sixth century B.C. on, yet the presence of Medea is unique to this vase, and the episode shown here has no direct parallel in literary sources. It is unclear whether the children sitting on the altar are Medea's or Herakles' children or whether the scene takes place before or after their death.

We saw one link between Medea and Herakles and the deaths of their children. In Diodorus's account, Medea flees to Thebes after killing her children, only to find Herakles raving mad, just after he slew his own children (4.55.4). Medea cures Herakles from his madness with drugs (*pharmaka*). But while these events take place in Thebes according to Diodorus's account, the Medea on the Dareios vase is clearly in Eleusis, as indicated by the inscription on the *naiskos* (ELEUSIS TO IERON). It is possible, though unlikely, that the different episodes depicted on the vase take place in different locations, as argued by Schmidt: Iris, Herakles, and the children are in Thebes, while Medea is in Eleusis; the figure of the *paidagōgos* is used as a go-between signifying the absence of unity of time and place.[13] The figure of the *paidagōgos* also appears on the vase by the Dareios Painter depicting the mourning for Opheltes-Arkhemoros, where he may play the same role of go-between between the different episodes shown on the two registers (cf. chap. 3). We have also seen the figure of the *paidagōgos* in the visual representations of the death of Medea's children, and more generally, his presence may signify childhood. Be that as it may, the circumstances of the meeting of Herakles and Medea at Eleusis remain unexplained.

Another visual tradition focuses on the children of Herakles and their mother, Megara, in the underworld. All these representations, like the ones above, are Apulian vases from approximately 340 to 320 B.C. The vases depict Megara and her children among other famous underworld figures, such as Orpheus, Hekate, Herakles, and Kerberos. Neither Megara and her children nor Herakles is ever the focus of such scenes, which always portray a *naiskos* with Hades and Persephone in their center.

One such example is a volute krater depicting Megara and her two sons (fig. 16). On the upper-left side, Megara (name inscribed) sits and addresses her two sons (inscribed HERAKLEIDAI), who stand, looking toward their mother. One of them, wearing a crown, leans upon a tree and gestures with his left hand; the other embraces his brother's shoulders with his right arm, and his left hand rests on his mother's right knee. This figure is not crowned, and he wears a bandage around his chest, a recurrent attribute of the Herakleidai in this type of representation. The Herakleidai and Megara are represented here—as on the many other vases on which they appear—next to other figures known for their association with the underworld: below them

FIGURE 16. Apulian volute krater. Trendall and
Cambitoglou, *Red-Figured Vases of Apulia*, 1.431, 82.
Naples, Museo Nazionale 81666. Photograph by Singer,
courtesy of Deutsches Archäologisches Institut, Rome,
negative number 71.447.

stands Orpheus (name inscribed), playing his lyre, with two female figures,
who are inscribed POINAI, personified goddesses of vengeance.

Herakles himself appears on this vase as well, and this is a common combination. When he appears on the same vases on which Megara and her children are represented, Herakles is always shown as he captures Kerberos. Thus
the motif of Herakles' labors occurs side by side with the motif of his chil-

dren in Hades, and on these vases, Herakles is never depicted as the murderer of his children. Yet their presence in Hades must point to his guilt, since it is possible for Herakles and Megara and their children to be in Hades at the same time only if the madness precedes the labors, which is, in fact, the chronology preserved in most of the written sources (with the exception of Euripides, Asklepiades, and Hyginus).

Finally, we should note that Philostratos describes a painting of the madness of Herakles in his *Eikones.* Philostratos acknowledges Euripides' version of the events, and the painting he describes follows the play in many points: Megara, holding the last surviving child, hides in a room, while the two children whom Herakles has just killed lie dead on an altar. They have both been killed by arrows, a slight variation on Euripides' version, and tears still drench their cheeks. Servants surround Herakles and attempt to bind him. Philostratos emphasizes the madness of Herakles and describes him foaming at the mouth and "smiling in a terrible and alien way" (*meidiōn de blosyron kai xenon;* 2.3), not unlike Euripides' description of his "deranged laughter" (*gelōti parapeplēgmenoi;* 935).[14] Philostratos then goes on to describe the physical symptoms of his madness: roaring, swelling neck, and pulsating veins.

Thus the few extant visual representations show both versions of the children's death. On the Asteas krater, we see mad Herakles throwing a child on a pyre. Many South Italian vases by contrast depict Megara and her children in Hades, where the children's wounds and bandages point to the tragic tradition of Herakles shooting arrows and smashing their skulls. Before their deaths, the children are depicted as small children (a baby, in the case of the Asteas vase), while they become adolescents in scenes taking place in Hades. The evidence is too scanty to make much of this here, but I want to stress this dichotomy, as this is something we will find again in other visual narratives of child heroes. The vases also emphasize mourning: we see it in the gestures of grief on the Asteas vase, for example, or in the context of Hades and its residents on the vases depicting Megara and her sons. Fear and violence are symbolized again by the fallen hydria on the Asteas vase, while the altar places the murder within sacred space and sacralizes the violence and fear expressed in the myth, as it does in depictions of the death of the children of Medea.

Before we examine the archaeological evidence, I digress for a moment and examine another narrative that can serve as a foil to the myth of Herakles killing his children. The story of Niobe's children, for example, superficially resembles the myth of the death of the children of both Medea and Herakles, yet there are intriguing differences.

Niobe, daughter of Tantalos and sister of Pelops, boasts that she is more fertile and blessed than Leto, who had only two children. This incites Leto to send her children, Apollo and Artemis, to kill her mortal challenger's children and, in this way, dramatically demonstrate to the hubristic mother who is the happier of the two. Sources disagree on the number of Niobe's children, and ancient authors themselves remark on the absurd number of variations:[15] yet Apollodoros, Diodorus Siculus, Ovid, Hyginus, Lactantius, and the First Vatican Mythographer all agree that there were seven sons and seven daughters, while Homer counted six sons and six daughters. Whatever the number, the children are usually shot according to their sex: Apollo aims at the sons, while his sister Artemis slays the daughters. The children are thus killed directly by gods, in order to punish their mother.

One interesting variant on the story found in Parthenios (first century B.C.) makes Niobe the daughter of Assaon, not Tantalos, and the wife of Philottos. Niobe quarrels with Leto about who has the more beautiful children, and Leto devises a complex punishment: Niobe's husband is killed while hunting, and her father, Assaon, develops a passion for her and wants to marry her. Niobe refuses, and to avenge what he perceives as a slight, her father invites her sons to a feast and burns them to death. When she learns of her children's death, Niobe throws herself from a rock, and her father belatedly realizes the evil he has wrought and commits suicide (*Erotika Pathēmata* 33). Stern argues that the burning of the children is not simply coincidental, but shows "rather that he too is engaging in a perversion of the sacrificial ritual" following the pattern of Tantalos's perverted sacrifice of his son Pelops, something we shall come back to in the subsequent chapters.[16] The burning is of course also reminiscent of Herakles throwing one of his children into fire and of how fathers in myth use fire as a means of destruction. In Parthenios's account, Leto's role is only indirect, and the focus is on love and its destructive powers, a theme central to all the stories collected in the *Erotika Pathēmata*.

The sources disagree on the location and manner of burial of the children. The gods themselves bury the children in Sipylos in the *Iliad* (24.610–11), while according to Statius, Niobe carries their funereal urns up the mountain (*Thebaid* 6.124); Pausanias, on the other hand, reports that, like the children of Herakles, they have their graves in Thebes:

Θηβαίοις δὲ ἐνταῦθα καὶ τὰ μνήματα πεποίηται τῶν Ἀμφίονος παίδων, χωρὶς μὲν τῶν ἀρσένων, ἰδίᾳ δὲ ταῖς παρθένοις.

A memorial was made there for the children of Amphion, with the boys and the girls separated.
—Pausanias 9.16.7

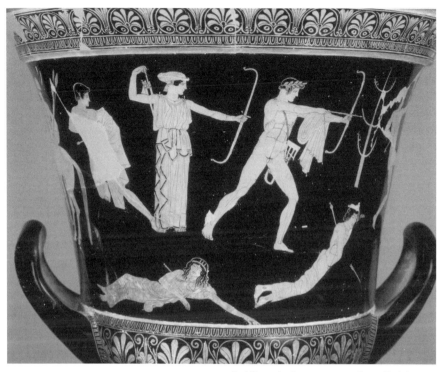

FIGURE 17. Red-figure krater, c. 450 B.C., from Orvieto. Louvre G 341. Musée du Louvre, Paris. Photograph by H. Lewandowski, © Réunion des Musées Nationaux / Art Resource, NY.

Whether the *mnēmata* for the children of Amphion in Thebes are literally their graves or cenotaphs commemorating their deaths,[17] Pausanias provides the intriguing detail that the *mnēmata* for the boys are separate from those for the girls. Most of the child heroes in this study are boys, but in some cases, like the children of Medea, there is a tradition that the children were of both sexes. The children of Medea, however, are always described as one group, and there were no different monuments according to their sex. The Theban separation of Niobe's sons and daughters could reflect that they had already reached puberty by the time of their death and thus had to be treated differently, in death as in life, than younger children would be.

On vases, the children of Niobe are typically depicted as adolescents. For example, on a red-figure krater of about 450 B.C., which might have been influenced by wall-painting (fig. 17), the gods are in the process of shooting the youths. A girl and a boy are lying dead on the lower register, while two others still stand on the upper part of the vase, on either side of Artemis and Apollo. The myth was also depicted on the throne of Zeus at Olympia, and it became popular on South Italian vases in the fourth century B.C.[18] Although the extant representations of this myth are few, the children of Niobe are consistently depicted as adolescents. The story has some similarities with that of Herakles, yet there are also obvious differences: the children are killed by gods, not by human parents. The stress is on the gods' power to destroy. Except for Parthenios's unique account, the children's death is understood as punishment. The mother is punished for her hubris, but the deaths does not involve any parental violence per se that needs to be atoned for.

When we turn back to the children of Herakles, compensation for their violent deaths is a key part of the myth. What do we know about the cult in their honor and the location of their graves? Pausanias refers to the tomb of the children several times in his guidebook to Greece. He first mentions it when he relates a controversy about where to bury Alkmene after her death at Megara: some want to carry her corpse back to Argos, while others want to bring her to Thebes, where her husband Amphitryon as well as Herakles' children by Megara are buried (1.41.1).

From Pausanias's description of his visit to Thebes, we know that the Thebans still displayed the *mnēma*—either their actual grave or a marker commemorating their deaths—of the children of Herakles and Megara (9.11.2). As we have seen above, Pausanias tells us most of what we know about the versions of the story by Stesikhoros and Panyassis, including those versions' essential similarity to what the Thebans still tell in Pausanias's day, with the exception that they now add the story of Herakles trying to kill his father Amphitryon.

According to the Thebans' account (which also happens to be similar to Euripides' version), the maddened Herakles also tries to kill his own father, but falls asleep after being struck by a rock. The Thebans have an explanation for the story and say that Athena herself threw the rock, which they nickname the Moderator (*Sōphronistēra*) (9.11.2). Right next to the tomb of the children, Pausanias describes a sanctuary of Herakles, the Herakleion (9.11.4). Beside the sanctuary is a gymnasium and stadium, both named after "the god" (*theos*) Herakles, as well as an altar of Apollo (9.11.7). Archaeologists have discussed the location of the site described by Pausanias, but have not excavated it to date.[19] The detail offered by Pausanias about the Sophronister (Moderator) stone is an important piece of information: the stone is placed by the gymnasium and stadium, thereby suggesting a link between the athletic games with the narrative of the madness of Herakles.

□

So far we have looked at a mother and a father who are responsible for their children's deaths. The children of Herakles, like those of Medea, die because of their parents: Medea's children are killed in revenge (be it by their mother or the citizens of Corinth), and the killing is powered by rage and anger; Herakles kills his children in a moment of madness, and here delusion, rage, and anger play a key role. Another link between the deaths of the children of Herakles and of Medea is the goddess Hera, who plays an important part in both myths, but is never directly involved with the children's deaths. By contrast, the gods themselves kill Niobe's offspring as punishment for their mother's hubris. Niobe is a helpless witness to her children's death, while Herakles (and Medea) are the direct (even if unwilling) cause of their children's deaths. Herakles is a masculine, distorted mirror image of Medea: where we had a mother motivated by the desire for revenge (or the desire for her children's immortality), we find a father who temporarily loses control. Herakles may not be entirely to blame for his madness, but madness (especially a father's madness, as we will see in coming chapters) is presented as a real danger.

Children suffer, at the mercy of their parents' desires and emotions. Madness leads to suffering and guilt, and the transgression of Herakles, like that of Medea, requires atonement. The literary narratives of the events ritualize the deaths of Herakles' children in terms of hunting, war, and sacrifice metaphors. In the visual representations, we find again the symbol of the fallen hydria as the visual equivalent of the ritualized emotion of fear in the face of violence and death. The madness and its dire consequences are memorialized with a ritual of mourning and athletic games: the citizens of Thebes compensate the children of Herakles for their violent deaths with a nocturnal fire ritual and athletic competitions. The Sophronister stone placed by the stadium ensures that the story of the death of the children is remembered by the athletes competing in the games. The madness of Herakles is thus commemorated and leads to mourning and remembrance of the children.

# CHAPTER 3

# Linos and Demophon

As we have seen in the preceding two chapters, children often attain heroic status through their indirect association with divine figures. Hera plays an important role in the heroization of the children of both Medea and Herakles, but the link can be even more direct, and in some myths, goddesses become explicitly involved with the process of heroization. Isis and Demeter in particular are associated with myths of children who die and become recipients of cult. In both cases, goddesses are entrusted with human babies, but, as they attempt to immortalize them, they cause the children's deaths and subsequent heroizations. Another child, Linos, the son of a god and a mortal woman, encounters a premature death and is avenged by his divine parent. I will start by looking at Baby Linos in more detail, then return to the myths of children who become heroes after they have failed to become gods, such as Demophon and the children of Astarte, and one child, Glaukos, who survives and therefore fails to become a child hero.

Let us start with Linos. Two heroes by the name Linos in Greek myth are sometime confused in the literary sources. The more renowned of the two, the Linos killed by Apollo because he tried to rival his singing, derives from Theban legend (see Hesiod fr. 305 Merkelbach and West; also Theokritos 24.105; Apollodoros 1.3.2; and Pausanias 9.29.3). The other, less well-known Linos, dies as a baby and becomes the recipient of a peculiar cult at Argos.

The grown-up Linos is a musician, but both he and the younger Linos are associated with mourning songs. Not only do these two heroes share the same name and the same association with music, but both were also buried in Argos (Pausanias 2.19.7).

The word *linos* describing a song appears in Homer (*Iliad* 18.570–71) and Herodotos (2.79), as well as in a fragment by Pindar (fr. 128c6 Maehler). Ancient authors associate the word with the cry *ailinon*. Chantraine notes that the only certainty about the word *linos* is precisely this association with the cry and with the singer of the same name, Linos.[1] While the word is often etymologically linked with the name of the mythic singer, the association between the song and the baby hero of the same name is often overlooked.

Farnell suggests an explanation for the existence of the two myths and two heroes of the same name. According to him, Baby Linos originally was "the young 'daimon' of verdure or vegetation who perishes in his prime, and is ceremoniously bewailed."[2] The *linos*-song originally sung to mourn Linos, Farnell argues, then becomes a song sung whenever any harvest is brought in, which explains its appearance in the *Iliad* 18.570–71,[3] where "the song grows ever in sweetness, till at last the name of Linos stands for the highest power of music; and a different story now arises, that his jealous art-rival Apollo slew him; he belongs no longer to the simple shepherd and bucolic folk, but to the company of the Muses who bewail him; and his name concerns the history of Greek lyric."[4]

This interpretation (and its reliance on the fertility motif) conflates the two figures and overlooks the two characters' happy coexistence in Greek myth and ritual. There is no need to postulate a chronological evolution in which one narrative transmutes into the other. This is, in fact, contradicted by the ancient evidence: the singer Linos already appears in Hesiod, and it is impossible to determine with any certainty to which Linos the *Iliad* passage refers. Moreover, the Argives show *both* tombs to Pausanias and feel no need to explain the reduplication of the names. Nevertheless Farnell makes an important point when he turns to the meaning of the name and its importance for the history of Greek lyric. I argue that the link with music and poetry is already present in the myth of Baby Linos, where death leads to mourning and, as we will see, to poetry.

The story of the death of Baby Linos survives in the mythographer Konon's *Diēgēseis* (first century B.C.) as well as in Pausanias (1.43.7).[5] In Konon's account, Psamathe, daughter of King Krotopos of Argos, gives birth to a child she conceived with Apollo. Because she is terrified of her father's reaction, she exposes the child in the countryside, where a shepherd finds him and starts to raise him as if he were his own son. The sheepdogs of Krotopos, however, soon come upon the baby and tear him apart. When Psamathe learns of her child's death, she is so overwhelmed that she cannot hide her grief from her father, who finds out what she did. Thinking that she behaved like a prostitute and lied to him about Apollo's role, he puts her to death. Apollo, angry at his lover's death, punishes the Argives with a plague.

In Pausanias's account, Apollo sends Poine, vengeance personified, to avenge his baby son's death.[6] Poine snatches children from their mothers and terrifies all the Argives, until a young man named Koroibos slays the monster. A second punishment in the form of a plague (*nosos loimōdēs*) falls upon the Argives. Koroibos then goes to Delphi to submit to Apollo's punishment for the killing of Poine, and the Pythia forbids him to go back to Argos and orders him instead to take a tripod and carry it away until the moment when the tripod falls from his hands and to build a temple of Apollo and live there. The tripod falls on Mount Geranion, near Megara, and there Koroibos founds the village called Tripodiskos.

I return now to Konon's account at the point where I left it, when the bane is sent by Apollo to punish the Argives for the death of Psamathe. The Argives consult the oracle, and they are told to conciliate (*ilaskesthai*) both Psamathe and Linos:

οἱ δὲ τά τε ἄλλα ἐτίμησαν αὐτοὺς καὶ γύναια ἅμα κόραις ἔπεμπον θρηνεῖν Λίνον. αἱ δὲ θρήνους ἀντιβολίαις μιγνῦσαι τάς τε ἐκείνων καὶ τὰς σφετέρας ἀνέκλαιον τύχας. καὶ οὕτως ἦν ἐκπρεπὴς ὁ ἐπὶ Λίνῳ θρῆνος, ὡς ἀπ' ἐκείνων καὶ τοῖς ἔπειτα ποιηταῖς παντὸς πάθους παρενθήκη Λίνος ᾄδεται. μῆνά τε ὠνόμασαν Ἀρνεῖον, ὅτι ἀρνάσι Λίνος συνανετράφη. καὶ θυσίαν ἄγουσι καὶ ἑορτὴν Ἀρνίδα, κτείνοντες ἐν ἐκείνῃ τῇ ἡμέραι καὶ κυνῶν ὅσους ἂν εὕρωσι. καὶ οὐ δ' οὕτως ἐλώφα τὸ κακόν, ἕως Κρότοπος κατὰ χρησμὸν ἔλιπε τὸ Ἄργος καὶ κτίσας πόλιν ἐν τῇ Μεγαρίδι καὶ Τριποδίσκιον ἐπικαλέσας κατῴκησεν.

[The Argives] honor Psamathe and Linos in various ways, and among other honors they also send women and young girls to sing the dirge for Linos. They mix the dirge with prayers, and they weep for Linos's and Psamathe's fate as well as for their own. And thus the dirge for Linos was so preeminent that beginning with them the Linos is sung in connection with all kinds of sufferings by later poets. They also called a month Arneios [the month of the Lamb], because Linos was raised among the lambs. And they perform a sacrifice and hold the Festival of Arnis, and on that day they kill all the dogs they can find. But even so their problem did not go away until Krotopos left Argos on order of the oracle, and founded and inhabited a city he called Tripodiskion in the Megarid.
—Konon 26 F 1.19 (*FGrH*)

Krotopos's dogs are responsible for the baby's death in both Konon's and Pausanias's accounts, but Konon reports that it is Krotopos, Psamathe's father himself, not Koroibos, who is ordered to leave Argos and found Tripodiskos. Unlike Pausanias's narrative, this account completely omits Poine, and Konon does not specify the nature of the bane (*loimos*)[7] sent by Apollo to punish the Argives. Although Pausanias does not include the death of Psamathe, most versions agree with Konon: Krotopos puts his daughter to death upon learning of the birth of his grandson.[8]

Konon gives more details about the ritual, describing it as a mixture of crying and prayers and relating the dirge, the Linos-song, to the story of Baby Linos, as well as to the Argive ritual of killing dogs during the month Arneios. The ritualized dirge (*thrēnos*) leads to weeping (*anaklaiein*), and the performance of the ritual in honor of Linos brings about the creation of a special song, which subsequently is sung "in connection with all kinds of sufferings by later poets." Here Konon makes explicit the link between the death of a child, his subsequent heroization, and the transmigration of the narrative of his death into poetry.

The Roman writer Statius gives a poetic version of the story in his *Thebaid* (first century A.D.). Although writing in Latin at a later period, Statius's narrative includes many details that reflect Greek concern with hero cult. He starts his account by linking Apollo's visit to Argos with his killing of the Python at Delphi, since Apollo comes to the house of Krotopos to seek purification for the murder. Once there, however, he falls in love with Psamathe and seduces her near the river of Nemea. It is noteworthy that the pastoral seduction in the countryside of Nemea foreshadows the story of the bucolic death of Baby Opheltes, which Statius relates later in the *Thebaid* (see chap. 5). Psamathe later gives birth to a son, but because she is terrified of her father's reaction—knowing he would never forgive such a union—she decides to expose the baby far away in the country. Psamathe leaves her son among the flock of sheep, hoping the shepherd will take care of him.

This *locus amoenus* of course turns out to be a dangerous spot. The bucolic cradle formed by the grass and branches is not worthy of such a child, Statius tells us, and, in fact, the baby does not survive his stay in the sheep-pen. He is soon torn apart by the shepherd's dogs (*Thebaid* 1.582–90). The horrific scene of the dogs attacking the defenseless baby contrasts with the seemingly innocent, beautiful surroundings.

Statius follows the main incidents we already know from Konon and Pausanias. In his account, like Konon's and Pausanias's, Psamathe's father sends his daughter to her death, and Apollo creates a monster to avenge her. Statius does not name the monster, but gives a detailed description of the

creature: she has the face and chest of a young woman, but on her head is a
hissing serpent that divides her dark brow into two parts. The monster
stealthily enters Argive bedrooms to steal and devour newborn babies
(*Thebaid* 1.601–4). As in Pausanias's narrative, a young man named Koroibos
kills the monster. Statius offers a slightly different version of the consequences
of Koroibos's actions: Apollo is angry at the killing and sends a new plague
to Argos. The oracle tells the king that the only way to put an end to the plague
is to sacrifice Koroibos. Koroibos accepts his punishment and asks Apollo to
take pity on the rest of the city. Apollo is so impressed by the young man's
courage that he spares his life. Ever since then, Statius adds, solemn feasts are
held every year, with new honors offered to the temple of Apollo (1.666–68).

The monster, even though nameless, is clearly similar to the Poine
described by Pausanias.[9] And while Apollo purportedly sends the creature to
avenge Psamathe's death, the method of punishment cannot fail to evoke the
baby's death. We see here a pattern already familiar from the narrative of
the death of the children of Medea: the entire community is punished for the
child's death, and this collective guilt is atoned for by the establishment of an
annual civic festival.

One other account of the same story deserves attention, that of the First
Vatican Mythographer. In this Romanized version, Apollo rapes the daughter
of Krotopos, who is a priestess of Vesta and should have always remained a
virgin. Krotopos kills his daughter because of her violation. The monster sent
by Apollo to avenge the young woman's death is named Lamia in this account,
and a brave young man, Koroibos again, kills it (First Vatican Mythographer
2.66). And Statius elegantly relates the same story, adds the mythographer,
whose account is more interesting for what it conceals than for what it reveals.
Here, the daughter of Krotopos is transformed into a Roman priestess and is
made to die immediately after being raped by the god. There is no mention of
pregnancy, birth, or exposing a baby. Yet, the monster that Apollo chooses to
send as his revenge is, again, famous for snatching newborn babies away from
their mothers and devouring them.[10] The story of Linos is entirely suppressed,
and yet the consequences of his death are still present: another monster associated with killing babies is substituted for the monster Poine, but the punishment, again, is wrought upon newborns.

A fragment from Callimachus's *Aitia* refers to the Argos ritual as well:

> Ἀρνεῖος μ[
> Ἀρνῆδας[
> καὶ θάνε.[
> τοῦ μενα[
> καὶ τὸν ἐπὶ ῥάβδῳ μῦθον ὑφαινόμενον

ἀνέρες ε[
πλαγκτὺν[
ἠνεκὲς ἀείδω δειδεγμένος
ουδεμενα[
νύμφης αι[
παιδοφόνω[
ἧκεν ἐπ᾿ Ἀρ[γείους
ἤ σφεων[
μητέρας ἐξεκένωσεν, ἐκούφισθεν δὲ τιθῆναι
οὐχ οὕτω[
Ἄργος ἀνα[

Arneios . . .
of the lambs . . .
and <u>died</u>
. . . and the <u>story woven on the rhapsode's wand</u>
. . . men . . .
wandering . . .
<u>I received and sing continuously</u>
. . . of the nymph . . .
<u>child-killer</u>
sent against the Argives
. . . which their
. . . <u>made mothers empty and lightened the nurses</u>
[<u>from their burden</u>] . . .
not thus . . .
Argos.
—Callimachus, *Aitia* I fr. 26 (Pfeiffer)

Although the fragment is short, it appears to include all the major episodes of the story as we know it from other written sources. The fragment starts with a mention of the month Arneios and the days of the Lamb, in which the Argives celebrate the festival in honor of Linos (cf. Konon above). There is a death (line 3), probably that of Linos, and a *mythos* woven by the rhapsode's wand, which the poet-narrator has received and will sing continuously (lines 5–8). The *nymphē* (line 10) may be Psamathe, and the child slayer, *paidophonos* (line 11), either her father or the monster subsequently sent by Apollo to avenge her death.[11] The end of the fragment seems to describe the bane sent against the Argives by Apollo: mothers are left empty, and nurses are lightened from their burdens (lines 12–16).

Here again the emphasis is on the punishment of the Argives through the death of the city's young children. Konon already described the ritual killing of dogs at Argos, and we find it in Callimachus as well as in other writers:

Aelian (c. A.D. 170–235) notices that the inhabitants of Argos refuse to kill snakes, but have no problem killing dogs when they come near the agora during the days of the Lamb (*Nature of Animals* 12.34); Athenaios (second–third century A.D.) also describes the *Kynophontis,* the dog-slaughter holiday celebrated at Argos (*Deipnosophistai* 3.99). The ritual killing of dogs during the days of the Lamb, while it may be linked to other (mostly initiatory) rituals involving wolves, also include an apotropaic element aimed at protecting mothers and their young children from a dangerous demon—be it Poine or Lamia—who is an essential element of the narrative of Linos's death.[12] Even when the monster is not personalized—as in Konon's version—we know that a *loimos* (bane) strikes Argos, and as we have seen with the case of the children of Medea (see chap. 1), *loimos* often strikes infants.[13]

Another Callimachean fragment describes a child among the lambs:

ἄρνες τοι, φίλε κοῦρε, συνήλικες, ἄρνες ἑταῖροι
ἔσκον, ἐνιαυθμοὶ δ' αὔλια καὶ βοτάναι.

Lambs, sweet boy, were your playmates, lambs were
your companions, sharing in the same folds and pastures.
—Callimachus, *Aitia* fr. 27 (Pfeiffer)

By analogy with Statius's description of Linos among the lambs, a nineteenth-century scholar identifies this *kouros* as Linos.[14] While the word *kouros* is commonly used to describe young boys or adolescents, it can also be used of younger children. In the *Iliad,* for example, a child who is still in the womb is described as a *kouros* (*hon tina gasteri mētēr kouron eonta pheroi;* 6.58–59); similarly, a young mother is described as giving birth to a *kouros* in a story related by Konon (*eteke koron; FGrH* 26.33). This fragment from the *Aitia* unfortunately lacks a context, but the bucolic description could hide the same mixture of dread and pleasure as Statius's description of the child left among the sheep in a cradle made of grass and branches, only to be devoured alive by dogs.

There are no visual representations of this episode, but we have a description by Pausanias of the tomb of Koroibos in Megara (1.43.7). This monument, inscribed with an elegiac inscription telling the story of Psamathe and Koroibos, also depicts Koroibos slaying Poine. Pausanias adds that the tomb is among the most ancient Greek images he has ever seen.

The *Greek Anthology* quotes another inscription that purportedly decorated the tomb of the monster killed by Koroibos:

κοινὸν ἐγὼ Μεγαρεῦσι καὶ Ἰναχίδαισιν ἄθυρμα
ἵδρυμαι, Ψαμάθης ἔκδικον οὐλομένης.

εἰμὶ δὲ <u>Κὴρ τυμβοῦχος</u>. ὁ δὲ κτείνας με Κόροιβος
κεῖται δ' ὧδ' ὑπ' ἐμοῖς ποσσὶ διὰ τρίποδα.
<u>Δελφὶς γάρ φάμα τόδ' ἐθέσπισεν, ὄφρα γενοίμαν</u>
<u>τᾶς κείνου νύμφας σῆμα καὶ ἱστορίης.</u>

I am set here, <u>an image common</u> to the Megarians and the Argives,
the avenger of accursed Psamathe.
I am <u>the Ker that occupies the tomb,</u> and Koroibos killed me,
and thus he lies under my feet, because of the tripod.
<u>For the voice of Delphi ordained that I should be</u>
<u>the monument of Apollo's bride and tell the story.</u>
—*Greek Anthology* 7.154

According to this inscription, the statue of the *daimōn* signals the tomb (*sēma*) of Psamathe, at the same time that it conveys the events that led to and followed her death. Again we see this concern with remembering and telling the story of what happened, although in this case, the focus is on the mother and no mention is made of Linos.

In the myth of Linos, we find again the motif of a mother's actions leading to her child's death. Psamathe only indirectly causes Linos's: she puts him in a dangerous situation, without any intention of harming him. This is not unlike most versions of the story of the death of Medea's children, in which she also puts her children (unwillingly) in a dangerous situation by "concealing" (*katakryptein*) them. Psamathe's actions, unlike Herakles', are rational. She does not kill her son in a moment of complete thoughtlessness or madness; she is distressed and fears her father's violent temper, which is reflected in that of his dogs, who behave like wild animals and do what he might have done himself had he been aware of the child's existence.

So far we have seen that child heroes, such as Linos and the children of Medea, can be honored with mourning festivals, often described as mixtures of rituals: mourning and initiatory in the case of the children of Medea (hair-cutting, special clothing, annual segregation); a nocturnal fire ritual and athletic competition in the case of the children of Herakles; and a mixture of mourning and prayers performed by women and girls for Linos. The dirge for Linos as described by Konon becomes a genre in itself: his mourning song is sung not only in commemoration of the child hero, but also by later poets in connection with other sufferings.[15]

Let us turn to children who are honored mainly through athletic competitions and festivals, which can also include heroic and initiatory-type rituals.

Several myths concern a goddess who tries to immortalize a child with disastrous consequences when the attempt is interrupted.[16] While this mythical pattern does not always coincide with narratives of heroization, one such story does include the death—and subsequent heroization—of a baby. This is the story of Demophon, who, in some versions of the myth, dies during an attempt at immortalization and whose death is commemorated at Eleusis through the establishment of athletic games. Although the myth of Demophon resembles the pattern of other stories of children's deaths followed by the institution of a mourning ritual, a few important differences are worth mentioning at the outset: unlike the human protagonists responsible for the deaths of the other child heroes, Demeter is a goddess. Demeter does not kill Demophon because of madness, neglect, revenge, or hubris; the death instead occurs accidentally because of the curiosity of the child's mother.

In the Homeric *Hymn to Demeter*, Metaneira entrusts her late-born and unexpected son (*opsigonon kai aelpton*; 219) to Demeter, who accepts the task of raising the boy and assures Metaneira that she will care for him and protect him from illness, magic, or the folly of a nurse. The boy's physical appearance quickly begins to change. Demophon grows "like a *daimon*" (*daimōni isos*), as Demeter prepares him for immortality. Daily, she anoints the child with ambrosia and breathes divine breath on him as she holds him in her lap. At night, she plunges the child into fire:

> νύκτας δὲ <u>κρύπτεσκε</u> πυρὸς μένει ἠΰτε δαλὸν
> λάθρα φίλων γονέων. τοῖς δὲ μέγα θαῦμ᾽ ἐτέτυκτο
> ὡς <u>προθαλὴς</u> τελέθεσκε, θεοῖσι δὲ ἄντα ἐῴκει.
> καί κέν μιν ποίησεν ἀγήρων τ᾽ ἀθάνατόν τε
> εἰ μὴ ἄρ᾽ ἀφραδίῃσιν ἐΰζωνος Μετάνειρα
> νύκτ᾽ ἐπιτηρήσασα θυώδεος ἐκ θαλάμοιο
> σκέψατο.

> And at night she <u>concealed</u> him in the fire like a firebrand
> unknown to his parents. To them it seemed a great marvel how he grew
> and <u>blossomed</u> forth, and he looked just like gods.
> And she would have made him ageless and immortal
> if well-girded Metaneira had not in her foolishness
> kept watch at night, looking from
> her fragrant chamber.
> —Homeric *Hymn to Demeter* 239–45

Demophon grows wonderfully, and his divine appearance is a wonder to his parents, who ignore what causes the transformation. He blooms (*prothalēs*), a state that evokes descriptions of other baby heroes, as well as of

Persephone herself at the beginning of the Homeric *Hymn to Demeter* (*glykeron thalos;* 66).[17]

Metaneira is overcome by curiosity, and she eventually discovers the nightly fire ritual performed by Demeter. While Demeter promised she would protect the child against the folly (*kakophradia*) of a nurse, the folly (*aphradia*) of the mother's spying and rushing in takes Demeter by surprise. Metaneira's sudden appearance puts an end to the process of immortalization of Demophon. Metaneira weeps and strikes at her thighs in a typical mourning gesture and accuses Demeter of trying to kill her son. Demeter responds angrily, snatches the boy out of the fire, and puts him on the ground. She then explains to the distraught mother that she was only trying to protect the child from old age and death and that this untimely interruption will result in his death.

At this point in the story, Demeter foretells that Demophon's death will be commemorated in a ritual that will be performed in his honor at Eleusis:

> νῦν δ᾽ οὐκ ἔσθ᾽ ὥς κεν θάνατον καὶ κῆρας ἀλύξαι.
> τιμὴ δ᾽ ἄφθιτος αἰὲν ἐπέσσεται οὕνεκα γούνων
> ἡμετέρων ἐπέβη καὶ ἐν ἀγκοίνῃσιν ἴαυσεν.
> ὥρῃσιν δ᾽ ἄρα τῷ γε περιπλομένων ἐνιαυτῶν
> παῖδες Ἐλευσινίων πόλεμον καὶ φύλοπιν αἰνὴν
> αἰὲν ἐν ἀλλήλοισι συνάξους᾽ ἤματα πάντα.

> But now it is impossible that he escape death and the fates.
> Yet there will always be <u>undying honor</u> for him because
> he lay on my knees and slept in my arms.
> In due season, for him, as time comes round,
> <u>the children of the Eleusinians will always</u>
> <u>wage war and dread battle with each other forever.</u>
> —Homeric *Hymn to Demeter* 262–67

Demeter's attempt at immortalizing Demophon is foiled by his careless mother; Demophon will never obtain a life free from death, but, as Nagy argues in his analysis of this episode, Demeter's actions do, in fact, prepare and destine him to become immortalized as a recipient of hero cult. Baby Demophon will die, but he will thereby obtain a *timē* that is unfailing (*aph-thitos*) in the form of ritual fights regularly held in his honor.[18] While Demophon survives in the Homeric *Hymn to Demeter,* the scholia attest to other versions in which Demophon does not survive his stay in the fire. The bungled immortalization becomes the cause of his death, and athletic funeral games in his honor are established at Eleusis.[19]

Before examining the rituals held in honor of Demophon, let us look at some other accounts of the same myth. Apollodoros also describes the death of Baby Demophon in his *Library* (first or second century A.D.). He follows the narrative of the Homeric *Hymn to Demeter* closely, but his account is brief and he omits mention of the ritual honors.

Most of the Roman accounts conflate Demophon and Triptolemos, traditionally a king and hero of Eleusis associated with the story of the invention of the plough, but sometimes identified as Metaneira's child (Homeric *Hymn to Demeter* 153, 474). Ovid retells the story of Demeter at Eleusis in his *Fasti* (early first century A.D.), where Metaneira entrusts the child Triptolemos to Demeter, who enjoins him to be the first to plough and sow grain (*Fasti* 4.549–60). Similarly Vergil's *Georgics* (first century B.C.) names Triptolemos as the boy-inventor of the plough (*puer monstrator aratri*), and the scholia identify him as the boy whom Demeter tried to immortalize with fire.[20] Hyginus (second century A.D.) also conflates Demophon and Triptolemos in his version of the same events. Both parents subsequently come upon Demeter as she is about to put the child on the fire, but this time it is the father's cry that puts an end to the immortalization process. Demeter gives Triptolemos a chariot with dragons to sow the earth (*Fabula* 147).

As we have seen, the Homeric *Hymn to Demeter* suppresses the child's death, yet it unmistakably refers to the heroic honors eventually given to Demophon. Hesychius (fifth century A.D.) and Athenaios (second–third century A.D.) also refer to a festival, the *ballētys* (pelting), in honor of Demophon that was taking place at Eleusis in Athenaios's time:

Ἐλευσῖνι γὰρ τῇ ἐμῇ οἶδά τινα πανήγυριν ἀγομένην καὶ καλουμένην Βαλλητύν.

I know of a festival held in my own Eleusis, which is called *Ballētys*.
—Athenaios, *Deipnosophistai* 406d

Is there any relationship between the mock fighting of the Homeric *Hymn to Demeter*, this *ballētys*, and the Eleusinian Games (also known as the Eleusinia)?[21] The Parian Marble tells us that the Eleusinian Games were the oldest games, established long before the Olympic Games, one hundred years before the Trojan War, during Pandion's rule. The scholia to Pindar's *Olympian* 9.150 also remark that the Eleusinian Games were said to be the first games (*touton de prōton agōnōn phasin einai*; Drachmann 3.301), though neither Demophon nor his death are mentioned. Finally, Ailios Aristeides (A.D. 117–81) mentions the antiquity of the Eleusinian Games, which he describes as being even older than the Panathenaia (*Panathenaic Oration* 362).

One anecdote in Aulus Gellius's *Attic Nights* (second century A.D.) gives us an important detail about the tragedian Euripides' participation and victory in the Eleusinian Games. At his birth, astrologers assured Euripides' father that he would be victorious in the games (*victorem in certaminibus*). His father understands this to mean that his son will become an athlete, and he conscientiously trains his son and then takes him to Olympia to compete in the games. The boy, however, is too young and is not allowed to participate. Instead he goes to the Eleusinian Games, where he wins (15.20). The Eleusinia, then, at some time must have included contests for boys younger than those allowed to compete at Olympia.[22]

What is the link between the *ballētys* and the Eleusinian Games? Did the latter evolve from the former or were they always distinct festivals? Scholars disagree and argue for both a direct link and complete absence of connection.[23] Nothing concretely links the *ballētys* with the Eleusinia, except for the resemblance of the Demophon story to that of other baby heroes honored with athletic games: child heroes, such as the children of Herakles (or, as we shall see, Pelops, Opheltes, and Melikertes), all die untimely and violent deaths, and all are honored through rituals that involve athletic competition. The link between Melikertes and Demophon is actually made explicit in the scholia.[24] In this context, the *polemon* (war) and *phylopin* (battle) that Demeter enjoins on the Eleusinians' children are to be understood as symbolic ritual fights in honor of Demophon, who is immortalized after death by his heroization.[25] By the time of Athenaios, the *ballētys* in honor of Demophon was clearly a separate, local festival, while the Eleusinian Games remained an important Panhellenic event.[26] Demophon thus was honored with an athletic competition, as were the children of Herakles, Pelops, Opheltes, and Melikertes (see below).

Richardson argues that the hymn itself might have been composed for recitation in an epic contest and that the most natural candidate is the Eleusinian Games.[27] What are we to make, then, of the hymn's suppression of the death of Baby Demophon? In the case of all the other baby heroes, the narrative of their deaths seems to be an important part of their cult (see especially chap. 6). It is therefore puzzling that the Homeric *Hymn to Demeter* includes an *aition* for a ritual, yet remains silent about the death of the very hero for whom the ritual was established. Of course, the story of Demophon in the context of the Homeric *Hymn to Demeter* is peripheral, and the focus is on the goddess rather than on the hero. The narrative avoids the mention of Demophon's death, perhaps unseemly in the context of a celebration of Demeter, yet the hymn includes the episode of Demeter putting Demophon in the fire and the reference to the rites in his honor, which evoke the baby's death and the games established in his honor.

Heroization is a process that can occur only after human death, and, as we saw, Demophon can obtain his unfailing honor only after he has died. One myth illustrates how survival, in the context of Greek myth, can be understood as a failure, an abortive attempt to achieve a different status. The myth I am referring to is the story of Glaukos, the young son of Minos, found in both Apollodoros's *Library* (3.17.1–21) and Hyginus's *Fabulae* (136).

Here is the essence of the story: Glaukos accidentally drowns in a jar of honey. After his disappearance, Minos consults the Kouretes (or Apollo) and learns that whoever can best describe or explain the three-colored cow in his flocks (i.e., a cow that changes color every few hours in Hyginus) will be able to find the child. The seer Polyeidos compares the colors of the cow to the fruit of the bramble (in Apollodoros) or the mulberry (in Hyginus) and subsequently finds the dead child in the honey jar. Minos is not satisfied and shuts the seer in with the corpse, requesting him to revive the boy. Polyeidos is at a loss, until a snake approaches the corpse. Polyeidos kills it in fear that it could harm the body, but a second snake revives the first with the help of an herb, which Polyeidos takes and uses to resuscitates Glaukos. In Apollodoros's version, Minos further compels Polyeidos to teach Glaukos the art of divination, but as the seer sails off, he asks Glaukos to spit into his mouth, and by doing so Glaukos forgets everything he has just been taught.

Muellner's analysis of this myth places it in the framework of Cretan initiation rituals as well as in the Panhellenic context of its performance in the Athenian theater. He argues that the Glaukos myth depicts a failed initiation and that the initiation fails because the boy is too young.[28] Muellner bases his interpretation partly on the words used in the literary sources to describe Glaukos (*eti nēpios*) and partly on the Sotades cup that shows Polyeidos and Glaukos, where the latter is obviously still a very young child.[29] Muellner suggests that stories of the Glaukos type "constitute a grammar of successful and unsuccessful passages. They conspire to show that the road to immortality and glory is on a mystical, wide-eyed path through death and beyond it, not by way of resurrection, which turns out to be a hollow victory or even a setback."[30]

Death, symbolic or real, is essential to any genuine change of status. In ritual, initiates metaphorically die the death that the recipient of heroic honor undergoes in myth. In the case of Glaukos, the myth's protagonist fails to achieve what the initiates seek to achieve in ritual. This myth provides us with a foil to the story of Demophon. Demophon goes through the ordeal of fire in vain; because of his mother's interruption, he fails to become an immortal, yet he is immortalized after his death by becoming the recipient of unfailing honor (*aphthitos timē*). Glaukos's story is a reverse initiation: he survives but loses his status of initiate when he spits into the seer's mouth.[31]

Although the story of Glaukos's death overturns the usual pattern, the concern in the ritual is clearly about passage into another age class. Cretan initiation rituals include mock battles fought to the sound of the pipe and lyre that resemble the mock battle (*ballētys*) honoring Demophon.[32] Muellner further links the myth of Glaukos with another Cretan ritual of ritual abduction (*harpagē*). Certain young boys, chosen for their nobility, are "captured" by an older man, in a staged abduction, in much the same way that Zeus carries off Ganymedes or Pelops after his revival in the cauldron.[33] After having undergone initiation in the countryside, the young abductees return to the city and are given special recognition in the form of various privileges and clothes; once they reach manhood, they become known as the *kleinoi*, "'famous, the subjects of undying *kleos*,' like the heroes of epic, for having been chosen and having passed through an 'ordeal.'"[34]

Let us go back to the mythical motif of a child's failed immortalization. Another myth that depicts a failed deification is that of Thetis and Achilles. According to Apollonios Rhodios's *Argonautika*, Thetis, like Demeter in the Homeric *Hymn to Demeter*, attempts to immortalize a mortal baby, her son Achilles.[35] Thetis submits Achilles to the same treatment Demeter used with Demophon:

ἡ μὲν γὰρ βροτέας αἰεὶ περὶ σάρκας ἔδαιεν
νύκτα διὰ μέσσην φλογμῷ πυρός. ἤματα δ'αὖτε
ἀμβροσίῃ χρίεσκε τέρεν δέμας, ὄφρα πέλοιτο
ἀθάνατος, καί οἱ στυγερὸν χροῒ γῆρας ἀλάλκοι.
αὐτὰρ ὅγ' ἐξ εὐνῆς ἀνεπάλμενος εἰσενόησεν
παῖδα φίλον σπαίροντα διὰ φλογός. ἧκε δ' αὐτὴν
σμερδαλέην ἐσιδών, μέγα νήπιος. ἡ δ' ἀίουσα
τὸν μὲν ἄρ' ἁρπάγδην χαμάδις βάλε κεκληγῶτα.

For she always burned his mortal flesh
at night by the flame of the fire. And again by day,
she anointed his tender frame with ambrosia, so that he might become
immortal and that she might ward off hateful old age from his body.
But Peleus leapt up from his bed and saw
his dear child gasping in the flame. And as he saw this,
he let go of a terrible cry, the fool. She heard it
and she snatched the baby and threw him screaming to the ground.
—Apollonios Rhodios, *Argonautika* 4.869–76

The basic elements of the mortal parent's surprise and horror function in the same way as Metaneira's shock in the Homeric *Hymn to Demeter*. Peleus shouts in horror, and Thetis, hearing him, catches the child and throws him on the ground. Thetis then jumps into the sea and disappears. Despite the violence of his mother's reaction, Achilles survives the interrupted ordeal, but his survival prevents his heroization at this point, although the bungled immortalization is an important component of Achilles' story: it is, in fact, what makes him thoroughly human, which in turns allows for his later death and heroization as an adult.

From an allusion to the same episode in Lykophron's *Alexandra*, we learn of a tradition in which, before Achilles, Thetis first unsuccessfully submitted six of her children to the same treatment and Achilles is the first and only one to survive (178–79). The episode is reminiscent of Medea's unsuccessful attempts to perform the *katakryptein* for several of her children, who all die.

□

Another variation on the same theme of a child entrusted to a divine maternal figure is found in the story that Plutarch tells of Isis and the child of Astarte in *Isis and Osiris*. Although the story of the children of Astarte is described as a foreign myth by the Greek sources, I include this narrative because the pattern it reveals is very much Greek: as Plutarch and Herodotos relate this purportedly Egyptian myth, both authors project Greek myths and rituals upon Egyptian practices. The episode occurs as Isis comes to Byblos, where the *larnax* containing her husband Osiris's body is hidden inside the trunk of a tree.

The story in Plutarch is strikingly similar to that of the Homeric *Hymn to Demeter:* Isis, like Demeter, searches for her loved one and comes to a fountain near the city, where the queen's servants find her. Later, the queen marvels at her servants' hairdos and perfumed bodies and summons Isis. The queen, like Metaneira, entrusts the stranger with one of her children to raise. The child remains anonymous, but Plutarch describes Isis's treatment of the baby:

τρέφειν δὲ τὴν Ἴσιν ἀντὶ μαστοῦ τὸν δάκτυλον εἰς τὸ στόμα τοῦ παιδίου διδοῦσαν, νύκτωρ δὲ περικαίειν τὰ θνητὰ τοῦ σώματος. αὐτὴν δὲ γενομένην χελιδόνα τῇ κίονι περιπέτεσθαι καὶ <u>θρηνεῖν</u>, ἄχρι οὗ τὴν βασίλισσαν παραφυλάξασαν καὶ ἐγκραγοῦσαν, ὡς εἶδε περικαιόμενον τὸ βρέφος, <u>ἀφελέσθαι τὴν ἀθανασίαν αὐτοῦ</u>.

Isis nurses the child with her finger instead of her breast, and at night she burns the mortal parts of his body. Transforming herself into a swallow, she flies around the column and <u>sings a dirge,</u> until the queen surprises her and

shouts in horror, as she sees her baby being burned in the fire, and <u>deprives him of immortality</u>.
—Plutarch, *Isis and Osiris* 357c

Isis, like Demeter, takes care of her young charge in unconventional ways and attempts to give him immortality by stripping off the mortal parts of his body. When she becomes a swallow, a bird associated with lament, she ostensibly mourns Osiris, whose body is contained within the column around which she flies.[36] Yet her lament also functions proleptically as a mourning song for the baby about to lose his chance for immortality (*athanasia*).

Isis then reveals herself as a goddess and cuts the trunk open to expose the *larnax* containing the body of Osiris. She throws herself on the coffin and wails in such a way that the youngest child of the king dies on the spot. Isis then takes the oldest child—is he the same child she was trying to make immortal?—and after having put the coffin into a boat, she sails away on the river.

In the first isolated spot she finds, Isis opens the coffin and embraces the body of Osiris, with her face pressed to his face, and cries. The child approaches in silence to observe the scene. Isis suddenly realizes his presence, turns toward him and looks at him with such a terrible (*deinos*) gaze that the child cannot endure the fear and dies. According to another version, the child would have died by falling into the sea. Be that as it may, he becomes the recipient of a cult and obtains his *timē* from the goddess. The Egyptians call this child Maneros and sing of him in their symposia. According to others, Plutarch adds, the child would have been named Palestrinos[37] or Pelousios and would have given his name to the city founded by Isis, while the Maneros celebrated in songs was the inventor of music (357d–e).

The Egyptian story is seen through Greek eyes: some details, such as Isis nursing the child with her finger—a gesture of adoption in Egypt[38]—are unique to the Egyptian tale; others, such as the meeting at the fountain and the queen entrusting the goddess with her baby, are very close to the Homeric *Hymn to Demeter.* The Egyptian child seems to survive the interrupted immortalization, as Demophon does in the Homeric *Hymn to Demeter,* yet after this episode, two children die in quick succession because of Isis. The first one, the youngest child of the king, dies because of her terrifying mourning cry, while the second one, the oldest, dies of fear after she looks at him in anger. It is unclear which, if either, of these children is actually the same one who underwent the attempted immortalization by fire.[39] But it is the second, older child who dies of fear and obtains *timē* from the goddess.

Herodotos also mentions the child Maneros in his description of Egyptian customs in his *Histories* 2.79 and—in a gesture of cultural appropriation—

assimilates him to the Greek Linos. According to Herodotos, Egyptians, in fact, sing the *linos*-song, which is also sung in Phoenicia, Cyprus, and elsewhere under different names, but is the very same song that the Greeks call the *linos*. While the link between the Greek Linos and the Egyptian Maneros may not at first be obvious, the two heroes—and their myths—are assimilated by Herodotos: Linos, the baby accidentally torn apart by dogs, and Maneros, the child killed by his own fear of the goddess Isis's anger, both ultimately receive their *timē* in the form of a mourning song. The story of Maneros, the only son of the Egyptians' first king, who died an untimely death (*anōros*) and whom they honor with *thrēnoi*, their first—and at that time only—song, is simply the Egyptian version of the Greek myth of Linos.

Neither Linos, Maneros, nor Demophon appear on extant images, perhaps because their myths and cults were restricted to a limited geographical area.[40] While these stories differ in details, they all follow the same pattern of failed immortalization, premature death, and eventual heroization. In the case of Maneros and Demophon, there is a doubling of the maternal figure, with a goddess playing the role of substitute mother. This combination of immortal and mortal mothers always ends in conflict and tragedy. In all these tales, maternal fear actually becomes the *cause* of children's death: Psamathe's fear brings about her son's death; in the case of Demophon and the children of Astarte, suspicion, fear, and surprise lead to conflict with the divine maternal figure.

In the Greek view, maternal fear is thus a destructive force in itself. Divine anger and grief can also be fatal to children. The narratives often represent shouting as the key moment that provokes the children's death, as if giving voice to fear was enough to bring about the dreaded outcome. These myths also focus on failed attempts at immortalization, and although they start out as depictions of failure, they in fact all focus on figures who are immortalized after death. The kind of heroic immortality granted to heroes is qualitatively different from the kind of immortality enjoyed by gods, who, by definition, never die.[41] Yet Linos, Demophon, and the children of Astarte—all need to be compensated for their deaths and are immortalized after their deaths.

We have seen how compensation often takes the form of heroic sacrifices and athletic competitions, as, for example, in the ritual in honor of Demophon; now we also see a focus on singing and poetry: Baby Linos is in fact the personification of *thrēnos;* similarly, the story of the children of Astarte functions, according to the Greeks, as an *aition* for the Egyptian lament. Mourning songs and *thrēnoi* are sung not only at the children's death, but become part

of the regularly held rituals established in their honor. The failed immortalization and heroization that form the core of these mythical narratives can
be understood as a metaphorical expression of the ordeal that worshipers
endure in the rituals performed in honor of heroes. The most demanding of
these ritual ordeals are athletic competitions. In the next three chapters, we
will examine three of the most important Panhellenic festivals, at Olympia,
Nemea, and Isthmia and the rituals of mourning and remembering dead children that are central to the establishment of these festivals.

# CHAPTER 4

# Pelops

The case of Pelops is complex. Many myths surround Pelops and the foundation of the Olympic Games, the most famous of which tells of Herakles' establishing the games in honor of his ancestor Pelops or of Pelops's founding the games in compensation for the death of Oinomaos during the chariot race.[1] In another myth, however, Pelops dies as a child. His father, Tantalos, cuts him up and serves him as a meal to the gods. The gods later revive Pelops, who therefore manages to embody two contradictory functions: he is a child hero who grows up to be an ancestor and who participates in the games established as a compensation for his own death.[2] Although the myth concerning Pelops at Olympia is not strictly parallel to other narratives of baby heroes, key elements of the myth and ritual in his honor echo those found in other narratives of child heroes. Pelops also provides an essential link between the local child-hero cults we have considered so far and the Panhellenic cults in honor of baby heroes we will look at in the next two chapters.

Pindar's *Olympian* 1 (476 B.C.), the most well-known extant version of the death of Pelops, is famous both for the tale it relates and the disclaimer that precedes it: humans should ascribe only beautiful deeds to the gods (35–36), and therefore the story of Pelops's being boiled by his father and served to the gods must be an invention (47–48).[3] The traditional story tells of Tantalos inviting the gods to a banquet on the same day on which his son, Pelops, disappeared. According to Pindar, this must have happened on the very day on which Pelops was abducted by Poseidon, and a jealous neighbor invented the story of Tantalos murdering his son and tricking the gods to explain the child's disappearance.

Although Pindar maintains the falsity of the myth, he uses one detail in his narrative that is influenced by the tradition he rejects. Pelops disappeared on the day of the feast because Poseidon, overcome by desire, abducted him and carried him off to Olympos to become Zeus's wine-steward (40–45). This seems to absolve Tantalos from all responsibility for his son's disappearance. A few lines earlier, however, Pindar describes how Poseidon first notices Pelops:

> τοῦ μεγασθενὴς ἐράσσατο Γαιάοχος
> Ποσειδάν, ἐπεί νιν καθαροῦ λέβη-
> τος ἔξελε Κλωθώ,
> ἐλέφαντι φαίδιμον ὦμον κεκαδμένον.

> Him [Pelops], with whom Poseidon the mighty holder
> of the earth fell in love, after Klotho
> took him out of the pure cauldron,
> furnished with a shining ivory shoulder.
> —Pindar, *Olympian* 1.25–27

The detail of the shining shoulder, of course, belongs to the story of the gods eating Pelops: Pelops has an ivory shoulder because Demeter ate his, just before the gods realized what Tantalos had served them. Later on, the gods put the boy back together and replace his missing shoulder with an ivory one.

There is also evidence that Pelops is still very young when he comes out of the cauldron, and, as Pindar describes it, he does not reach maturity until much later. The presence of Klotho evokes birth—or rather rebirth here— and again summons images of a very young Pelops. Later on in Pindar's *Olympian* 1, Pelops is cast off from Zeus's palace and sent back to the world of mortals as a punishment for his father's theft of ambrosia and nectar from the gods (60–66). Pelops is subsequently described as reaching the bloom of manhood, with the first appearance of a downy beard on his face (67–68). As Pelops starts exhibiting the physical signs of manhood, he also begins to think about marriage, another sign that he has now reached maturity. The story of the abduction of Baby Pelops by Poseidon can in fact also be understood in terms of a mythical initiation into adulthood.[4] The transition from baby to ephebe, or the failure thereof, is central to many myths of child heroes.

Poseidon's ardor for the infant Pelops need not be troubled by considerations of age: Kassel shows that it is not uncommon for gods to be attracted to very young children, even newborns. He argues that the episode in Pindar refers to the infant's first bath: "Baby Pelops was so radiant with beauty after his first bath that Neptune was seized by passionate desire."[5] He also cites the example of Adonis:

γεννηθῆναι τὸν λεγόμενον Ἄδωνιν, ὃν Ἀφροδίτη διὰ κάλλος ἔτι νήπιον κρύφα θεῶν εἰς λάρνακα κρύψασα Περσεφόνῃ.

And Adonis, as he is called, was born, whom Aphrodite, because of his beauty and even though he was still an infant, hid in a chest unknown to the gods and entrusted him to Persephone.
—Panyassis fr. 27 (Bernabé = Apollodoros, *Library* 3.14.4)

The infant Adonis's beauty mesmerizes not only Aphrodite, but Persephone as well, who, after taking only one look at him, refuses to give him back to Aphrodite. When called upon to decide the case, Zeus decides that Adonis should spend one-third of the year by himself, one-third with Aphrodite, and one-third with Persephone (Apollodoros, *Library* 3.14.4).[6]

Toward the end of *Olympian* 1, Pindar describes the tomb and altars for Pelops standing at Olympia:

νῦν δ᾽ ἐν αἱμακουρίαις
ἀγλααῖσι μέμικται,
Ἀλφεοῦ πόρῳ κλιθείς,
τύμβον ἀμφίπολον ἔχων πολυξενω-
τάτῳ παρὰ βωμῷ τὸ δὲ κλέος
τηλόθεν δέδορκε τᾶν Ὀλυμπιάδων ἐν δρόμοις
Πέλοπος, ἵνα ταχυτὰς ποδῶν ἐρίζεται
ἀκμαί τ᾽ ἰσχύος θρασύπονοι.
ὁ νικῶν δὲ λοιπὸν ἀμφὶ βίοτον
ἔχει μελιτόεσσαν εὐδίαν
ἀέθλων γ᾽ ἕνεκεν. τὸ δ᾽ αἰεὶ παράμερον ἐσλόν
ὕπατον ἔρχεται παντὶ βροτῶν.

Now he [Pelops] shares
in splendid blood sacrifices,
resting beside the bed of the Alpheos,
where he has his much-frequented tomb next to the altar
that is visited by many strangers. The fame of Pelops
shines afar from Olympia in the races
where they vie for swiftness of foot
and the strong heights of harsh labor.
And the winner throughout the rest of his life
enjoys honey-sweet calm,

so far as games can give it. But day-by-day excellence
is the highest that comes to every mortal man.
—Pindar, *Olympian* 1.90–100

The poet has shifted from myth to ritual. Pelops is no longer described in terms of what happened to him while he was alive, but as a recipient of cult. The participle *klitheis* (resting) evokes reclining at feasts, an essential aspect of hero cult.[7] The word *haimakouria* (blood sacrifices) is interesting in this contest: it is a Boeotian word similar to the word used by Plutarch in his description of the rituals for the heroic dead at Plataia. The verb *memiktai* also evokes images of the hero mingling with his worshipers at the feast (Plutarch, *Aristeides* 21.5).[8] Already in the fifth century B.C., then, Pelops is central to the Olympic Games.

The story of Pelops and the cauldron is also part of Bacchylides' repertoire (c. 518–450 B.C.). A fragment preserved in the scholia to Pindar's *Olympian* 1.40 records that Bacchylides' version was different from Pindar's:

ὁ δὲ Βακχυλίδης τὸν Πέλοπα τὴν Ῥέαν λέγει <u>ὑγιάσαι</u> καθεῖσαν διὰ <u>λέβητος</u>

Bacchylides says that Rhea <u>restored</u> Pelops to <u>health</u> by putting him in the <u>cauldron</u>.
—Bacchylides fr. 42 (Snell and Maehler)

Whereas Pindar had Klotho taking Pelops out of the pure cauldron, Bacchylides has Rhea put him down into the cauldron to restore him to health. In both cases, a female figure uses the cauldron, always represented as means of transformation, as a means of reviving Pelops.

Iphigeneia in Euripides' *Iphigeneia in Tauris* (413 B.C.) echoes Pindar's incredulity toward the tale of Tantalos and Pelops (386–91). Iphigeneia does not believe stories of gods delighting in human flesh, and like Pindar, she thinks gods can have no part in anything evil. But Iphigeneia's words are vague when it comes to Pelops. While the emphasis shifts a little depending on which translation we choose for the word she uses (*pais*), the horror of the story is stressed by both: the gods would never delight in eating the child of a human being, and the gods would certainly never take pleasure in eating the flesh of a child.

Lykophron's *Alexandra* (second century B.C.) alludes to the prophecy that Troy could be captured only with the help of the bones of Pelops. Kassandra predicts Troy's destruction and lists the three conditions necessary for the Greeks to achieve this end: Achilles' son Neoptolemos, the bones of Pelops, and Herakles' bow.[9] Lykophron refers to the flame that devoured (*katabrōthein*)

Pelops's body, but without explicitly mentioning the cauldron in which Tantalos boiled his child (*Alexandra* 53–55). The scholia add that Pelops was devoured by fire and reduced to ashes as he was being made into a meal for the gods:

καταποθέντος δηλαδὴ τοῦ Πέλοπος ἐν τῇ αἰθάλῃ καὶ τῇ σποδιᾷ ὁπότε πρὸς εὐωχίαν τῶν θεῶν ἐτύθη.

And Pelops was cooked by the soot and ashes, when he was prepared into a feast for the gods.
—schol. Lykophron, *Alexandra* 55

Here the mention of soot and ashes evokes images of roasting rather than boiling. Be that as it may, both Lykophron and the scholia depict the tradition of the infant Pelops being cooked and eaten by the gods. Lykophron mentions Pelops once more in the *Alexandra,* but this time as an adult and an ancestor, Menelaos's grandfather, who was devoured by Demeter (152–55). Lykophron then goes on to tell the traditional story of Pelops winning the hand of Hippodameia and killing of Oinomaos. He describes Pelops with the expression *dis hēbēsas* (twice young), an expression also found in an epigram quoted by Tzetzes in his life of Hesiod, where Hesiod's first youth might be understood as his human life, while the other is the second life he enjoys through the eternal fame of his poetry.[10] Thus, *dis hēbēsas* does not so much evoke being young in the chronological sense, but, in the case of Pelops, it refers to his being revived after having been dismembered and boiled by his father, which is how the scholia to Lykophron understands it (schol. Lykophron, *Alexandra* 156). The expression could also refer to Pelops's living again as a hero at Olympia after his death.

Diodorus Siculus includes the later adventures of Pelops winning the hand of Hippodameia in his *Library of History* (first century B.C.). After closing the story of Pelops, he notes that he might as well tell the story of his father, Tantalos, "in order to omit nothing worthy of being known" (4.74.1). Yet Diodorus remains silent about the episode of the feast of the gods and the cauldron. He relates how Tantalos was especially dear to the gods, on account of his father Zeus, and how he shared their meals and conversations, but he was ultimately unable to behave in a way becoming to a human being (*anthrōpinōs*): he divulged to human beings things heard among the gods that should never have been repeated (*aporrēta*). He was subsequently punished both in life and after his death (74.2–3).

Pelops and his adventures in the cauldron are briefly mentioned in Apollodoros's *Epitome* (first or second century A.D.):

ὅτι Πέλοψ σφαγεὶς ἐν τῷ τῶν θεῶν ἐράνῳ καὶ καθεψηθεὶς <u>ὡραιότερος</u>
ἐν τῇ ἀναζωώσει γέγονε, καὶ κάλλει διενεγκὼν Ποσειδῶνος <u>ἐρώμενος</u>
γίνεται, ὃς αὐτῷ δίδωσιν ἅρμα ὑπόπτερον.

Pelops, after being slaughtered and boiled at the banquet of the gods was
<u>more beautiful</u> after being revived, and because of his beauty, he became
Poseidon's <u>beloved,</u> who gave him a winged chariot.
—Apollodoros, *Epitome* 2.3

We find here again the same connection between the reviving of Pelops
and his subsequent beauty. After he comes out of the cauldron, Pelops is more
beautiful than ever, and that is when, as in Pindar's version, Poseidon falls in
love with him. The word *hōraioteros* has both aesthetic and age connotations,
and it implies that Pelops was not only beautiful, but also had reached his
prime. The word also evokes its opposite, *aōros*, which is often used of cult
heroes who die an "untimely" death: the word can refer both to premature
death and to "the nature and appropriateness of the individual's death";[11] in
Pelops's case, both his young age and the horrific nature of his death at his
father's hand put him in the category of *aōroi*. Pelops becomes more attrac-
tive after being revived, something that is also true of heroes after death (a
point we will return to in chaps. 5–6).

Hyginus (second century A.D.) also tells the story of Tantalos killing his
son in *Fabula* 82. The details about the shoulder and the revival of the boy
are the same we already saw in Pindar. Pelops is also mentioned in Hyginus's
list of those for whom games were established (273.5); according to the
mythographer, Herakles founded the games at Olympia in honor of Pelops,
the son of Tantalos. Here we find again the elements of the story already present in Pindar and Bacchylides.

❑

Several *lēkythoi* depict unidentified adolescents emerging from cauldrons,
but no extant representations can be linked to the episode of Pelops in the
cauldron with any certainty.[12] An Etruscan mirror in the Bibliothèque
nationale, for example, shows an ephebe coming out of a cauldron (fig. 18).[13]

Two women stand behind a cauldron, from which a young man emerges.
On the left, two men, one sitting and the other standing, observe the scene.
The two women look toward the men, rather than toward the cauldron. The
youth who comes out of the cauldron looks fully grown and muscular. The
man sitting is older than the other two: he has a beard and his musculature
is less defined. The participants remain anonymous, and there is no easy way
of identifying the scene. By analogy with the iconography of child heroes, it

FIGURE 18. Etruscan mirror, Bibliothèque nationale 1329. Photograph courtesy of Bibliothèque nationale de France, Paris.

would not be surprising to see young Pelops emerge from the cauldron as an
ephebe like the one in figure 18. Yet we will have to wait until the next two
chapters to explore this subject more. As it stands, we have no firmly docu-
mented visual representation of the story of Baby Pelops.[14]

Although the connection between the infant Pelops and Pelops as a hero is
not as direct as in the case of the other children I examine in this study, it is
instructive to consider the shrine in honor of Pelops at Olympia. Pausanias
describes the *temenos* of Pelops in book 5 of his *Periēgēsis* (second century A.D.).
According to him, the Eleans honor Pelops more than the other heroes at
Olympia, just as they honor Zeus most of all the gods (5.13.1), and the Pelopeion
is located near the temple of Zeus, but far enough away to leave space for statues and other offerings in between. Pausanias describes the enclosure:

καὶ λίθων τε θριγκῷ περιέχεται καὶ δένδρα ἐντὸς πεφυκότα καὶ
ἀνδριάντες εἰσὶν ἀνακείμενοι, ἔσοδος δὲ ἐς αὐτὸ πρὸς δυσμῶν ἐστιν
ἡλίου.

It is enclosed by a stone wall and has trees growing inside it, and there are
statues there; the entrance to it faces the setting sun.
—Pausanias 5.13.1

The enclosure consists of an open space, filled with trees and statues.
According to Pausanias, Herakles himself established the *temenos* for his
great-grandfather, Pelops. Pausanias also tells how Herakles first sacrificed to
his ancestor in a pit (*bothros;* 5.13.2).

The Pelopeion is ostensibly in honor of the hero who had a part in the
establishment of the games, and therefore it plays an important part in their
celebration. There is still a sacrifice to Pelops in Pausanias's day, when those
in power for the year sacrifice a black ram. The *bothros* sacrifice—a typical
sacrifice for heroes—is offered to Pelops exclusively: no part of the sacrifice
goes to the prophet (*mantis*), with the exception of the neck of the ram, which
goes to the so-called woodman, who is responsible for gathering white poplar
wood for sacrifices. Anybody else who eats of the victim sacrificed to Pelops
is forbidden to enter the temple of Zeus (5.13.2–3).[15]

Heroic shrines are often located on the site of a hero's grave, and the hero's
bones can be desirable commodities. Pausanias tells the story of how the
shoulder bone of Pelops was moved during the Trojan War and lost on
the return trip when the ship bringing the bone back was shipwrecked off the
coast of Euboea. Eventually the bone is found and returned to Olympia,

where, however, it is no longer on display in Pausanias's time because of the damage it had incurred by its long stay in the depths of the sea (5.13.4–6). Although Pausanias omits the episode of the cauldron, the story of the shoulder blade of Pelops cannot fail to evoke it, and we see in his account the same conflation of clashing traditions we already saw in Pindar.

Archaeological evidence confirms Pausanias's account of the heroic shrine at Olympia. The Pelopeion is located between the Heraion and the temple of Zeus, west of the stadium. Because the areas reserved for cult and for athletic activities were separated by the hundred-meter-long Echo Colonnade in the fourth century B.C., some scholars argue that the cult preceded the athletic festival or that the athletic festival started as part of the worship of Pelops, later transferred to the cult of Zeus.[16] The dating of the Pelopeion is controversial. Dörpfeld, excavating at the beginning of the twentieth century, posits the existence of three different stages, starting with Pelopeion 1 in the prehistoric period.[17] Although this is a controversial hypothesis,[18] and the beginnings and early function of the Olympia sanctuary remain mysterious, Kyrieleis argues that "Dörpfeld's observations were in principle perfectly correct."[19] There is also evidence for a prehistoric child burial to the northeast of the Pelopeion, whose later accidental discovery could have given momentum to the cult of Pelops at Olympia.[20]

Despite the lack of physical evidence for an early cult of Pelops, and no matter when exactly the ritual in his honor was established, it is clear from the written sources that the figure of Pelops was central to the Olympic Games from Pindar's time on. Furthermore, Burkert shows a direct link between the myth of dismemberment and perverted sacrifice of Pelops and the sacrifice of a black ram that was the culmination of the footrace competition at Olympia. The shoulder—the ivory shoulder of Pelops in the myth and the ram's shoulder in the ritual—are key elements that link the death of Baby Pelops with the ritual in his honor at the Olympic Games.[21]

As we can see in the case of Pelops, the cauldron can be a means of both destroying and reviving: his father kills him, and a female figure revives him using the same means.[22] The story of the boiling of Pelops follows a common pattern found in other tales of boiled children, such as Learkhos and Melikertes (more on them in chap. 6), and the child (Nyktimos, Arkas, or an unidentified victim) served to the gods by Lykaon. This Arcadian myth is strikingly similar to that of Tantalos: the gods come to visit the mortal Lykaon, who slaughters a young boy and prepares a cannibalistic sacrificial meal in a cauldron for his immortal guests. When he realizes the nature of the feast, Zeus overturns the table and transforms Lykaon into a wolf.[23] Like Baby Pelops, the Arcadian boy is later revived by the gods in the same cauldron in which he was boiled.

There are many parallels between the Arcadian athletic festival of the Lykeia and the Olympic Games. Yet the Lykeia is a local festival restricted to a specific age class that remains closer to a ritual of initiation into adulthood. The child killed by Lykaon is revived in the cauldron just as Pelops is, but the focus of the myth is on the act of cannibalism, which is transferred onto the ritual, in which participants partake of a stew purportedly composed of both animal and human meat. As Burkert reconstructs it, this local ritual functions as a rite of initiation for boys whose notional cannibalism subsequently requires them to be segregated (as "wolves") for a period of time.[24] The focus of both myth and ritual is thus on transgression and segregation as a means of atonement and transformation.

By contrast, the initiatory dimension of the Olympic Games survives in some of its mythical aspects such as the death and rebirth of Pelops in the cauldron, but its ritual function becomes more generalized as the games are open to different age classes and to athletes from all over Greece.[25] Yet the myth of Pelops in the cauldron focuses on the child: from the perspective of child-hero cults, Pelops gets to have a child cult and to grow up to obtain even more honors. He remains a child hero at Olympia at least in the context of the sacrifice ending the footrace, and the ritual in his honor stresses his experience in the cauldron, rather than the cannibalism associated with the episode. While the myth of Lykaon's emphasis on cannibalism and transgression—which in some versions cause the destruction of most of the human race via the flood (see Apollodoros 3.98)[26]—is indeed gruesome, as Burkert puts it, the myth of Pelops by contrast consistently highlights the baby's beauty—Pelops's sojourn in the cauldron, in fact, is responsible for the feature that makes him irresistible to Poseidon, the ivory shoulder—survival, and successful transition to manhood.[27]

Pelops has the distinction of being a hero who not only lives twice (*dis hēbēsas*), but who also dies twice. The foundation of the Olympic Games is explained through many layers of different myths, and the connection between the death of the infant Pelops and the establishment of the games is problematic, yet, the baby hero is clearly central to the rituals held at Olympia. In the story of Pelops and the cauldron, we have the elements of a familiar pattern: a violent parent, the brutal death of a child, religious transgression, a shrine, and the establishment of funerary games that ultimately become Panhellenic festivals. There are unique elements as well, such as Pelops's ultimate survival and the absence of a maternal figure. With the myths of Baby

Opheltes at Nemea and Baby Melikertes at Isthmia, we will examine two other cases in which the premature death of a child leads to athletic *agōnes* that perpetuate the narratives of their deaths and heroization through mourning and celebration. The myth of Pelops differs from the narratives of these two other child heroes because he eventually becomes an adult, yet Baby Pelops is remembered, fragmentarily as it were, in the form of his ivory shoulder, an object of wonder and worship for the ancient Greeks.

# Opheltes-
# Arkhemoros

Although the myth most often associated with the founding of the Nemean Games is the story of Herakles overcoming the lion of Nemea,[1] there is another, earlier, foundation myth for the same games.[2] From the fifth century on, the story of Opheltes-Arkhemoros is a popular subject among Greek authors. The myth relates the story of the accidental death of Baby Opheltes and its aftermath. The story at its simplest tells the death of a child attacked by a serpent and the subsequent foundation of funeral games in his honor.

Like other child heroes, such as the children of Medea, Opheltes enters sacred space with dire consequences. He is left alone in the bucolic and sacred domain of a snake and suffers a dreadful death. The dangers of flower-picking and falling asleep emerge as important themes in the narrative of the death of Opheltes. At first sight, the two activities do not seem to be related, but they are traditionally linked in Greek myth, and Opheltes is often described as falling asleep (and ultimately dying) as he picks flowers. As we shall see, motifs of flowers and falling asleep are often included in popular songs such as lullabies, in which maternal fears express themselves. These fears in turn converge with the sacred and become ritualized in the narrative of the death of Opheltes. Similar to the visual clues seen in the ritual dimension of the story of the children of Medea and of Herakles, here too we find the emotion of fear symbolized by the fallen hydria consistently shown at the foot of

Hypsipyle on visual representations of the death of Opheltes. In this myth we encounter the same anxieties expressed in other narratives of child heroes: the dangers awaiting babies in the world, grown-ups who make mistakes, the risks involved in entering sacred space, violence in the wilderness, and the need for atonement and compensation.

A fragment of the poet Simonides (c. 556–468 B.C.) may be the oldest extant literary reference to Opheltes. The two lines describe someone crying over a small child who just lost his life:

> ἰοστεφάνου γλυκεῖαν ἐδάκρυσαν
> ψυχὰν ἀποπνέοντα γαλαθηνὸν τέκος

> They wept for the tender baby of the violet-crowned
> [mother] as it breathed out its sweet soul.
> —Simonides fr. 553 *PMG* = Athenaios 9.396e

Athenaios quotes the lines and reports that Simonides is recounting the story of the death of Opheltes. The plural subject of *dakryein* could refer to the parents and the Seven against Thebes.

Pindar uses the very same phrase, *psykhan apopneein,* in *Nemean* 1 when he describes Baby Herakles smothering the serpents sent by Hera to kill him:

> ἀγχομένοις δὲ χρόνος
> ψυχὰς ἀπέπνευσεν μελέων ἀφάτων.

> And as they were strangled, time
> breathes out their souls from their unspeakable bodies.
> —Pindar, *Nemean* 1.46–47

In Pindar's periphrasis, time itself causes the death of the snakes, as the duration of Herakles' throttling forces the life out of the serpents' immense bodies. The phrase *psykhan apopneein*[3] doubtless evokes images of death by strangulation that fit both contexts: while Baby Herakles throttles the serpents trying to kill him and emerges from the encounter unscathed, the serpent of Nemea smothers Opheltes and the baby does not survive this all-too unequal fight.[4]

The first undisputable mention of Opheltes is found in an epinician of Simonides' nephew, Bacchylides (c. 518–450 B.C.), in honor of the victory of Automedes of Phlios at the Nemean Games.[5] The allusion is succinct and shows that the story of Opheltes' death is traditional enough by Bacchylides' time that it needs no introduction or explanation to be understood by his audience. Bacchylides starts by locating his poem geographically through an allusion to the great Panhellenic hero Herakles: the poet will celebrate the victor Automedes as well as the plain of Nemea where Herakles performed his first labor. Although the story of Herakles overcoming the lion, probably one of the oldest myths associated with Nemea, is already attested in Hesiod's *Theogony* 327–32,[6] the link between this myth and the foundation of the Nemean Games is not mentioned in ancient literature until the first century A.D., and Bacchylides does not connect the two events.[7]

The parallels between Herakles and Automedes are obvious: both the hero and the athlete face their trials in the same place, and both win their struggle. Like Automedes later on, Herakles emerges victorious out of his *athlos,* a word that, in epinician poetry, can denote both the mortal combats of heroes and athletic contests.[8] The story of Herakles functions not only as a geographical point of reference, but also reflects the ritual in which Automedes and the other athletes take part.

Another series of parallels is established through the image of Herakles and the lion: first, between Herakles and those heroes who established and participated in the original Nemean Games; second, between the lion and another destructive monster, the yellow-eyed, child-eating snake; and, finally, between Herakles and Opheltes, the Nemean nursling.

Bacchylides goes on to describe the foundation of the Nemean Games:

κε[ῖθι φοι]νικάσπιδες ἡμίθεοι
  πρ[ώτιστ]ον Ἀργείων κριτοί
ἄθλησαν ἐπ᾽ Ἀρχεμόρῳ, τὸν ξανθοδερκής
πέφν᾽ ἀωτεύοντα δράκων ὑπέροπλος,
σᾶμα μέλλοντος φόνου.

There, the demigods with the red shields,
the choicest of the Argives, were the first
to compete in the athletic games in honor of Arkhemoros,
who was killed [while sleeping? picking flowers?] by a monstrous
    yellow-eyed serpent,
a sign of the ruin to come.
—Bacchylides 9.10–14

Bacchylides tells the story tersely, but his narrative is nevertheless rich in veiled meaning, and his laconic manner clearly implies that the myth was well known to his audience. As there is no need to explain who Herakles is in the first lines of the epinician, there is no need to introduce Arkhemoros because the name in itself is enough to evoke his story. Everybody knows who he is, and there is no need to mention the circumstances of the accident, the identity of his parents, or his age.

Bacchylides' account of the death of Opheltes also abounds in words that conjure the cultic dimension of the story: "demigods" (*hēmitheoi*), the phrase *epi* plus a proper noun in the dative case, and "sign" (*sama*)—all belong to the ritual vocabulary of hero cult. The first to compete at the Nemean Games were "the demigods," "the choicest of the Argives." The word *hēmitheos* is much discussed, and its exact connotation much disputed. I follow Nagy and take the word to have a ritual connotation referring to the status of heroes in cult.[9] The use of *hēmitheos* in epic makes explicit the difference in perspective between looking at heroes as protagonists of the epic narrative in the past or as cult recipients in the present of the audience. I argue that this switch in perspective is at work in Bacchylides' poem: it is indicated in the Opheltes passage not only by the use of the word *hēmitheoi* but also by the content, which clearly refers to both the myth (past) and the ritual (here-and-now of the audience).

The construction *epi* with the dative case also belongs to traditional ritual syntax: the phrase is attested in literary sources and inscriptions from the beginning of the seventh century on.[10] The idiom is used in epic narrative when heroes establish a once-only funeral athletic festival to honor the death of one of their comrades (cf. *Odyssey* 24.91). Similarly, it is used in real life when relatives institute a once-only festival in honor of the deceased.[11] Perhaps by extension, the same idiom comes to be used in the context of seasonal athletic contests in honor of recipients of hero cult. The institution of ritualized fight or athletic contest as a way to appease the anger of the dead and atone for the guilt of the living is well attested in ancient Greek society.[12] The Seven are responsible—even though only indirectly, as we shall see—for Baby Opheltes' death, and they establish athletic games as a way of atoning, or as a compensation for, his death. Furthermore, Bacchylides says that the games are established in honor of Arkhemoros: the poet uses Opheltes' new name acquired after his death, the name that denotes him as a recipient of cult.

The third detail with ritual undertones used by Bacchylides in this passage is the word *sama* (= *sēma*). This word has several meanings, among which are "sign or signal," "tomb," or "memento."[13] In Bacchylides 9, the word denotes at least three different things: the "sign" intended for Amphiaraos and the Seven against Thebes; the "tomb" of Baby Arkhemoros upon which the Seven institute the Nemean Games; and the "sign of the ruin to come" (*sama mellontos phonou*), which also functions as a gloss on Arkhemoros's new name and a "memento" that makes the event of Opheltes' death present in the mind of the audience by recreating the episode at the time of a performance.

Bacchylides' brief account of the death of Opheltes and the first Nemean Games nevertheless conveys a complex picture of the events. One word in the manuscript remains a puzzle: *asageuonta* (line 13), itself a correction from *asageronta* in the manuscript, appears nowhere else in Greek literature or in the testimony of lexicographers. Both Kenyon and Jebb accept R. A. Neil's conjecture, *aōteuonta,* the meaning of which Hesychius explains by the verb *apanthizesthai* (to gather honey from flowers, to pick flowers, or to cull the best).[14] Kenyon takes the emendation literally as "while he was picking flowers,"[15] while Jebb argues that the word might be a variation on the use of another verb *aōteein* (to sleep), a rare form found twice in Homer and once in Simonides in the lullaby that Danaë sings to her son Perseus.[16]

One possible link between the two forms is the language of childhood: picking flowers in Greek poetry is conventionally associated with juvenile activities. Persephone, for example, is described as *paizousan* as she takes hold of flowers, right before she is engulfed in the earth and carried off by Hades (Homeric *Hymn to Demeter* 5–6).[17] Turning to other versions of the death of Opheltes, the motif of flower-picking emerges as an important one: as Persephone's plucking the narcissus precipitates one chain of events, so Opheltes' plucking of flowers precedes the serpent's attack and opens up the door to Hades, as it were. There seems to be a thematic connection between flower-picking and death.[18] As we will see in Euripides' and Statius's narratives, Opheltes plucks flowers right before he falls deep into a sleep from which he will awaken only with the appearance of the serpent and death. If Neil's conjecture is indeed correct, Bacchylides here uses language associated with childhood, and there is a shift from the epinician genre toward that of the lullaby (I will come back to this point below).

Bacchylides 9, the earliest certain reference to the death of Opheltes and the founding of the Nemean Games, alludes not only to a myth, but refers to the ritual of the athletic contest as well. The death of Opheltes, first commemorated by the Seven in the myth, is then commemorated by the athletes participating in the ritual surrounding the Nemean Games, as well as by the poet composing a poem in honor of the victor. Thus the epinician itself is a memento, or a *sēma,* in honor of Arkhemoros, a hero who needs no introduction to Bacchylides' audience.[19]

The tragedians also chose the death of Opheltes as subject matter for their plays: both Aeschylus (525–456 B.C.) and Euripides (c. 480–406 B.C.) composed trilogies dealing with the Nemean events, though unfortunately only fragments remain. Aeschylus's trilogy probably comprised the *Lemniai, Hypsipyle,* and *Nemea,*[20] but the only information we have about these plays comes from the scholia to Pindar's *Nemeans.* According to one scholar, Aeschylus's trilogy transmitted a Lemnian version of the story in which the Seven against Thebes played no role at all: in this version, Hypsipyle's sons, Euneos and Thoas, kill the serpent and establish the games for Opheltes,[21] the son of Nemea, a rather shadowy figure, who plays no role in the death of

Opheltes in any of the extant literary sources (hypothesis to Pindar's *Nemeans,* Drachmann 3.3). The eponymous nymph of Nemea, however, occurs in visual representations (see discussion of Ruvo amphora below).

Until the early twentieth century, Euripides' tragedy *Hypsipyle* was known through only a few fragments published by Nauck.[22] More substantial fragments from a second-century papyrus were published in 1908, and it is here that Hypsipyle makes her first appearance as a nurse on the literary scene: for the first time in extant literary sources, Hypsipyle herself and the role she plays in Opheltes' death are made explicit, and Opheltes is clearly described as a small baby.[23] The play tells the story of Hypsipyle, the encounter with Amphiaraos and the Seven against Thebes, the death of Baby Opheltes, and the reunion between Hypsipyle and her two sons by Jason, Thoas, and Euneos. Euripides' version comes about a half-century after Bacchylides' mention of Opheltes, but it is the earliest detailed account of the myth:[24] the fragments provide details about the death of Opheltes omitted from the earlier version.

The vocabulary of childhood is present throughout the play: the different words used to describe Opheltes consistently depict him as a very young child, an infant placed in the care of a nurse who carries and cares for him. Activities associated with childhood recur through the play: at the beginning, Hypsipyle comforts the crying Opheltes by mentioning toys (*athyrmata*) that will soothe his heart (*Hypsipyle* fr. I.1.2–3 Cockle). A little later, in the *parodos*, Hypsipyle talks about singing a lullaby for Opheltes:

ἰδοὺ κτύπος ὅδε κορτάλων
<        >        ἄν(ω)
οὐ τάδε πήνας, οὐ τάδε κερκίδος
ἱστοτόνου παραμύθια Λήμνια
Μοῦσα θέλει με κρέκειν, ὅ τι δ' εἰς ὕπνον
ἢ χάριν ἢ θεραπεύματα πρόσφορα
[π]αιδὶ πρέπει νεαρῶι
τάδε μελωιδὸς αὐδῶ.

Behold, the din of the castanets
· · · · · · · · · · · · · · · · · · · · · · · · · · · · · ·
neither with the woof here, nor with the weaver's shuttle
here stretched on the loom does the Muse
want me to weave Lemnian songs,
but I shall sing melodiously
the kind of delight or soothing offering
appropriate to lull a young child to sleep.
—Euripides, *Hypsipyle* fr. I.ii.9–16

Hypsipyle tells the chorus about her desire to sing to comfort Baby Opheltes. The reference to the accompaniment of castanets (*kortala*) is spoofed in Aristophanes' *Frogs* (1305–7). Dover argues that having Hypsipyle sing to the music of castanets was probably an innovation by Euripides, perhaps signaling "down-market music" in Athens, although one black-figure amphora in Copenhagen shows the Muses playing castanets as they accompany Apollo playing the lyre and Hermes to the throne of Zeus.[25] Yet we should note that the motif of Hypsipyle singing comforting songs, lullabies, is central to this passage, and the emphasis is on the youth of the baby.

As in the other versions of the myth, the encounter between Hypsipyle and the Seven against Thebes is at the origin of the accident. In Euripides' version, Amphiaraos approaches Hypsipyle and tells her he needs clean running water to perform a sacrifice for his army (fr. I.iv.29–36). After Amphiaraos's request, the text is very fragmentary, until the next connected passage, which describes Opheltes in the meadow:

> εἰς
> τὸν λειμῶνα καθίσας ἔδρεπεν
> ἕτερον ἐφ᾽ ἑτέρῳ † αἰρόμενος
> ἄγρυμ᾽ ἀνθέων ἡδομέναι ψυχᾶι
> τὸ νήπιον ἄπληστον ἔχων

> Sitting in the meadow, he plucked flowers,
> lifting one after the other,
> delighted in his soul by the flowery booty,
> behaving like an insatiable baby.
> —Euripides, *Hypsipyle* fr. 754N

These words, probably part of one of Hypsipyle's speeches, describe Baby Opheltes seated in the meadow and picking flowers, a description that further supports Neil's emendation in Bacchylides 9. The contrast between the inherently peaceful scene of the small child playing with grass and flowers and the sudden attack of the serpent is striking. The parallel between Opheltes' and Persephone's fate is once again unmistakable: meadows are peaceful places where the most dangerous events take place; the flowery *leimōnes* of ancient Greece, moreover, are often found close to, or even in, the underworld.[26]

The snake is described in another fragment, which may be part of another speech by Hypsipyle or of a messenger's speech (fr. 60.ii.9–19). The snake (*drakōn*) inhabits and guards the spring to which Hypsipyle leads Amphiaraos and the Seven against Thebes.[27] The danger is well known, since shepherds fear it, and the monstrosity of the snake's appearance is emphasized (*gorgōps*, savage-looking), as it was in Bacchylides 9. Here also, the contrast is marked between the serene atmosphere of the shady spring and the silent and horrific danger it conceals: the more bucolic and peaceful the scene, the more ominous and dangerous.[28]

The rest of the fragments deal with Hypsipyle's defense to Eurydike and the reunion with her two long-lost sons. Hypsipyle defends herself to Eurydike and remembers how she used to carry the baby in her arms; she describes her own pain at Opheltes' death, which affects her in the same way as her own child's would (fr. 32 and 60). Hypsipyle uses the words *teknon* (child) and *tithēnēma* (nursling), two terms that evoke early childhood (as well as motherhood). Amphiaraos comes to her help and explains the circumstances of the accident to Eurydike. He relates how he needed water in order to perform a sacrifice on behalf of the army and gives more details (unfortunately the text is badly damaged) about the death of Opheltes:

> [δρ]άκων ασ[
> ἠκόντισ' ἁ[
> καί νιν δρομ[
> εἵλιξεν ἀμφ[ὶ
> ἡμεῖς δ' ἰδό[ντες
> ἐγὼ δ' ἐτόξευσ['
> <u>ἀρχὴ</u> γὰρ ἡμῖν [
> Ἀρχέμορος ε . [
> σύ τ' οὐχὶ σαυτὴ[ν
> <u>ὄρνιθα</u> δ' Ἀργείο[ισι
> καὶ μὴ στολ[
> —Euripides, *Hypsipyle* fr. 60.ii.9–19

Although incomplete, this passage offers a vivid depiction of the episode. Rather than attempting a fragmentary translation, let me offer a paraphrase: Amphiaraos and his men suddenly see the serpent coiling around Baby Opheltes. Amphiaraos attempts to shoot (an arrow?) at the snake, but it is too late. There follows an etymological explanation for the new name of Opheltes: his death is a "beginning" (*arkhē*) for the Seven (*hēmin*) and an omen (*ornis*) for the Argives, and they rename the child Arkhemoros.

After comforting Eurydike with a digression on the fleeting nature of human life, Amphiaraos goes on to tell about the foundation of games in honor of Arkhemoros:

> ἃ δ' εἰκὸς Ἀργο[
> <u>θάψαι</u> δὸς ἡμ[ῖν
> οὐ γὰρ καθ' ἡμ[
> ἀλλ' <u>εἰς τὸν ἀε[ι</u>

τοῖ[ς σο]ῖς βρότε[
<u>κλεινὸς</u> γὰρ ἔσ[ται
<u>ἀγῶνα</u> τ᾽ αὐτῶ[ι
<u>στεφάνους</u> διδ[
<u>ξηλωτὸς</u> ἔστ[αι
ἐν τῷδε με .[
<u>μνησθήσετα</u>[ι
<u>ἐπωνομάσθη</u>[
Νεμέας κατ᾽ ἄλσ[ος
—Euripides, *Hypsipyle* fr. 60.ii.35–47

Again, the passage is too broken for continuous translation. It is clear, however, that many key words evoke the funeral and ritual context of the games.
*Thaptein* (to honor with funeral rites) deals with an appropriate funeral for the
dead body, while *kleinos* (famous) and *zēlōtos* (envied, blessed) signal the status of the child after heroization; *agōn* (contest, struggle) and *stephanoi*
(crowns) refer to the athletic competition at Nemea; and *mnēsasthai* (to be
remembered) and *eponomasthēnai* (to be named) allude to remembrance and
the change of name of Opheltes, who will be remembered as Arkhemoros. *Eis
ton aei* (forever), in the fourth line, evokes the permanence of the institution.

To sum up, the story that was only hinted at in Bacchylides 9 is given in
all its details in Euripides' play: this passage relates not only the death of
Opheltes, but all the circumstances surrounding it. More elements of the
myth are present: Opheltes' death is caused by his nurse's negligence, which
is provoked by the Seven's arrival in Nemea and their need for water. The baby
is placed down in a meadow, where he plays with flowers and is attacked by
a monstrous serpent. The Seven attempt to save him, but too late. Amphiaraos
interprets the death as a bad omen and establishes funeral games in honor of
the dead baby.

The so-called Lille papyrus, discovered at the beginning of the twentieth
century, was not published until 1977: used as mummy cartonnage, it consists
of several fragments of Callimachus's poetry and can be dated to the late third
century b.c., within a generation after Callimachus's death.[29] The first fragment (254–55) announces that the poem is dedicated to Berenike in honor of
her victory at Nemea,[30] and the poet mentions the tomb of Opheltes:

παρ᾽] <u>ἠρίον</u> οὔ[νεκ᾽] Ὀφέλτου
. . . . . . . . .] Ἀρχέμορος ἐκαλεῖτο [

By the <u>grave</u> of Opheltes
. . . he was called Arkhemoros.
—Callimachus, *Aitia* PLille 82.13–14, *Supplementum Hellenisticum* 254.13
and 255.7

The reference, like the one in Bacchylides 9, is concise, and the story behind Opheltes' death is not developed.

Fragment 257 tells of the encounter between Molorkhos and Herakles and describes the havoc created by the lion in the region around Nemea. Callimachus is the first extant source to mention Molorkhos and his hospitality, and some argue that he, in fact, invented the story.[31] In fragment 260, Herakles predicts that Molorkhos will have plenty of cattle if he kills the lion. Fragments 264 and 265 (Pfeiffer 57 and 59) describe another conversation between Herakles and Molorkhos that takes place after Herakles has killed the lion. Herakles says he will relate what Athena told him about the future Nemean Games (Pfeiffer 57). The following fragment is badly damaged, but still offers a wealth of information about the ritual of the Nemean Games:

```
                         ].υ.[
    ].στέφος [
     ]λλ' ὅτεμ[
     ]χρύσοιο.[
    καί μιν Ἀλητεῖδαι πουλὺ γεγειότερον
    τοῦδε παρ' Αἰγαίωνι θεῷ τελέοντες ἀγῶνα
    θήσουσιν νίκης σύμβολον Ἰσθμιάδος
    ζήλῳ τῶν Νεμέηθε. πίτυν δ' ἀποτιμήσουσιν,
    ἢ πρὶν ἀγωνιστὰς ἔστεφε τοὺς Ἐφύρῃ.
             ].νωητετεοί, γέρ[ον
              ].οὐδ' ἱερὴ π.[
             ]σεμοι προμ[
              ]ον Παλλὰς ἔ[
             ]αρενῳ τοδ[
               σ]ὴν κατ' ἐπω[νυμίην.'
             ]υς τε Μολόρ[χειος
             ].θυμὸν ἀρε[σσάμενος,
    ν]ύκτα μὲν αὐτόθι μίμνεν, ἀπέστιχε δ' Ἄργος ἑῷος.
    οὐδὲ ξεινοδόκῳ λήσαθ' ὑποσχεσίης,
    πέμψε δέ οἱ τὸ[ν] ὀρῆα, τίεν δέ ἑ ὡς ἕνα πηῶν.
    νῦ]ν δ' ἔθ' [ἀ]γι[στείη]ν οὐδαμὰ παυσομένην
             ]..Πελοπη.[
             ]..ἔσχον ἀνα[
             ]έστησαν ὅς[
             ]παισὶν ἀνας[
```

And the sons of Aletes holding games much older
than these at the sanctuary of the god Aigaion
will put it [the crown of celery] as a token of the Isthmian victory

in rivalry with the Nemean Games. And they will remove the pine tree,
which before <u>crowned the competitors</u> in the games of Ephyra. . . .
He spent the night there and walked away to Argos at dawn.
And he did not forget his promise to his host,
but he sent him the mule, and he honored him as if one of his own kin.
And still now the <u>holy rites will not cease</u>. . . .
—Callimachus fr. 59.1–25 (Pfeiffer)

The beginning of the passage describes how the Corinthians—descendants
of Aletes and therefore of Herakles—became envious of the Nemean Games'
wild celery crowns and decided to switch from the pine crowns they traditionally awarded at the Isthmian Games and to adopt the Nemean custom
(lines 1–9).[32] Herakles seems to address Molorkhos as gerōn (10–15).
Molorkhos welcomes Herakles into his home, and after eating and sleeping,
the hero returns to Argos and sends a mule to his host as a gift or payment,
honoring him as if he were one of his relatives (16–20). If the reading *agis-
teiēn* is correct, the fragment concludes with the observation that the "holy
rites" have never stopped up to the present (21). Callimachus's description is
reminiscent of Euripides' aetiology for the games in *Hypsipyle* (cf. underlined
words with fr. 60.ii.35–47 above). The last four lines, apart from an allusion
to Pelops and to some children (*paides*), are too badly damaged to be of use.

Competing aetiologies for athletic contests are by no means uncommon,
as Nagy notes in his study of the Olympic Games, and different traditions
may be used to explain the origins of the different competitions included in
the games and reflect the evolution of the relative importance of different
competitions.[33] Traditionally, in fact, the association of Herakles' first labor
with the Nemean Games seems to have functioned as an *aition* for a particular athletic contest, the *pankration*. A passage in Bacchylides 13 may have
been the inspiration behind both the form and content of Callimachus's
*aition* for the Nemean Games.[34]

In Apollodoros's version of the story (first or second century A.D.), the Seven
come to Nemea seeking water. Hypsipyle shows them the way to a spring, leaving behind Opheltes, *nēpion paida*, whom she was nursing (*etrephen*). While
Hypsipyle and the Seven are gone, the baby is killed by a serpent. Adrastos and
his men come back, kill the serpent, and bury the boy. Amphiaraos interprets
the death as a sign of things to come, and they rename the child Arkhemoros
and celebrate the Nemean Games in his honor. Amphiaraos's companions
divide the victories among themselves: Adrastos wins the horse race, Eteokles
the footrace, Tydeus the boxing, Laodokos the javelin-throwing, Polyneikes the
wrestling, and Parthenopaios the archery match.

The Roman mythographer Hyginus (second century A.D.) adds a few details to the story in his *Fabula* 74: from his account we learn of the oracle's command never to put Opheltes on the ground before he is old enough to walk. When the Seven come to Nemea and ask Hypsipyle for water, she puts the child (*puerum*) down where celery grows, and while she draws water for the Seven, the serpent who is the guardian of the source kills the baby. Adrastos and his companion kill the serpent and institute funeral games for the boy, in which the winners are crowned with wild celery.

Statius's account (first century A.D.) of the death of Opheltes is remarkable in many ways: it is longer than any other, includes a direct address to Baby Opheltes, and dwells lovingly on descriptions of the child playing in the meadow as well as on the lugubrious details of the serpent's attack. It also describes in detail the funeral games for Arkhemoros and the different athletic contests. Inasmuch as Statius's account is highly derivative and resembles the earlier ones, not much, and certainly no new, information about the rituals surrounding the death of Opheltes can be gleaned from it. Statius is further removed from its subject matter than an author like Bacchylides, who flourished less than a century after the formal institution of the games. Nevertheless, Statius's version is clearly steeped in the Greek tradition and helps illuminate many details of the story.

In Statius's *Thebaid*, Bacchus dries up all the rivers and springs, except for one, as a way of delaying the Seven on their way to Thebes. By the time they arrive in Nemea, the Seven are desperate for water and beg Hypsipyle to help them. The first mention of Opheltes occurs in Statius's description of the one river that is left flowing by Bacchus, the Langia. Like Bacchylides, Statius begins with the end of the story—the funeral games—and first describes the consequences of events he has yet to relate. Statius uses the two names, Arkhemoros and Opheltes, without explanation.

Later in the narrative, the Seven finally come upon Hypsipyle and Opheltes in the forest and ask her to show them where to find water. Hypsipyle puts the baby down so that he may not delay them on the way to the spring: Hypsipyle places the child on the ground in a field and comforts his crying with tender words and by giving him flowers gathered in a bunch. It is impossible to determine exactly what sources Statius had at his disposal, but he stands at the end of a long tradition, and the association between babies and flowers is clearly a traditional one, which here finds its most detailed expression, as we will see shortly. Statius then describes Opheltes alone in the grass, at times crying for his nurse or smiling and babbling (*Thebaid* 4.786–93). Statius emphasizes the bucolic elements of the story and also gives a charming description of the ease and swiftness with which infants change their emotional states. Yet the combination of child, meadow, and flowers also spells danger, and the reader knows that the bucolic setting is more threatening than reassuring.

Baby Opheltes remains alone on the ground, as Hypsipyle tells her story (in close to five hundred lines) to the Seven; the narrative then switches back to what is happening to Baby Opheltes, unbeknown to Hypsipyle or the Seven:

> Immemor absentis—sic di suasistis!—alumni,
> ille graves oculos languentiaque ora comanti
> mergit humo, <u>fessusque diu puerilibus actis</u>
> <u>labitur in somnos,</u> prensa manus haeret in herba.

> [You, Hypsipyle,] forgetful—thus did the gods compel you—of your
>     absent charge,
> and he, with heavy eyes and drooping head,
> sinks in the luxuriant earth, <u>wearied by his long childish play,</u>
> and <u>falls asleep</u> with one hand still holding the grass tight-clutched.
> —Statius, *Thebaid* 5.501–4

In these four lines, we find all the elements present in the earlier Greek narratives: the child alone on a patch of green, picking flowers and playing with the grass, soon overcome by sleep. While Statius does not specify what the *puerilibus actis* pursued by the child were, the phrase may very well describe the activity of picking flowers, in which Baby Opheltes is still engaged as he falls into a torpor. As Lactantius notes, the way in which the child suddenly falls asleep is an indication of Opheltes' young age since, "when a baby falls asleep, he does not let go of whatever he was holding" (*cum somno requiescit infantia, quicquid tenuerit non reliquit;* schol. Statius, *Thebaid* 5.503–4 [Lactantius]). Thus we find again the themes that are also central to Bacchylides and Euripides' versions of the story: flower-picking and falling asleep as a prelude to death.

We saw in Euripides how Hypsipyle uses songs to comfort the baby into sleep. While there is no actual lullaby in Euripides or Statius, I suggest that the theme of the death of Arkhemoros contains many elements that belong to the lullaby genre, and I will focus for a moment on representations of lullabies in Greek literature and see how their themes connect with the myth of Opheltes.[35] Greeks nurses, Plato tells us, lull children to sleep and calm their fears by a combination of song and dance:

> ἡνίκα γὰρ ἄν που βουληθῶσι κατακοιμίζειν τὰ δυσυπνοῦντα τῶν
> παιδίων αἱ μητέρες, οὐχ ἡσυχίαν αὐτοῖς προσφέρουσιν ἀλλὰ τοὐναντίον
> κίνησιν, ἐν ταῖς ἀγκάλαις ἀεὶ σείουσαι, καὶ οὐ σιγὴν ἀλλά <u>τινα</u>

μελῳδίαν, καὶ ἀτεχνῶς οἷον καταυλοῦσι τῶν παιδίων, καθαπερεὶ τῶν
ἐκφρόνων βακχείων, ἰάσει ταύτῃ τῇ τῆς κινήσεως
ἅμα χορείᾳ καὶ μούσῃ χρώμεναι.

Thus when mothers have children suffering from sleeplessness and want to
lull them to rest, the treatment they apply is to give them, not quiet, but
motion, for they rock them in their arms; and instead of silence, they use a
kind of singing; and thus they charm the children with the *aulos* (like the
victims of Bacchic frenzy) by employing the combined movements of dance
and song as a remedy.
—Plato, *Laws* 790e

Plato's description includes many elements traditionally associated with
lullabies: rocking, music, and singing. Lullabies can also be used in the context of ritual. The Phrygians, for example, according to Plutarch, think that
their god sleeps through winter:

Φρύγες δὲ τὸν θεὸν οἰόμενοι χειμῶνος καθεύδειν, θέρους
δ' ἐγρηγορέναι τοτὲ μὲν κατευνασμούς, τοτὲ δ' ἀνεγέρσεις
βακχεύοντες αὐτῷ τελοῦσι.

The Phrygians, believing that the god sleeps in the winter and is awake in the
summer, sing lullabies for him in one season and rousing songs in the other
with Bacchic frenzy.
—Plutarch, *Isis and Osiris* 378e

Thus they help the god fall asleep by singing lullabies (*kateunasmoi*). These
ritual lullabies are so powerful that they have to be counteracted in the spring
by way of "rousing" (*anegerseis*) songs. Death is indeed the twin brother of
Sleep (*Iliad* 14.231), and while sleep poses no real danger for immortal gods,
this traditional thematic association is of great concern to human beings:[36]
sleep is a perilous state—particularly for small children—and death is a pervasive motif in ancient lullabies.

We have seen how the story of Opheltes and the serpent offers a distorted
mirror image of another baby's encounter with a similar threat. In
Theokritos 24, Alkmene sings a lullaby to her twin sons, Iphikles and
Herakles. Alkmene's song is very explicit, and, with her plea to her children
to fall asleep, she includes a demand that they wake up:

εὕδετ', ἐμὰ βρέφεα, γλυκερὸν καὶ ἐγέρσιμον ὕπνον·
εὕδετ' ἐμὰ ψυχά, δύ' ἀδελφεώ εὔσοα τέκνα·
ὄλβιοι εὐνάξοισθε καὶ ὄλβιοι ἀῶ ἵκοισθε.

Sleep, my babies, sleep sweetly and the kind of sleep from which one
    wakes up,
sleep, my souls, my twins, happy babes.
Be blessed in your sleep, and wake up blessed at dawn.
—Theokritos, *Idyll* 24

Alkmene's lullaby is pervaded with fear of death: she begs her children to
sleep the kind of sleep from which one can wake up (*egersimon hypnon*) and
bids them both to sleep and to reach dawn "blessed" (*olbioi*). Baby Herakles,
unlike doomed Opheltes, will indeed wake up in time (with the help of Zeus)
and successfully carries out his first (unofficial) labor by strangling the two
snakes sent by Hera to kill him.

While Alkmene's lullaby overtly states its benign ends, others are more
ambivalent and incorporate themes that are threatening and troubling,
rather than reassuring and somniferous. In an earlier example, Simonides
relates the story of Danaë and her baby, Perseus, after they are put into a
wooden chest and thrown into the sea by Akrisios. Embedded in Danaë's
lament is a lullaby that she sings to calm her child as they are tossed about
by the winds and waves:

ἀμφί τε Περσέι βάλλε φίλαν χέρα
εἶπεν τ᾽· ὦ τέκος οἷον ἔχω πόνον·
σὺ δ᾽ ἀωτεῖς, γαλαθηνῷ
δ᾽ ἤθεϊ κνοώσσεις
ἐν ἀτερπέι δούρατι χαλκεογόμφῳ
<τῷ> δε νυκτιλαμπεῖ,
κυανέῳ δνόφῳ ταθείς·
ἄχναν δ᾽ ὕπερθε τεᾶν κομᾶν
βαθεῖαν παριόντος
κύματος οὐκ ἀλέγεις, οὐδ᾽ ἀνέμου
φθόγγον, πορφυρέαι
κείμενος ἐν χλανίδι, πρόσωπον καλόν.
εἰ δέ τοι δεινὸν τό γε δεινὸν ἦν,
καί κεν ἐμῶν ῥημάτων
λεπτὸν ὑπεῖχες οὖας.
κέλομαι δ᾽, εὖδε βρέφος,
εὑδέτω δὲ πόντος, εὑδέτω δ᾽ ἄμετρον κακόν·

She put her loving arms around Perseus
and said, "My child, what grief I bear!
But you sleep, you slumber
like a tender baby,
in this joyless brass-bound box, stretched out

in the dark night
and murky gloom.
You pay no attention
to the deep swell of the waves
rushing by above your hair
nor to the voice of the wind,
lying wrapped in your purple blanket, a lovely face.
If this danger were indeed danger to you,
then you would turn
your delicate ear to my words.
<u>But I order you, sleep, little baby</u>;
and let the sea sleep, and let the measureless evil sleep.
—Simonides 543.6–22 *PMG*[37]

Danaë's lullaby to Baby Perseus evokes images of corpses, coffins, and death. While Perseus peacefully sleeps, he is also, as Rosenmeyer argues, facing his "first trial, as his rites of manhood are compressed into the ritual of birth and exposure."[38] Danaë ends her lullaby with a direct command, "I order you, sleep little baby" (line 21), and metonymically gives her plea cosmic proportions by similarly commanding the sea and "measureless evil" (*ametron kakon*) to go to sleep. The threatening elements in her song ostensibly function apotropaically, and Baby Perseus escapes death and survives his long night at sea. Danaë uses several verbs meaning "to sleep," among which are *aōteein* and *knōssein*, two unusual forms. The verb *aōteein* is of course related to the form *aōteuein*, as discussed above in the context of Bacchylides 9.13. Again images of flowers and sleep mix in the metaphorical language of childhood.

Lullabies in Greek poetry—whether narrated or alluded to—often occur at moments of crisis when the child, with or without its mother, faces great dangers. The very presence of a lullaby in ancient literature is indeed in itself a sign of menace. The boundary between threatening and apotropaic elements sometimes gets blurred, and it becomes difficult to distinguish what is warded off from what is sought after. I argue that motifs belonging to lullabies can also function as danger markers, just as do the lullabies themselves. Activities linked with sleeping, such as flower-picking, thus are also closely associated with danger and death.

Lullabies extant in ancient literature share many features with songs used to lull children to sleep in later periods. The flower motif is found in modern Greek songs, as well as in many other European folksong traditions.[39] There are celebrated adaptations in "high" art as well. We find similar elements, for example, in a poem by Goethe:

Du liebes Kind, komm, geh mit mir!
Gar schöne Spiele spiel' ich mit dir:
Manch' bunte Blumen sind an dem Strand,
Meine Mutter hat manch' gülden Gewand.

. . . . . . . . . . . . . . . . . . . . . . . . .
Meine Töchter sollen dich warten schön;
Meine Töchter führen den nächtlichen Reihn,
Und wiegen und tanzen und singen dich ein.

. . . . . . . . . . . . . . . . . . . . . . .
In seinem Armen das Kind war tot.

You sweet child, come, come with me!
We shall play lovely games together,
there are flowers of many colors by the water's edge,
my mother has many garments of gold.

. . . . . . . . . . . . . . . . . . . . . . . . .
My daughters shall be your lovely attendants;
every night my daughters dance a round dance,
and they will rock you and dance you and sing you to sleep.

. . . . . . . . . . . . . . . . . . . . . . .
In his arms, the child was dead.
—Goethe, *Elfking*

Goethe's vivid description of the Elfking, who seduces children into following him—to their death—includes promises of flowers of many colors, dancing, and singing. Death comes, again, in the trail of flowers and lullabies.

While the Phrygians' ritually performed songs ensure their god's well-being, no rousing songs can wake up human beings once they are dead. Lullabies for children embody mothers' concerns for their child's safety and attempt to avert disaster by facing it. The well-known lyrics of a traditional English song, in fact, illustrate the many functions of the lullaby: "When the bough breaks, the baby will fall, and down will come baby, cradle and all." Lullabies—both ancient and modern—allude to death as a way of warding it off, expressing a mother's unspeakable fears. The kind of maternal fears expressed in lullabies are similar to the anxieties contained in the story of the death of Opheltes, but in the case of Opheltes, the horror and fear transmutes to become part of a sacred narrative that culminates with the baby's heroization.

Let us go back to Statius's account of the death of Opheltes, which includes many more details, including a protracted description of the serpent's approach. To Bacchylides' three-word description of the snake, Statius answers with thirty lines of gory details: the huge serpent's appearance, the greenish poison in his fangs, his three-pronged tongue and triple row of teeth.

As the snake starts moving toward Opheltes, his every coil and swirl are described. Even the serpent's putrid breath has its dangers, as it kills off the grass along the snake's route (*Thebaid* 5.527–28).

Between the description of the serpent and its attack, Statius interrupts his narrative with a direct address to Baby Opheltes:

> Quis tibi, <u>parve,</u> deus tam magni pondera fati
> sorte dedit? Tune hoc vix prima ad limina vitae
> hoste iaces? An ut inde <u>sacer per saecula</u> Grais
> gentibus et tanto dignus morerere sepulcro?
> occidis extremae destrictus verbere caudae
> ignaro serpente puer, <u>fugit</u> ilicet <u>artus</u>
> <u>somnus et in solam patuerunt lumina mortem.</u>

> What god, <u>little one</u>, gave you the burden
> of such a terrible fate? Hardly on the first threshold of life
> are you slain by such an enemy? Was it so that you might be <u>sacred
>     forever</u>
> to the Greek people and did you die so that you might be worthy of
>     such a burial?
> You died, struck by the end of the unaware
> serpent's tail, and at once <u>sleep left your limbs</u>
> <u>and your eyes open only for death</u>.
> —Statius, *Thebaid* 5.534–40

Statius refers to Opheltes as a cult recipient: Baby Opheltes is *sacer* (sacred) to the Greeks throughout the centuries, and his special status explains why he was granted such a burial. The serpent strikes the baby with his tail, and death replaces sleep. In Statius's account, the serpent is unaware (*ignaro serpente*) of killing Opheltes, although the description of Opheltes' mutilated body later in the narrative seems to indicate a certain degree of malice in his assailant (cf. 5.596–98; 6.35).

There follows the return of Hypsipyle and the Seven to the palace and a sad and violent scene between them and the grief-stricken parents. Adrastos successfully defuses the situation, and Amphiaraos offers an interpretation of the events to the parents and the crowd that has gathered (5.733–53). In his speech, Amphiaraos relates a prophecy given to him by Apollo, in a way that is very much reminiscent of Herakles relating the prophecy given to him by Athena in Callimachus's poem dedicated to the victory of Berenike. In both cases, the prophecies concern the foundation of the Nemean Games. According to Amphiaraos, all the events leading to, and including, the death of Baby Opheltes, are in fact meant only as a warning, the signal of the beginning of the ruin, hence his new name, destined for the Seven. Amphiaraos announces that the child deserves lasting honors.

In book 6, Statius describes the preparations for the funeral of Arkhemoros as well as the foundation of the games in his honor. He begins by mentioning the other three Panhellenic Games, Olympia, Delphi, and Isthmia, and connecting them with Pelops, the Python, and Palaimon, the games where warriors begin to practice and nurture their martial valor (6.3–4). Statius here makes clear the connection between baby heroes and Panhellenic festivals. Opheltes' body is then placed on a bier with several levels: the first is decorated with grass from the fields, while the second is decked with a more sophisticated arrangement of flowers; a pile of luxurious goods from Arabia is heaped on the third; and finally gold and jewels are placed on the topmost level. Among these jewels is one showing another baby hero, Linos, with the dogs who killed him, a story that has always been an object of horror for Opheltes' mother (see Statius 1.557–672; see chap. 3). Statius is keenly aware of the links between various baby heroes, as this allusion to the narrative of the death of Linos makes explicit (6.54–248).

Eurydike speaks during the funeral and accuses Hypsipyle of having killed Opheltes by her negligence (6.139–76). Crushed by Opheltes' death, Eurydike gives vent to her resentment of the role that Hypsipyle played with the baby. Eurydike confesses that she had no real relationship with her son and that Hypsipyle was his de facto mother. When Hypsipyle abandons Opheltes on the meadow, a mother's worst nightmare is realized.

The *Thebaid* then goes on to relate how a temple to Arkhemoros is built nine days after the funeral. The temple is decorated with scenes of the child's brief life and death. (6.242–48). Again, we find echoes of the Greek tradition here: heroic shrines were often decorated with statues (and perhaps paintings) reenacting the narrative of heroization (see, for example, Pausanias's and Ailios Aristeides' descriptions of the shrine of Melikertes in the next chapter). The rest of book 6 describes the different athletic contests that the Greek warriors engage in during the funeral games for Opheltes. At the end of the funeral, Adrastos gives a last speech and pours a libation in honor of Opheltes. Adrastos's speech echoes that of Amphiaraos at 5.733–53. The same themes appear in both: the necessity of establishing games for the dead baby and the divinity of Arkhemoros are emphasized. If Arkhemoros helps the Seven, he will be worshiped not only around Nemea, but he will have temples and a cult as far as Thebes (*Thebaid* 7.90–104). It is not uncommon for the Greeks to describe their heroes in divine terms, even as they make an essential distinction between gods and heroes.[40] By Roman times, heroization, and even deification, of dead human beings has become commonplace, and categories are even more flexible.[41]

When we turn away from Roman poetry to the prose of Pausanias's guide-book to Greece, we find an eyewitness account of the sanctuary of Opheltes at Nemea. By Pausanias's time, in the second century A.D., the games were held at Argos, in the winter rather than in the summer (2.15.2; 6.16.4). Nemean Zeus and Opheltes were still the focus of the rituals, and the games included a race for men in armor. When Pausanias visited Nemea, he found the temple of Nemean Zeus in ruins, with the roof caved in and the statues gone. The shrine of Opheltes, however, seems to have been intact, and Pausanias gives a detailed description of the site.

Interestingly, he starts with the patch of grass near the temple where Baby Opheltes was put down by Hypsipyle:

κυπαρίσσων τε ἄλσος ἐστὶ περὶ τὸν ναόν, καὶ τὸν Ὀφέλτην <u>ἐνταῦθα</u> ὑπὸ τῆς τροφοῦ τεθέντα <u>ἐς τὴν πόαν</u> διαφθαρῆναι λέγουσιν ὑπὸ τοῦ δράκοντος.

There is a <u>grove of cypresses</u> around the temple, <u>there</u> where they say that Opheltes was killed by the serpent when he was put down <u>on the grass</u> by his nurse.
—Pausanias 2.15.2–3

Pausanias does not give many details about the circumstances of the death. He does not name Hypsipyle, but otherwise, Pausanias's version of the story is similar to the earlier ones: Opheltes is placed on a grassy patch where he is attacked by the serpent. Pausanias gives several details about the physical lay-out of the shrine: the tomb (*taphos*) of Opheltes is surrounded by a fence of stones (*thrigkos lithōn*) very much like—indeed perhaps imitating—the one surrounding the Pelopeion at Olympia (Pausanias 1.42.8).[42] Altars are placed beside the tomb inside the enclosure. And a mound of earth (*khōma*) signals the tomb (*mnēma*) of Lykourgos, Opheltes' father.

Opheltes remained central at Nemea, and the Christian writer Clement of Alexandria (c. A.D. 160–215) mentions him in his *Protreptikos*, when he exhorts the Greeks to stop participating in the games held around the tombs of dead heroes. He mentions the four Panhellenic Games and describes the Nemean Games:

Νεμέασι δὲ ἄλλο παιδίον Ἀρχέμορος κεκήδευται καὶ τοῦ παιδίου ὁ ἐπιτάφιος προσαγορεύεται Νέμεα.

Another small child [*paidion*], Arkhemoros, is mourned at Nemea, and his tomb is where the games of Nemea are held.
—Clement of Alexandria, *Protreptikos* 2.29

The use of the word *paidion* (small child) is interesting: in the preceding sentence, Clement was speaking of the Isthmian Games in honor of Melikertes, and he clearly thinks of both Melikertes and Opheltes as small children of about the same age. Clement then decries all the Panhellenic Games because they resemble mysteries and oracles:

μυστήρια ἦσαν ἄρα, ὡς ἔοικεν, οἱ ἀγῶνες ἐπὶ νεκροῖς διαθλούμενοι, ὥσπερ καὶ τὰ λόγια, καὶ δεδήμευνται ἄμφω. . . . αἶσχος δὲ ἤδη κοσμικὸν οἵ τε ἀγῶνες καὶ οἱ φαλλοὶ οἱ Διονύσῳ ἐπιτελούμενοι, κακῶς ἐπινενεμημένοι τὸν βίον.

It seems that <u>the games</u> held <u>in honor of the dead</u> are in fact <u>mysteries,</u> just like oracles, and both are public. . . . This is now a <u>cosmic shame,</u> both the games and the phalluses made for Dionysos, spreading over life in an evil manner.
—Clement of Alexandria, *Protreptikos* 2.29

Clement concludes by asserting that the games are a "cosmic disgrace." While Clement—a pagan who converted to Christianity—is a late, prejudiced, and thus not a very reliable source, the link between mysteries and the games is one that Philostratos makes in his *Heroikos,* when he compares the rituals for the children of Medea and Melikertes with those in honor of Achilles and describes all of them as a mixture of initiatory and mourning rituals, something we will come back to in the next chapter (see also chap. 1 on the same passage).

When we turn to the visual tradition for the myth, the oldest possible representation of the myth of Opheltes is also one of the most controversial. A white-ground cup made by the potter Sotades and painted by the Sotades Painter in Athens in the second quarter of the fifth century depicts a man who throws a stone at a snake, which rears up and exhales smoke. Traces of a fallen figure are discernible on the bottom left (fig. 19).[43] The earliest publications on the cup describe it as the death of Opheltes.[44] Burn, however, notes several problems with this interpretation: the man in the hat is dressed more like a peasant than a hero, and there is no baby in the scene (although so much of the cup is missing that this is a difficult claim to sustain). The toe formerly believed to be the baby's, moreover, is probably the man's.

Burn argues that since the cup and other vases were found in the same tomb, "their iconography may be deliberate, significant, and linked" and that it is "extremely likely that they were executed as a special commission."[45] Using this principle, she analyzes the Sotades cup showing the man and snake

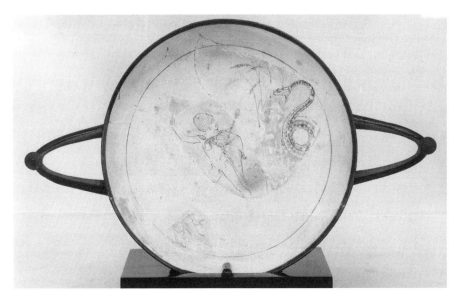

Figure 19. Attic red-figure, white-ground cup, attributed to the Sotades Painter, c. 475–450 B.C. London D 7, British Museum. Photograph courtesy of the Trustees of the British Museum.

in relationship with two other London cups. Both the Glaukos cup and the Melissa cup depict scenes that have to do with honey, which in turn is often linked with themes of initiation, death, and life after death. By identifying the man on the third cup as Aristaios and the woman as Eurydike just after she is bitten by the snake, Burn connects the third cup with the other two via the honey and initiation themes. Aristaios taught the art of beekeeping to humans, and Eurydike is often understood as the ultimate bride, perpetually poised on the brink between girlhood and womanhood.

One of the problems with the identification of the scene on the cup is the man's identity. Burn refers to two contradictory assessments by Beazley: first, that the attire of the man is not appropriate to a hero and thus he cannot be identified as one of the Seven against Thebes; second, that in a few cases this same costume is worn by "light-armed warriors," which would fit the story of the Seven and Opheltes perfectly.[46] To confuse matters more, Burn notes that Aristaios *was* in fact "a hero, the son of Apollo and the nymph Kyrene."[47] The argument from the clothes, then, is not convincing either way. The absence of Baby Opheltes in itself does not constitute ground enough to dismiss the identification of the scene with his death, since in at least one of the literary versions—Statius's—of the events, Hypsipyle first discovers the serpent and no trace of the baby. The death of the serpent, moreover, is an integral part of the story of the death of Opheltes.

Thus many of Burn's arguments for the identification with Aristaios and the death of Eurydike could just as well support the thesis that the cup shows the death of Opheltes. The cup appears to be part of a set that was commissioned for a funeral, and thus the iconography of the cups is probably deliberate. The thematic tie between the three, which Burn identifies as honey, and more particularly honey as a symbol of initiation rituals and a symbol of death and life after death, could just as well apply to the myth of the baby hero. As Eurydike's death can be seen as a failed initiation ritual, so can the death of Opheltes. Of course, the episode of the death of Opheltes does not have the same obvious links with honey as the myths surrounding Aristaios, but if the connection is acknowledged to be symbolic rather than literal, the same theme of initiation as death is certainly present in the story of Opheltes.[48]

A third way of interpreting the cup might solve the problem of the man in the hat, while preserving the link with honey. Perhaps the Sotades cup depicts a variant on the theme of the death of Opheltes, and the man killing the serpent is not one of the Seven, but Hypsipyle's son, Euneos (see discussion of Aeschylus's *Nemea* above). In classical Athens a *genos* Euneidai claimed to be descended from Euneos and had strong connections with Dionysos Melpomenos.[49] In Euripides' *Hypsipyle,* Euneos claims that Orpheus himself taught him in the art of music (fr. 64.98). Thus if the Sotades cup shows a Lemnian version of the death of Opheltes, with Euneos attacking the serpent, we could find the same elements linking it to the other Sotades cup that Burn sought: the "honeyed music" of Orpheus[50] and a failed initiation that ends in death.

Hoffmann interprets the three cups in terms of mystery rites. He argues that each cup embodies a fundamental aspect of initiation. The figure attacking the snake is deliberately depicted in an ambiguous way: we do not know whether he is protecting or has just killed the woman. While he does not identify the people on the cup, Hoffmann argues "that the serpent, the woman, and the stranger symbolize the fundamental paradox of Greek mystery religion" and that what remains obscure to us would have been common knowledge among initiates.[51] This interpretation is in tune with an identification of Baby Opheltes since heroization in myth (i.e., the change of status from mortal to hero) can be understood in terms of initiation in ritual (see chap. 3).

The first undisputable representation of the death of Opheltes dates from around 360 B.C. Only a few fragments of the Paestan chalice krater now at the

Bari Museum remain (fig. 20).[52] The scene is extremely dramatic: a huge snake lies across an altar on the left and is in the process of swallowing a small boy; already the boy's entire right arm is inside its mouth. The boy turns toward his left and holds his left arm up toward a woman's dress, presumably Hypsipyle's. The boy is chubby and looks like a young child. Toward the right is a hydria that looks like it has just been dropped by the woman who rushes to the baby's rescue. Here we find the combination of altar and hydria—signifying violence, sacred space, and fear—which we have seen in other depictions of heroic deaths such as the death of the children of Medea (see fig. 2).

The Apulian amphora from Ruvo of about 350 B.C. by the Lykourgos Painter, now at the Hermitage Museum, shows the scene right after Opheltes has been killed by the serpent (fig. 21).[53] The child lies on the ground in the middle. He looks too big to be a baby, and Simon goes as far as to describe him as an ephebe.[54] Hypsipyle runs toward him from the left, while a female figure (perhaps the eponymous nymph Nemea) stands on the right side. On the upper register the serpent coils around a tree in the center. Two warriors attack it from the right side, one with a rock, the other with a javelin that is just about to pierce the serpent's throat. On the left side, a third warrior threatens the snake with a sword, while a fourth man, presumably Amphiaraos, stands at the upper-left corner, calmly observing the scene.

FIGURE 20. Paestan red-figure chalice krater, c. 360 B.C. Bari Museum 3581. Photograph courtesy of Deutsches Archäologisches Institut, Rome, negative number 1480.

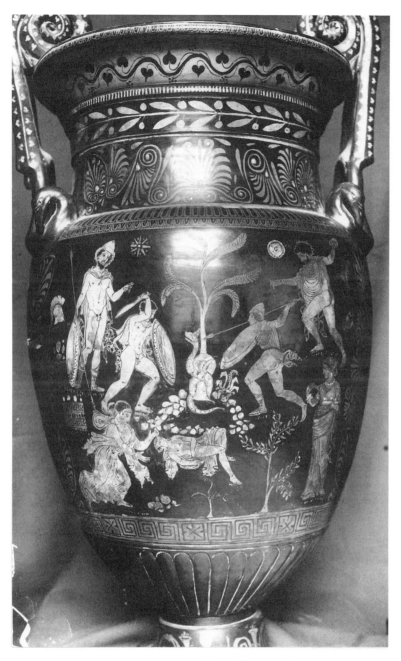

FIGURE 21. Apulian red-figure amphora B.1714, c. 350 B.C.
by the Lykourgos Painter. St. Petersburg, The State
Hermitage Museum, B.1714. Photograph courtesy of The
State Hermitage Museum, St. Petersburg.

Both the Bari krater and the St. Petersburg amphora depict events sur-rounding the death of Opheltes. The Bari krater shows the serpent as it is swal-lowing Baby Opheltes, while the St. Petersburg amphora shows the immediate aftermath of Opheltes' death, with Hypsipyle rushing to his side—two scenes that could not have been part of a staged version of the story but contain ele-ments crucial to the narrative of the baby's heroization.[55] The Bari krater depicts Opheltes during the attack, and he is still depicted as a young baby. The St. Petersburg amphora is rich with details that fit a ritual context: Opheltes looks like an older boy; he is lying dead, as the woman on the right side approaches carrying a plate that could represent offerings for the heroized boy.

The St. Petersburg amphora, in fact, encompasses both the present of the death of Opheltes and his future as recipient of hero cult. The serpent is coiled around a tree planted in the center of a triangular perimeter. The stone wall also evokes sacred space: both (a) the space that the serpent guards and that the baby transgresses and (b) the sacred space of the heroic shrine that will be built in honor of Opheltes. The shape of the triangular shrine echoes Pausanias's eyewitness description of the shrine of Pelops at Olympia and that of Ino-Leukothea at Megara.

Another Apulian amphora of about 340 B.C. from Ruvo by the Dareios Painter, now in the Naples Museum, shows an elaborate mourning scene (fig. 22).[56] At the center of the image is a *naiskos* containing three figures identi-fied with inscriptions. Eurydike stands in the middle with her head slightly turned toward our left, where Hypsipyle stands with her arms extended toward her. On the right side is Amphiaraos, who gestures toward Eurydike and comforts her. On the upper-left corner, next to the *naiskos*'s roof, Dionysos lies on a panther skin under ivy branches and holds a lyre with his left hand, extending a cup toward a figure to the left. "Dionysos" is Hypsipyle's first word in the opening monologue of Euripides' play, as she traces her ancestry back to him, which could explain his presence here. Dionysos with the lyre may also be an allusion to Dionysos Melpomenos, the god served by the Euneids, the descendants of Euneos in Athens. Euneos, in fact, stands right below Dionysos on the left, leaning on his lance and addressing a figure on the left who also leans on his lance (perhaps Thoas). Zeus sits on the upper-right side, holding his scepter in the right hand, with Nemea sitting below him to the right. Zeus has his sanctuary at Nemea, and Nemea herself may further symbolize the location of the events depicted. On the right, below Zeus and Nemea, are two other figures closely associated with the myth of Opheltes, Kapaneus and Parthenopaios, two of the Seven against Thebes.

On the lower register, a mourning scene shows various characters caring for the corpse of Arkhemoros. A woman stands on the left, holding a parasol

FIGURE 22. Apulian red-figure volute krater, c. 340 B.C.,
by the Dareios Painter. Naples, Museo Nazionale 81394
(H3255). Photograph by Singer, courtesy of Deutsches
Archäologisches Institut, Rome, negative number 71.439.

over Arkhemoros's head. Arkhemoros lies on a bed, and a veiled female figure tends him and crowns him with a garland. Immediately to the right of
the bed is a figure identified as a *paidagōgos* with a lyre in his left hand, and
to his right are two figures carrying low tables loaded with various offerings.
As on the St. Petersburg amphora, Arkhemoros looks like an ephebe rather
than a baby. The presence of the *paidagōgos* is interpreted as a sign that the
child depicted here is old enough to be taught how to play the lyre,[57] although

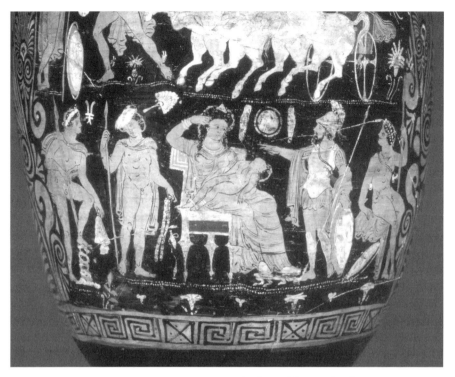

FIGURE 23. Apulian red-figure volute krater, c. 340 B.C. Louvre K 66 (N3147, K 790), Paris, Musée du Louvre. Photograph by H. Lewandowski, © Réunion des Musées Nationaux / Art Resource, NY.

we do not have to understand the figure quite so literally. The Dareios Painter also often uses the *paidagōgos* figure to signify a lack of unity of time and space in the scene depicted.[58] Thus the teacher depicted here could mediate between the scene in the *naiskos* and the mourning scene below. The image of the *paidagōgos* is also a tragic reminder of Opheltes' short and violent life. The teacher finds himself in the dreadful position of mourning his young charge.

Another Apulian vase of around 340 B.C. now in the Louvre, the Lasimos krater, depicts a mourning scene (fig. 23).[59] On the lower register, a woman sits in the center. She holds her right hand to her hair in a gesture of mourning, and a dead or unconscious child with a wound on his chest lies across her lap. She has let her distaff and spindle drop to her right side. In front of her, to the right, an armed warrior addresses her. Several decorative objects and plants in the background are difficult to identify (a shield and greaves on the wall behind the seated woman? a fan or palm frond to her left?).

Séchan argues that the scene is a "Dolorosa" inspired by Euripides' tragedy showing the death of Opheltes. According to him, the visible wound on the child shows that this is a specific story and not a type scene.[60] Séchan suggests that the vase shows the moment when Eurydike receives the body of her dead son. The warrior standing by her side may be Amphiaraos comforting her and telling her about the sign given by the death of Opheltes and the games that he and the Seven established in honor of the dead baby. The two young men on the left could be Hypsipyle's sons, asking Eurydike for forgiveness for their mother.[61]

The vases thus can be divided into three groups: one showing Opheltes being killed by the serpent, one showing the moment right after the serpent's attack, and mourning scenes. The age of Opheltes in the visual representations is not always in accord with literary sources that portray him as a baby. He does look like a baby on the Bari krater, where he is half-swallowed by the snake, and on the Lasimos krater, where he lies on his mother's knees.

Besides representations of the story on vases, one fresco and several marble reliefs depict the death of Opheltes. An Attic sarcophagus from A.D. 160, in the Corinth Museum, shows the death of Opheltes (fig. 24). On the front, the child looks to the right, where Hypsipyle looks back toward him in horror, her right arm raised. On the left, a naked warrior charges the serpent with a sword.

A first-century A.D. fresco from Herculaneum shows a snake in the center attacked by two warriors, while a female figure stands on the right.[62] The painting is difficult to read, but a child is barely discernible in the coils of the snake, and the scene recalls that on the St. Petersburg amphora and Attic sarcophagus. Similarly, several later Roman marble reliefs depicting the death of Opheltes all seem to go back to an earlier Greek model and are therefore useful for our discussion.[63]

Two grave altars from Nicephorus from the late first century A.D., now at the Detroit Institute of Arts, show the death of Opheltes (fig. 25). The scene is sculpted under a laurel wreath below an inscribed plaque. On the right the serpent attacks the child, his body upside down; in the middle stands a warrior with a cloak; to the left, Hypsipyle, whose water pot has rolled to the warrior's feet, flees the scene in terror. This altar belongs to the same tradition as the Attic sarcophagus in the Corinth Museum.[64]

A second-century A.D. relief from the Palazzo Spada also depicts Opheltes and the serpent (fig. 26). The baby is again upside down, with his right arm

FIGURE 24. Attic sarcophagus, c. A.D. 160, Corinth Museum. Photograph by H. Wagner, courtesy of Deutsches Archäologisches Institut, Athens. Neg. Corinth 55.

extended over his head as if he were asking for help. Two armed men attack the serpent and attempt to save the baby. A woman stands to the left; her face turns toward the scene on the right, but her body faces the other direction as if she were fleeing. She has let her water pot drop to the ground, where it lies between the legs of the warrior standing to her right. The relief has been partially restored, and the man in the top right corner, perhaps Kapaneus, might have been given a spear instead of the traditional rock by mistake.[65]

Another marble relief is found on an Attic sarcophagus from around A.D. 150–60 (fig. 27). Traditionally, the scene is identified as Baby Herakles killing the snakes sent by Hera, but like Simon I take it to be a depiction of the death of Opheltes.[66] Baby Opheltes is sitting on the ground, his right arm and leg

FIGURE 25. Funerary monument, first century A.D., Roman. Detroit Institute of Arts 38.107. Gift of Mrs. Standish Backus. Photograph © 1986 The Detroit Institute of Arts.

FIGURE 26. Roman relief, second century A.D. Rome, Palazzo Spada 1812. Photograph by Schlechter, courtesy of Deutsches Archäologisches Institut, Rome, negative number 85.429.

already encircled by the serpent. A naked bearded man, perhaps Lykourgos, stands behind him, holding a sword.

The myth of Opheltes and Hypsipyle also appears on coins from the Peloponnese. While these examples are all from the Roman period, they emphasize the same key elements we saw in the written sources and the vase-paintings. On one coin, Hypsipyle is running toward the boy, already prisoner of the serpent (fig. 28). On another example, we can see a male figure

FIGURE 27. Attic sarcophagus, A.D. 150–60. Athens, National Museum 1457. Photograph by G. Hellner, courtesy of the Deutsches Archäologisches Institut, Athens, negative number 1974/91.

FIGURE 28. Bronze coin from Argos (Hadrian, A.D. 117–38). Line drawing from *Archäologische Zeitung* 1869, pl. 23, 12.

FIGURE 29. Bronze coin from Argos (Lucius Verus, A.D. 161–69). Line drawing from *Archäologische Zeitung* 1869, pl. 23, 13.

FIGURE 30. Bronze coin from Argos (Plautilla, A.D. 198–217). Line drawing from *Archäologische Zeitung* 1869, pl. 23, 11.

FIGURE 31. Roman contorniat, fourth century A.D. Line drawing by Z. Lafis.

on the left (fig. 29). The body of Opheltes lies in the center, under the serpent, while a man, presumably one of the Seven, rushes toward him from the left. Finally, another coin from Argos shows the body of Opheltes (fig. 30). The serpent rears on the left as if about to attack the boy on the right, who is lying on what looks like a pile of rocks, maybe an altar.

Hypsipyle also appears on a fourth-century A.D. contorniat (fig. 31).[67] Hypsipyle (name inscribed) runs toward the right, carrying her baby on her arm. The way in which she is depicted recalls another woman running with a baby on her arm, Ino-Leukothea, of whom we will see much more in the next chapter. What is fascinating here is that another scene appears on the lower left of the coin, where a small figure strangles two snakes. Since Opheltes is always described as a passive victim of the snake, the child depicted here is most likely Herakles. We have seen above how poets depict the story of Herakles and the serpents in much the same way that they sing about Opheltes and his encounter with the serpent. The stories have very different consequences of course, but poets seem to be conscious of each story mirroring and distorting the other, and they use the same vocabulary to tell both stories. Here we have a visual conflation of the two themes, with Hypsipyle carrying Opheltes (just before his encounter with the serpent?) and Herakles strangling the serpent that attacks him. As we will see, the pose of Hypsipyle is also very reminiscent of the figure of Ino holding Melikertes in the same way. In both cases, we see a maternal figure in a dangerous moment, just before the babies' deaths and subsequent heroization.

As we have seen, there is an evolution in the themes preferred by the artists. All the marble reliefs are similarly dramatic and focus on the horror and violence of the scene. Simon traces these elements back to the iconography on an archaic bronze shield band found in Olympia that depicts a fight between Amphiaraos and Lykourgos (figs. 32–33).

The relief dates from the second quarter of the sixth century B.C., close to the date of the refounding of the Nemean Games. The band shows a quarrel between two armed men. Between them stands a third man who intervenes to stop the fight. On either side of both fighters stand two more warriors who also attempt to restrain them. The central figure is identified by inscription as Adrastos. The other two central figures are more problematic. Using Pausanias's description of a similar scene on the throne of Amyklai (3.18.12) and the few letters still legible on the shield band, Simon identifies the two fighting men as Amphiaraos and Lykourgos.[68] Although it does not show the death of Opheltes per se, the relief clearly depicts an event involving the Seven against Thebes at Nemea and the institution of the games.

FIGURE 32. Bronze shield band, early sixth century B.C. Olympia, Archaeological Museum 1654. Photograph by W. Wagner, courtesy of Deutsches Archäologisch Institut, Athens, negative number Olympia 1986.

FIGURE 33. Line drawing by Z. Lafis.

The Olympia shield band emphasizes precisely what Meuli argues is the catalyst for instituting athletic *agōnes* in honor of a dead person: the fight between Lykourgos and Amphiaraos can be understood as a struggle between a killer and the victim's avenger. Athletic *agōnes* are a ritualized form of such a fight and a stylized type of revenge by which the angry spirit of the dead can be appeased.[69]

It is perhaps not surprising that a shield band be decorated with such a scene of conflict. While it does not directly depict Opheltes, Simon uses the Olympia shield band as an example of a particular strand in the iconography of the myth: the archaic shield band and the later depictions it may have influenced focus on the military, agonistic side of the story; men and the public ritual of the athletic games take center stage. By contrast, the classical representations tend to center on mourning rather than fighting and on the private rituals surrounding the death of a loved one; the spotlight is on women and more particularly on the mother (or the nurse). The iconography of the fourth-century vases is heavily influenced by classical tragedy, while the later tradition goes back to an earlier, archaic model that emphasizes the military and agonistic elements of the story.[70]

We have seen that the Ruvo amphora by the Lykourgos Painter placed the dead Opheltes within a triangular precinct surrounded by stones (see fig. 21) that resembles the sanctuary described in the written sources. Iconography and literature here rejoin archaeology, and when Stephen Miller of the University of California at Berkeley excavated the area around the temple of Zeus at Nemea in the early 1980s, he came upon a heroic precinct very much like the one described by Pausanias.[71] The *hērōon* of Baby Opheltes is located at the edge of the sanctuary for Nemean Zeus. Nevertheless, Miller argues that "the scale of the Heroön and the quantity of the dedications discovered within it show that the cult of Opheltes enjoyed a fair popularity" (fig. 34).[72]

Remains from the first half of the sixth century B.C. coincide with the traditional date for the foundation of the Nemean Games. Foundations of ashlar stone were found in the southwestern corner, and a heap of unworked rocks lie in the northwestern corner of the *hērōon*. It remains unclear whether those different remnants were part of two different structures or whether they shared one same function. Starting in the second half of the sixth century B.C., the sanctuary took the shape of a lopsided pentagon. The foundations consist of rough unshaped stones that might have supported a mud-brick wall, protected above by tiles. In a "rectangular structure made of large boulders placed on edge" large quantities of ash, bone, and votive deposits were

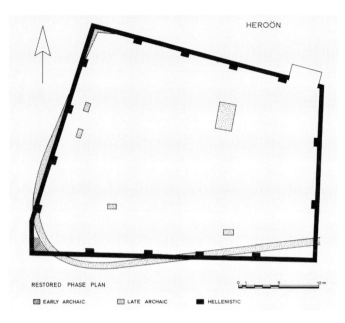

FIGURE 34. Plan of the *hērōon.* From S. Miller, *Nemea,* 105. Courtesy of the Nemea Excavations Archives, University of California, Berkeley.

FIGURE 35. Reconstruction of the *hērōon.* From S. Miller, *Nemea,* 106. Courtesy of the Nemea Excavations Archives, University of California, Berkeley.

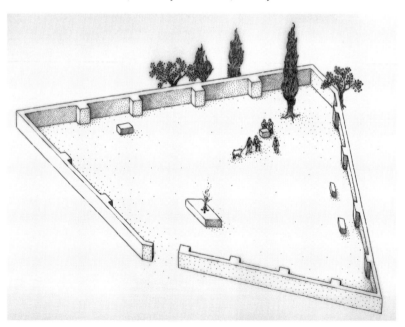

found. This might have been an altar or possibly the tomb of Opheltes.[73] The Hellenistic structure follows the shape of the late archaic foundations. The asymmetric shape of the structure and the absence of any supports suggest that the *hērōon* was unroofed.[74]

The entrance to the precinct was in the northeastern corner, facing the temple of Zeus. There was probably a gate roofed with the curved Laconian tiles whose fragments were found nearby. There is also evidence that trees grew inside the precinct. Several stone blocks placed in the *hērōon* could have been altars, corresponding again to Pausanias's description. Ruins of a rectangular edifice about 1.40 × 3.15 m lie northeast of the center of the *hērōon*. This structure might be Opheltes' tomb, and it was probably built during the late archaic stage and kept in use during the fourth century and later (fig. 35).

The precinct seems to have been renovated in the late fourth or early third century B.C. The enclosure was cleared, and remains of a ritual inauguration can be detected in the burial of a krater against the northeastern corner of the wall.[75]

Objects found inside and around the shrine also confirm the religious function of the site from the second half of the sixth century B.C. on.[76] Deposits of ash and burnt bones for sacrifice, as well as miniature votive vessels and libation cups, were discovered within the enclosure. Objects with magical association also suggest the religious nature of the site: a cup-skyphos with a magical inscription and several lead curse tablets were found. Miller argues that an iron caduceus, symbol of Hermes Psykhopompos, denotes the site as a chthonic and heroic shrine.[77]

Statuettes were found within the shrine, including a terracotta figurine of a baby boy (fig. 36). Miller argues that the boy holds a mask to his face, "a gesture of chthonic significance."[78] The significance of the statuette (or mask) is difficult to establish, but clearly the image of the baby is important not only in the literary and visual sources, but also has a ritual dimension.

Another statuette was found outside the shrine (fig. 37). The bronze figurine dates from the Hellenistic period and depicts a small boy raising his right hand. The baby's pose is very similar to the one depicted on the Corinthian sarcophagus and the Spada relief. Despite the gaps in the evidence, the archaeological record clearly confirms the existence of a flourishing baby-hero cult starting in the early sixth century B.C. and corresponding to the myths preserved in the literary and visual sources.[79]

The narrative of the death of Opheltes contains many elements we have seen in other myths of child heroes: sacred space and its dangers, the ritualization

FIGURE 36. Terracotta statuette of Opheltes
with mask (TC 117). From S. Miller,
"Excavations at Nemea," pl. 25 g. Photograph
courtesy of the Nemea Excavations Archives,
University of California, Berkeley.

FIGURE 37. Bronze figurine of Opheltes,
Hellenistic period (BR 671). From S. Miller,
*Nemea, 27.* Photograph courtesy of the Nemea
Excavations Archives, University of California,
Berkeley.

of maternal fears, the establishment of athletic games in compensation for the
death of a child, and the emphasis on mourning and songs. The emotion of
fear is visually symbolized by the fallen hydria, which we also saw in depictions of the children of Medea and of Herakles. Opheltes is consistently
depicted as a baby before death and as an adolescent after heroization. In the
myth of Opheltes and the serpent, maternal fears typically expressed in popular songs such as lullabies become reality and converge with the sacred.

# CHAPTER 6

# Melikertes-
# Palaimon

Many authors from Pindar to Ailios Aristeides and the Christian father Clement of Alexandria have retold the story of Melikertes, one of the most intriguing baby heroes.[1] Many different narrative strands found in isolation in the myths and rituals surrounding other child heroes come together in the story of Melikertes' violent death. As with the children of Medea or those of Herakles, here is a child who falls victim to his parents. His mother, Ino, for different reasons in different sources, throws herself into the sea with her small son. Prior to the fatal plunge of Melikertes, there is a story of god-induced madness, reminiscent of Herakles', and of a cauldron used to boil a child, reminiscent of Tantalos boiling his son Pelops. After their jump into the sea, the paths of mother and son diverge. Ino is welcomed by the Nereids and made into a goddess, while the child's body is rescued by a dolphin and brought ashore at the Isthmus. There, Sisyphos (the brother of Athamas) finds the corpse and establishes funeral games in honor of the dead baby, renamed Palaimon.[2]

Although the myths and cults associated with Ino-Leukothea are much discussed, there are few discussions of Melikertes alone, and the myths surrounding the child are often subsumed into those concerning Ino.[3] This trend changed in the more recent past, especially when it comes to the archaeological evidence for a hero cult in honor of Melikertes at Isthmia.[4]

The first appearance of Ino in extant literature is in the *Odyssey,* when she finds Odysseus struggling in the sea, barely holding on to his raft:

τὸν δὲ ἴδεν Κάδμου θυγάτηρ, καλλίσφυρος Ἰνώ,
Λευκοθέη, ἣ πρὶν μὲν ἔην <u>βροτὸς</u> αὐδήεσσα,
νῦν δ᾿ ἁλὸς ἐν πελάγεσσι θεῶν ἔξ ἔμμορε <u>τιμῆς</u>.

And the daughter of Kadmos, Ino of the fair ankles,
the White Goddess, saw him. Before, she had been one who spoke as a
    <u>mortal,</u>
but now in the depths of the sea, she has won <u>her share of honor</u> from
    the gods.
—Homer, *Odyssey* 5.333–35

While Homeric epic does not specify how Ino came to be the White Goddess, it is clear that she used to be mortal (*brotos*) before she obtained her *timē,* her "share of honor," from the gods. The reference to her mortal life before her present circumstances functions as a cue to the audience to remember the events that brought Ino to the sea in the first place: her leap with her baby son Melikertes when she was trying to escape the murderous fury of her husband and the subsequent death and heroization of the child and deification of the mother.[5]

The scene in the *Odyssey* is also thematically linked to the story of Ino jumping into the sea with her child: Ino comes upon Odysseus as he is about to drown, just as she herself and her son did before their deification and heroization. Ino, however, has now become a goddess, and she has the power to rescue Odysseus. She appears to him in the shape of a seabird and gives him detailed instructions: Odysseus must get rid of his clothes, abandon the raft, and swim to land. She also gives him her veil, with directions to keep it tied on until he reaches the mainland (*Odyssey* 5.346–47). Once he takes hold of the mainland with both his hands, she tells him, he should untie the veil and throw it back into the sea, turning his face away. Odysseus follows her instructions, and, as soon as he is safe on land, he throws the veil back into the sea, where Ino takes it back into her hands (5.462). We are left with this powerful image of Ino, alone in the sea, holding her beautiful, immortal veil, a veil that subsequently appears on many visual representations of Ino and Melikertes, as we shall see below. While Homer does not mention Melikertes, his existence is presupposed by the presence of Ino-Leukothea in the depths of the sea.[6]

The first direct mention of Melikertes in Greek literature is from the early fifth century B.C., in a fragmentary Isthmian epinician by Pindar. Only three lines are extant, and the context is unclear:

Αἰολίδαν δὲ Σίσυφον κέλοντο
ᾧ παιδὶ <u>τηλέφαντον</u> ὄρσαι
<u>γέρας</u> φθιμένῳ Μελικέρτᾳ

They ordered Sisyphos, the son of Aiolos,
to establish an <u>honor that can be seen from afar</u>
for his dead child Melikertes.
—Pindar, *Isthmian* fr. 5 (Maehler)

We do not know who is giving orders to Sisyphos or any details about his discovery of the child's body.[7] The language used in the lines evokes concerns that are typically associated with the appropriate treatment of Greek cult heroes: Melikertes has perished (*phthimenos*), and he must be compensated by an honor (*geras*) that will be visible far and away (*tēlephanton*). The problematic *ho* implies that the child is Sisyphos's son, but there is no extant tradition that links the two figures in this way.

Both words used by Pindar, *geras* and *tēlephanton*, bring to mind the memory of another famous hero, Achilles, whose grave is described by Agamemnon in the *Odyssey* with the same vocabulary of conspicuous visibility that transcends both space and time:

ὥς κεν <u>τηλεφανὴς</u> ἐκ ποντόφιν ἀνδράσιν εἴη
<u>τοῖς οἳ νῦν</u> γεγάασι καὶ <u>οἳ μετόπισθεν</u> ἔσονται.

So that it can be <u>seen from afar</u> from the sea
both by men who are <u>now</u> alive and those who will be <u>afterward</u>.
—Homer, *Odyssey* 24.83–84

The word *tēlephanēs* clearly goes beyond the purely geographical scope. The tomb of Achilles will be visible "from afar" to people both in the present and in the future. By being able to see Achilles' tomb, people in the future will also be able in some sense to "see" the past, just as worshipers will be able to connect with the hero Melikertes by seeing his *hērōon* and hearing the poet sing his story. Pindar's poem about Melikertes is, in fact, in itself a *tēlephanton geras*.[8]

The Indo-European root *\*bha-* from which *tēlephantos* is derived means "to shine" or "to illuminate." A similar root meaning "to speak" gives rise to words of the *phēmi* family. Chantraine argues that the two roots can be conflated and that many Greek words, such as *phasis*, which can mean "appearance" or "denunciation," actually carry both meanings.[9] In the case of Pindar's *Isthmian* fragment, the *tēlephanton geras* belongs to the rhetoric of cult: I suggest that it refers both to the poetic narrative of the hero's death and to the concrete visible heroic shrine built in his honor.

The scholia to Pindar's *Isthmians* provide more details that help explain the fragment: the Nereids receive Ino and her baby after their plunge into the sea. They transform Ino into the White Goddess, Leukothea, while a dolphin brings the body of Baby Melikertes ashore at the Isthmus:

τὸ δὲ τοῦ παιδὸς <u>σῶμα ἐκκομισθὲν</u> ὑπὸ <u>δελφῖνος</u> εἰς τὸν Ἰσθμὸν εὗρε Σίσυφος

And Sisyphos found the <u>body</u> that had been <u>brought</u> to the Isthmus by a <u>dolphin</u>.
—schol. Pindar, *Isthmians* (Drachmann 3.194)

Both *sōma* and *ekkomizein* again belong to the specialized vocabulary of hero cult.[10] The body of the hero is not only brought to the Isthmus, but brought home to the site of the heroic shrine. Here we also have the first extant source describing the dolphin that brings the body of Melikertes back to shore.

The scholia then describe how a group of dancing Nereids appear to Sisyphos:

<u>χορεύουσαι</u> τοίνυν ποτὲ αἱ <u>Νηρείδες</u> ἐπεφάνησαν τῷ Σισύφῳ καὶ ἐκέλευσαν εἰς τιμὴν τοῦ Μελικέρτου ἄγειν τὰ Ἴσθμια

And then, <u>dancing, the Nereids</u> appeared to Sisyphos and told him to establish the Isthmian Games in honor of Melikertes.
—schol. Pindar, hypothesis *Isthmians* (Drachmann 3.192)

The Nereids who appear to Sisyphos in Pindar's poem are dancing—just as the members of a chorus would dance—and their presence adds a tragic flavor to the scene. It is even possible to imagine that Ino herself is present in this group, as Pindar's *Pythian* 11.1 describes her as living with the Nereids.

The Nereids often appear in scenes of mourning, as when, for example, they come out of the sea to mourn the death of Achilles and to attend the funeral games held in his honor by his mother Thetis, another striking scene in which we see gods mourning for a mortal:[11]

μήτηρ δ' ἐξ ἁλὸς ἦλθε σὺν ἀθανάτῃς ἁλίῃσιν
ἀγγελίης ἀίουσα· <u>βοὴ</u> δ' ἐπὶ πόντον ὀρώρει
<u>θεσπεσίη</u>, ὑπὸ δὲ τρόμος ἔλλαβε πάντας Ἀχαιούς·

His mother, after hearing the news, came out of the sea
with the immortal sea goddesses at her side. <u>Divine crying</u>
rose all over the sea, and trembling seized all the Achaeans.
—Homer, *Odyssey* 24.47–49

The divine crying (*thespesiē boē*) functions as a cry of mourning. Alkaios (c. 600 B.C.) uses the same words in a poem about Lesbian ritual choral contests:

> ὄππαι Λ[εσβί]αδες κριννόμεναι φύαν
> πώλεντ᾽ ἐλκεσίπεπλοι, περὶ δὲ βρέμει
> <u>ἄχω θεσπεσία</u> γυναίκων
> <u>ἴρα[ς ὀ]λολύγας</u> ἐνιαυσίας

> Where Lesbian women go to and for
> with their trailing robes as they are judged for their beauty,
> and the <u>divine sound</u> of the women's
> yearly <u>sacred shout</u> rings around.
> —Alkaios fr. 130b

Alexiou shows the commonality of themes between lament and love songs, and here the epic mourning of the Nereids finds a parallel in Alkaios's choral lyric poetry.[12] In both passages, we also find a ritualization of songs. The shouts of the Nereids and the shout of the Lesbian women can be described as "divine" because both happen in the context of cult: the mourning ritual performed by Thetis and the Nereids and the festival of the Lesbian women.

While Homeric epic generally suppresses direct references to hero cult,[13] Pindar's epinician poetry refers to both the myth and the ritual surrounding the cult of Melikertes. A fragment starts with the story of Ino snatching her baby out of a fire and leaping into the sea, where she is received by the Nereids, the fifty daughters of Doris (fr. 128d Maehler). In his *Nemean 6*, Pindar describes the sacrifice of a bull at the Isthmian Games:

> πόντου τε γέφυρ᾽ ἀκάμαντος ἐν ἀμφικτιόνων
> ταυροφόνῳ τριετηρίδι Κρεοντίδαν
> τίμασε Ποσειδάνιον ἂν τέμενος.
> βοτάνα τέ νίν ποθ᾽ ἁ λέοντος
> νικάσαντ᾽ ἤρεφε δασκίοις
> Φλειοῦντος ὑπ᾽ ὠγυγίοις ὄρεσιν.

> And the bridge of the tireless sea honored Kreontidas
> in the biennial games of those who live around, where
> a bull is sacrificed in the sacred precinct of Poseidon.
> And the herb of the Nemean lion once
> crowned him when he won beneath
> the shady ancient mountains of Phleious.
> —Pindar, *Nemean* 6.39–44

Pindar here gives some information about rituals performed at the Isthmian Games: there is a sacrifice of a bull, and the winner at Isthmia is crowned with the lion-herb.[14] The Isthmian Games are officially dedicated to Poseidon, but they are also held in honor of Melikertes.

The hypothesis to the *Isthmians* offers accounts of the foundation of the Isthmian Games that differ in details, yet some elements are ubiquitous: Ino's and her son Melikertes' plunge into the sea, and the games at Isthmia as funeral games for the dead boy. The games are established in compensation for the death of the child, and wild celery crowns are given as prizes. Celery (*selinon*), which is associated with death (see below), is later replaced by pine garlands, and the scholia emphasize that pine is a symbol of barrenness.[15] Another recurrent element is the motif of the cauldron of boiling water: Athamas and Ino alternately are depicted as intending to throw one of their children into a cauldron of boiling water, a pattern that we will examine more thoroughly below when we turn to the evidence for the cult.

The story of Ino and Melikertes was also the focus of several tragedies, all lost. We know that Aeschylus and Sophocles each composed an *Athamas* (actually Sophocles authored two separate plays of the same name). Sophocles also composed a *Phrixos,* whose content is unknown, and there were two *Phrixos* plays by Euripides.[16]

Hyginus (second century A.D.) is the only extant source for Euripides' *Ino.* In *Fabula* 4, Ino disappears, and Athamas, thinking that she is dead, marries Themisto, with whom he has two children. Later on, he learns that Ino is actually alive on Mount Parnassos, where she went to perform Bacchic rites. He sends for her and hides her from Themisto, who eventually learns that her rival is alive, but ignores her whereabouts. She decides to kill Ino's children and unwittingly confesses her plan to Ino herself. She tells how she will differentiate between the children by dressing hers in white and Ino's in black; Ino exchanges the children's clothes, and Themisto is tricked into killing her own children.[17] When she realizes what she has done, Themisto kills herself. Athamas later is struck with madness and kills his son Learkhos while hunting, while Ino jumps into the sea with her younger son Melikertes and is made into a goddess. In this account, Ino is both wicked stepmother (to Themisto's children) and the good mother who prefers to die with her son rather than abandon him to his crazed father.[18]

Euripides also alludes to the story elsewhere. As Medea is killing her children off stage, the chorus sings:

μίαν δὴ κλύω μίαν τῶν πάρος
γυναῖκ' ἐν φίλοις χέρα βαλεῖν τέκνοις,

Ἰνὼ μανεῖσαν ἐκ θεῶν, ὅθ' ἡ Διὸς
δάμαρ νιν ἐξέπεμπε δωμάτων ἅλαις.
πίτνει δ' ἁ τάλαιν' ἐς ἅλμαν φόνῳ τέκνων δυσσεβεῖ,
ἀκτῆς ὑπερτείνασα ποντίας πόδα,
δυοῖν τε παίδοιν ξυνθανοῦσ' ἀπόλλυται.
τί δῆτ' οὐ γένοιτ' ἂν ἔτι δεινόν; ὦ γυναικῶν λέχος
πολύπονον, ὅσα βροτοῖς ἔρεξας ἤδη κακά.

I have heard of one other woman alone
of those of old, who laid her hands on her children,
Ino, driven mad by the gods when the wife of Zeus
drove her out of the house and made her wander;
she fell into the sea, the wretched one, impiously murdering her
    children.
She stepped over the sea's edge
and perished with her two children.
What more dreadful thing can be? Oh the love of women
so full of pains, how many evils has it already caused for mortals.
—Euripides, *Medea* 1282–91

Why the chorus has such a limited knowledge of Greek precedents is in itself intriguing since there is no shortage of infanticidal mothers in the ancient tradition: Prokne immediately comes to mind, whom Euripides in fact mentions in his *Herakles*.[19] In the *Medea* version of the events, Ino is driven mad by Hera, and she falls, rather than jumps, into the sea with her two children—a variant of the traditional story, perhaps used to make a closer parallel between Ino and Medea, who kills her two sons in the play.[20] Both women kill their children, and in both cases, as we know from other sources, their children become the recipients of hero cult.

Although Euripides does not refer to the cult of Melikertes in this allusion in the *Medea*, it is clear from another play that he knew of it. In his *Iphigeneia in Tauris*, a passage describes a herdsman's prayer that includes an invocation of "Lord Palaimon, guardian of ships, son of the sea goddess Leukothea" (270–71). This function of protector of ships and sailors will later on be emphasized by the Romans, who assimilate Melikertes-Palaimon to Portunus, the god of harbors.

Callimachus (third century B.C.) alludes to an intriguing variation on the story. Ino throws herself into the sea, but with very different consequences. According to the *Diēgēseis* (*Aitia* IV fr. 91 Pfeiffer), after Ino throws herself in the sea with her son, Melikertes, the body of the boy washes ashore in Tenedos. The Lelegians, who once dwelled there, make an altar for him, upon which the city performs sacrifices whenever it fears some great danger: a woman sacrifices her own infant (*brephos*) and is immediately struck blind. This ritual was later discontinued, when the descendents of Orestes came to live in Lesbos. Thus according to Callimachus's *Aitia,* there used to be a cult of Melikertes in Tenedos that required sacrifice of infants. This type of sacrifice is reminiscent of the child sacrifices performed in the Phoenician colonies, in Carthage in particular.[21]

A similar story appears in Lykophron (second century B.C.), who describes Melikertes as *brephoktonos* (the baby slayer). He depicts Melikertes watching the Greek fleet arriving in Tenedos, on its way to Troy:

καὶ δὴ Παλαίμων δέρκεται βρεφοκτόνος

And there Palaimon the <u>Baby Slayer</u> is watching.
—Lykophron, *Alexandra* 229

A scholion comments on Palaimon "the Baby Slayer" and describes a cult in Tenedos that includes baby sacrifices. It is likely that the body of Melikertes was claimed to be found in different locations and that several cults were devoted to him, though it is less easy to see why such cults would ever require child sacrifices. This is inconsistent with everything we know about Greek hero cult and sacrifice: while it is frequent for the spirits of young victims to take revenge on their living counterparts—as in the case of the children of Medea causing all Corinthian infants to die—there is no evidence of hero cults requiring human victims. The function of such myths may be apotropaic. Be that as it may, this seems to be a late development in the myth of Melikertes, and the earlier sources echo neither Callimachus's *Aitia* 4 nor the scholia to Lykophron.[22]

Ovid (43 B.C.–A.D. 17) draws on the story of Melikertes in both his *Metamorphoses* and the *Fasti.* In the *Metamorphoses,* Juno exacts her revenge after Athamas and Ino raise the child Dionysos. She sends the Fury Tisiphone, who drives the couple mad by throwing snakes and poison at them. Athamas loses his mind and starts pursuing Ino and their two sons, believing them to be a lioness with her two cubs. He seizes Learkhos and kills him in a gruesome manner:

<u>Utque ferae</u> sequitur vestigia coniugis <u>amens</u>
deque sinu matris ridentem et parva Learchum
bracchia tendentem rapit et bis terque per auras
more rotat fundae <u>rigidoque infantia saxo</u>
<u>discutit ora ferox.</u>

<u>In his madness</u> he follows his wife's footsteps <u>as if she were a wild beast,</u>
and he snatches Learkhos, smiling in his mother's bosom
and holding forth his tiny arms, and whirls him twice and three times
in the air like a sling, and <u>he savagely</u>
<u>dashes the baby headfirst against a hard rock</u>.
—Ovid, *Metamorphoses* 4.515–19

This description of Athamas violently smashing his child on a rock is very similar to the way in which Herakles kills some of his children, as we saw above in chapter 2. We find here the same comparison between killing the children and hunting wild beasts—and the same senseless brutality. Ino, maddened with pain or with the poisons of Tisiphone, starts howling and flees, holding Melikertes in her arms (*Metamorphoses* 4.521–22).

Ovid addresses Melikertes, *parvum Melicerta,* stressing the smallness and vulnerability of the child. The *Metamorphoses* goes on to describe the cliff hung high over the sea from which Ino leaps into the water. Venus takes pity on the mother and son and asks Neptune to transform them into gods. Neptune assents and gives them their new divine names, Palaimon and Leukothea. The story of Ino and Melikertes ends with two transformations. Ino's female companions are so distressed that they attempt to replicate her jump into the sea: some are transformed into statues, while others become seabirds.

Ino and Melikertes also appear in Ovid's *Fasti,* on June 11, the day of the *Matralia,* the festival in honor of Mater Matuta. Ovid first identifies the recipient of the festival as the "Theban goddess" and describes how Ino came to Rome from Thebes and came to be known as Mater Matuta.[23] The story thus starts at Thebes, with the traditional tale of Ino and Athamas raising Dionysos after Semele's death. In this account, as in the *Metamorphoses,* Ino is not pursued by Athamas, but is driven mad by sorrow, and, after snatching Baby Melikertes from his cradle, she leaps into the sea (6.493–94).

Here again, Ovid makes his narrative more vivid by addressing Baby Melikertes directly in the vocative, as he does in the passage in the *Metamorphoses* examined above. The direct address stresses the tragic fate of the baby, but also can be seen as a gesture of appropriation: Ovid addresses a character that he understands as part of his own tradition. Although the story of Melikertes and Ino is clearly derived from Greek sources, Ovid presents these figures as Roman, and in his version, mother and son come ashore in Italy. Panope and her hundred sisters rescue Ino and Melikertes after their leap and carry them safely to the mouth of the Tiber. As they reach the Tiber, their names have been changed to Leukothea and Palaimon (6.501–2). There Ino is attacked by maenads, who try to snatch the baby boy away from his mother.

Ino invokes the local gods, whom she does not know yet, and her plea for help is heard and heeded by Herakles, who is pasturing his cows by the riverbanks, and he puts the savage maenads to flight. Later on Ino takes refuge with the priestess Carmentis, who prophesies that Ino will become a goddess: Ino and her son will be divinities of the sea, and Portunus will be in charge of ports. They will take on new names, different ones for the Greeks and for the Romans, and with the change of names, they will effectively become gods (*Fasti* 6.541–50).

We see here elements both old and new. The madness of Athamas and the death of Ino and her baby son in the sea is familiar enough, as is the emphasis on the young age of the child, whom Ino snatches from his cradle, but Ino and Melikertes become Roman gods, whose functions are linked with their stay in the sea. In the *Fasti*, Ovid's focus is on a Roman festival, and he is interested in explaining only the ritual of the *Matralia*. In both the *Metamorphoses* and the *Fasti*, Ino and Melikertes become Roman, as it were, as soon as they enter the sea, where the story starts to diverge from the Greek sources. Ovid passes over Melikertes' role in the Isthmian Games and his role as a cult hero in Greek religion. Melikertes becomes Portunus, a god associated with both gates (*porta*) and harbors (*portus*), whose past as a hero of Greek myth and ritual has no bearing on his Roman function.[24]

Plutarch (c. A.D. 50–120) includes the story of the foundation of the Isthmian Games in his *Theseus*. While Plutarch presents Theseus as the founder of the Panhellenic festival at Isthmia, he also mentions the ritual in honor of Melikertes:

ὁ γὰρ ἐπὶ Μελικέρτῃ τεθεὶς αὐτόθι <u>νυκτὸς</u> ἐδρᾶτο, <u>τελετῆς</u> ἔχων μᾶλλον ἢ θέας καὶ πανηγυρισμοῦ τάξιν.

For the contest established in honor of Melikertes was taking place there <u>at night,</u> organized like an <u>initiation ritual</u> [*teletē*] rather than like a spectacle or public festival.
—Plutarch, *Theseus* 25.5

With this observation, Plutarch simultaneously admits that some ritual existed *before* Theseus, while he denies that they were real games. There was indeed already an *agōn* in honor of Melikertes—and here Plutarch uses the familiar ritual syntax *epi* with Melikertes in the dative case. Plutarch differentiates between the Panhellenic athletic games founded by Theseus and the rites in honor of Melikertes, which he describes as already in place by the time that Theseus comes to the Isthmus. This *agōn*, however, is not a simple public athletic festival, but rather it is organized like mystery rites (*teletē*).[25]

Statius (c. A.D. 45–96) wonders at the beginning of his *Thebaid* how far back he should go in the history of Thebes before he starts the story of the war between Oedipus's sons. Ino and Palaimon appear in the list of famous Theban episodes taking place before what is of immediate concern. It would take too much time, Statius enticingly tells us, to include such things as whom unhappy Athamas attacked with his bow and why Ino was not afraid of jumping into the Ionian Sea with her son Palaimon (*Thebaid* 1.12–14). Here Ino is depicted as a savior, who fears nothing when it comes to protecting her son.

Lactantius comments on this passage and gives the background of the story (schol. Statius, *Thebaid* 12–14 [Lactantius]). He tells of Ino nursing Liber Pater when he was still a baby and of Juno's subsequent wrath and vengeance. Athamas kills his son Learkhos with the arrows of Herakles; Ino, when she sees her husband's madness, throws herself into the sea with her son Palaimon. There she eventually turns into a maritime goddess and is called Mater Matuta, while her son becomes the god Portunus, who is mentioned in Vergil's *Aeneid* (without any reference to his Greek origins). Both Statius and Lactantius favor the name Palaimon rather than Melikertes.

Although he says he does not want to tell the story of Ino and Palaimon, Statius is very fond of these two characters and alludes to them several times in the course of the *Thebaid*. As the Fury Tisiphone approaches Thebes and gets ready to sow the seeds of the conflict between Oedipus's two sons, the horned serpents that cover her head hiss so loudly that the whole country is shaken with terror. Their hissing is heard from Mount Parnassos to Olympia, and the top of Mount Oeta falls off; Ino also hears the serpents. Statius presents Ino and her son as frozen in time at that moment after their plunge into the sea: Palaimon's body forever being carried on the wandering dolphin's back, with his mother standing nearby in the water.

In a fascinating passage at the beginning of book 6, Statius tells of the Panhellenic Games founded before those for Opheltes-Arkhemoros, which he is about to describe. He starts with the Olympian and the Pythian Games. About the Isthmian Games, he notes:

> Mox circum tristes servata Palaemonis aras
> nigra superstitio, quotiens animosa resumit
> Leucothea gemitus et amica ad litora festa
> tempestate venit: planctu conclamat uterque
> Isthmos, Echioniae responsant flebile Thebae.

> Then the dark cult of Palaimon is performed
> around the sad altars, as often as proud
> Leukothea renews her crying and in the time of the festival

comes to the welcoming shores: the Isthmus resounds with her lament
on all sides, and Echionian Thebes answers tearfully.
—Statius, *Thebaid* 6.10–14

This is a remarkable description: the Isthmian Games are not only founded
in honor of Palaimon, but Leukothea's mourning and laments are incorpo-
rated into the games. The games for Leukothea's son, just as the games for
Opheltes—to which Statius devotes most of book 6—are recurring funeral
rites for the baby killed by the serpent.

Statius also alludes briefly to Palaimon in book 7 as the Argives approach
Thebes. A series of omens warning of the terrible outcome of the expedition
of the Seven includes one sent by Palaimon himself. The inhabitants of the
Isthmus report that Palaimon has been heard crying over the entire sea
(*Thebaid* 7.420–21). This omen comes last in a series of countless supernatu-
ral signs, all unheeded by the Seven.

In book 7, Statius also includes Palaimon in a lovely description of the
waters of the river Ismenos. The river's gentle behavior is compared to that
of the sea whenever Palaimon visits his mother. Palaimon comes hurriedly
to his mother for kisses and strikes the dolphin who carries him too slowly
(*Thebaid* 9.330–31). These are charming images of a small boy who rushes to
his mother for affection and of a mother and son living in the sea happily
ever after, as in a fairy tale.

This contrasts starkly with the last mention of Palaimon in the *Thebaid*.
The hero Dymas attempts to secure protection for the body of Parthenopaios,
and when he sees the boy being dragged away by his hair, he begs:

> Serus tunc denique supplex
> demisso mucrone rogat: "Moderatius, oro,
> ducite, fulminei per vos cunabula Bacchi
> Inoamque fugam vestrique Palaemonis annos!
> si cui forte domi natorum gaudia, si quis
> hic pater, angusti puero date pulveris haustus
> exiguamque facem! Rogat, en rogat ipse iacentis
> vultus: ego infandas potior satiare volucres,
> me praebete feris, ego bella audere coegi."

> At last, too late a suppliant
> having let go of his sword, he begs: "Carry him more gently,
> I beg you, by the cradle of lightning bolt Bacchus
> and the flight of Ino and the years of your own Palaimon!
> If any of you has the joy of children at home, if any
> here is a father, grant the boy some dust

and a little fire! He himself begs you with mute
face; it would be better if I sated the accursed birds,
cast me to the wild beasts, I pushed him to dare wage war."
—Statius, *Thebaid* 10.422–30

Parthenopaios is described as a *puer,* a Latin word that shares all the ambiguities and vagueness of the Greek *pais.* Although Parthenopaios cannot, of course, be quite as young as the comparison with Baby Bacchus and Palaimon entails, Statius clearly presents his death as premature and underlines this fact with Dymas's plea for a substitute parent to take care of the youth's body. Clearly, there is much anxiety about age and the moment of transition between childhood and adulthood. Parthenopaios himself is self-conscious about his lack of beard and youthfulness (7.701–3), and his opponents in war make fun of his young age (9.784–86). When Parthenopaios is finally mortally wounded, Statius exclaims on his young age, *heu simplex aetas!* In his last speech, Parthenopaios once again refers to his youth and confesses that he took up arms against his mother's wishes (9.892). While Parthenopaios is not a baby like Palaimon, both belong to the same world of childhood, and both die premature deaths that make appropriate the comparison between the two.

Statius's allusions to Palaimon have a picturesque quality: the child is often pictured riding a dolphin in the sea or being comforted and taken care of by his mother Ino-Leukothea. The passage in book 6 describing the games at Isthmia, however, stands out by mentioning the rituals performed in honor of Melikertes (we will come back to this below). Another interesting characteristic of Statius's references to Melikertes is the emphasis on the extended geographical span of the myth: the Isthmian Games are an occasion for mourning from the Isthmus to Thebes, covering the same ground that Ino covered in her escape from Athamas.

Apollodoros's *Library* (first or second century A.D.) mentions the story of Ino and Melikertes twice. In book 1, Apollodoros starts with the story of Athamas and Ino, and, here, as in Hyginus's summary of Euripides, we encounter Ino as wicked stepmother again: Ino tries to destroy her husband's children, Phrixos and Helle, from his first marriage (1.9.1). Later, we learn that Athamas also loses his children by Ino:

Ἀθάμας δὲ ὕστερον διὰ μῆνιν Ἥρας καὶ τῶν ἐξ Ἰνοῦς ἐστερήθη παίδων. αὐτὸς μὲν γὰρ μανεὶς ἐτόξευσε Λέαρχον, Ἰνὼ δὲ Μελικέρτην μεθ' ἑαυτῆς εἰς πέλαγος ἔρριψεν.

Athamas was later deprived of his children by Ino because of Hera's wrath. Driven mad, he shot his son Learkhos with an arrow, while Ino threw herself and Melikertes into the sea.
—Apollodoros, *Library* 1.9.2

Apollodoros's succinct version offers no explanations for Hera's wrath and no details about what happens to Ino and Melikertes after their plunge into the sea. Apollodoros goes on with the story of Athamas and his subsequent remarriage and successful fathering of more children. The explanation for Hera's wrath comes in book 3: Zeus entrusted Baby Dionysos to Hermes, who persuaded Ino and Athamas to rear him as a girl. Irritated by their acceptance, Hera sent *mania* to them, and Athamas hunted his oldest son Learkhos as if he were a deer and killed him. Then, Apollodoros describes Ino's actions:

Ἰνὼ δὲ τὸν Μελικέρτην εἰς <u>πεπυρωμένον λέβητα ῥίψασα</u>. εἶτα βαστάσασα μετὰ νεκροῦ τοῦ παιδὸς <u>ἥλατο κατὰ βυθοῦ</u>.

After <u>throwing</u> Melikertes <u>into a boiling cauldron,</u> then carrying it with the corpse of her child, Ino <u>leapt into the depths</u>.
—Apollodoros, *Library* 3.4.3

A superficial reading of the passage might give the impression that Ino puts Melikertes in the cauldron to kill him, but the act of throwing Melikertes in the cauldron more probably represents an attempt to revive the already dead Melikertes, in all likelihood killed by his father. Using the cauldron as a means to resuscitate her son, Ino tries to escape the mad Athamas. While men use cauldrons in myths to boil and kill children, as we saw in chapter 4, women use cauldrons for different ends, such as rejuvenating and reviving.[26]

After Ino leaps into the sea, Apollodoros describes how she comes to be called Leukothea and her son Palaimon on account of their helping sailors taken in storms. Later the Isthmian Games are founded in honor of Melikertes (3.4.3). Here again, no details about the circumstances of the foundation of the games are provided by the author of the *Library*. The expression *epi* with the dative form of Melikertes shows that the games were established as compensation for his death. Although the *Library* recounts the more famous episodes associated with the legend of Melikertes and the foundation of the Isthmian Games, the different elements of the story are presented in isolation, and Apollodoros does not explicitly make the connections between them.

Hyginus (second century A.D.) records many variants of the story. We have already looked at *Fabula* 4, which records the plot of Euripides' *Ino*. *Fabula* 1 is also about Themisto and retells the same story of deception and inadvertent killing of her own children. In this version, however, Themisto is Athamas's first wife and resolves to kill Ino's children after Ino deprives her of her husband; she is deceived by the children's nurse and kills herself when she realizes her mistake. *Fabula* 2 concerns Ino's plotting against Phrixos and

Helle, her husband's children from his marriage to Nephele (*Nebula*). This is essentially the same version that we also find in Apollodoros. Ino and her women companions roast seeds so that they will not produce any plant. When the grain fails to grow and famine threatens, Athamas sends a messenger to Delphi to ask for advice; Ino bribes the messenger, who brings back the oracle that Phrixos must be sacrificed to Jupiter. Athamas refuses to sacrifice his own child, but Phrixos is willing to sacrifice himself on behalf of the city. After Phrixos, wearing the sacred fillets, is led to the altar, the messenger is overcome by pity for the young man and discloses Ino's plan to Athamas. Athamas gives Ino and Melikertes over to Phrixos to be killed, but Dionysos intervenes and sends a mist that allows him to snatch Ino away.

We also know from *Fabula* 3 that Dionysos strikes Phrixos and Helle with madness and that they wander helplessly in the woods until their mother saves them by sending the golden ram to take them away. Later on, Athamas is struck with madness by Jupiter and kills his son Learkhos. Ino throws herself into the sea with Melikertes. Hyginus also explains the new names of Ino and Melikertes, as well as their Roman equivalents, Mater Matuta and Portunus. In this version, it is Dionysos himself who chooses Ino's new name. Hyginus links Ino's and Melikertes' plunge into the sea and the foundation of the Isthmian Games, held every four years in honor of Melikertes.

Gantz notes that "much of this smacks of tragedy" and that some elements of the story were indeed part of Euripides' second *Phrixos*. We know that the play mentioned grain bins and that the hypothesis refers to Ino's escape, Dionysos's attempt to drive Phrixos and Helle mad, and Nephele's rescue; the tale of Athamas's madness and Ino's plunge into the sea were probably not part of Euripides' *Phrixos* since this story was included in the *Ino*.[27]

Although Hyginus likens Palaimon to the Roman god Portunus, Portunus seems to have had little in common with the boy hero of Isthmia. As we have seen above, Portunus is an ancient deity, probably initially a god of doors, who then becomes a god of the sea and harbors. Yet while Ovid also used the story of the deification of Baby Melikertes as an *aition* for the Roman Portunus, he did not link him with the Isthmian festival, which Hyginus does. The two authors have of course different aims and it is not surprising to find a version very close to the Greek sources in the mythographer, while the poet draws on this account to create a Roman tradition. We also find in the versions retold by Hyginus many familiar elements of heroization narratives: madness, killing (and killing one's own children), famine, establishment of cult as compensation, and athletic games.

There are two different threads in the stories told about Ino, which are not explicitly linked with one another. One tells of Ino's rivalry with Athamas's other wives and includes two variants: Ino versus Nephele and her children Phrixos and Helle, and Ino versus Themisto and her children. The other thread tells of Athamas's god-sent madness and Ino's attempt to escape him by leaping into the sea with Melikertes. One of the few extant sources in which the connection is made explicit between the story of Ino's jealousy of Athamas's second wife, Nephele, and Athamas killing his children is the scholion to Homer's *Iliad* 7.86 (see Pausanias below, for a similar version). There Ino plots against the children of Athamas's second wife with the same scheme of factitious famine and spurious oracle. Athamas, after he learns of Ino's plot, tries to kill Ino and her children. Hyginus and Pausanias provide the only other versions in which the story of Ino and Melikertes jumping into the sea is logically connected to the story of Ino trying to kill her husband's other children.

The special divine status of Melikertes is asserted not only in Hyginus's *Fabula* 2, in which the boy Melikertes becomes the god Palaimon, but also in *Fabula* 224, *qui facti sunt ex mortalibus immortales,* where Melikertes comes last in the long list of human beings who were granted immortality. *Fabula* 273 focuses on those who established games. The games in honor of Melikertes at Isthmia are the tenth games mentioned, right after those for Arkhemoros at Nemea: Eratokles, a rather mysterious figure (*plane ignotus,* as a commentary to the *Fabulae* puts it),[28] says that the Isthmian Games were established for Melikertes the son of Athamas and Ino, while other poets say that Theseus founded the games (*Fabula* 273.8). Hyginus is clearly aware of the coexistence of Corinthian and Athenian versions of the foundation of the games.

Ino was also worshiped as a heroine. In the first book of his second-century A.D. guidebook to Greece, Pausanias describes several monuments associated with the cult of Melikertes and Ino around the Isthmus of Corinth.[29] Although most Greeks worship Ino as a goddess, this is not true in Megara, where the Megarians claim that the corpse of Ino washed up on the beach and was found by two girls, Kleso and Tauropolis, who buried it. They worshiped her as a heroine and were also the first to name her Leukothea. While my main focus is on Melikertes, this mention of Ino and her cult is of interest because Pausanias describes her *hērōon*:

Ἰνοῦς ἐστιν ἡρῷον, περὶ δὲ αὐτὸ θριγκὸς λίθων.

And there is the *hērōon* of Ino, and it is surrounded with a wall of stones.
—Pausanias 1.42.7

These are the same words that Pausanias uses to describe the shrine of Opheltes at Nemea and the Pelopeion at Olympia (*thrigkos lithōn;* 1.42.8;

5.13.1). All three shrines are described as being surrounded with a fence of stones, an observation confirmed by archaeological evidence, which indicates that the shape of the Pelopeion may have influenced that of the heroic shrines at Nemea, which subsequently would have influenced the layout at Isthmia.[30]

Pausanias also describes the Molourian rock on the road from Megara to Corinth from which Ino throws herself into the sea. The rock is sacred because of its role in Ino's and Melikertes' transformation, but the rocks underneath it are thought to be cursed because of their association with Skiron, who used to throw travelers into the sea from the same place (1.44.7).

Parental figures play an important role in all the narratives of child heroes, yet Ino's role is unique. She chooses death rather than abandoning her son, paradoxically saving him by killing him, with the result that she too undergoes metamorphosis into a cult figure. Ino-Leukothea's double status as goddess and heroine reflects different perspectives: at Megara, she is a heroine because her body washes ashore there, while elsewhere she becomes a goddess. Even in Homer's *Odyssey,* it is Ino's former status as a mortal that is emphasized rather than her divinity (only present in her new name, Leukothea, the white goddess).

Pausanias reports two versions of the story of the madness of Athamas, either sent by a god or caused by Ino's own actions (1.44.7). According to Pausanias, the body of Melikertes was brought by a dolphin to the Isthmus:

ἐξενεχθέντος δὲ ἐς τὸν Κορινθίων ἰσθμὸν <u>ὑπὸ δελφῖνος</u> ὡς λέγεται τοῦ παιδός, τιμαὶ καὶ ἄλλαι τῷ Μελικέρτῃ δίδονται μετονομασθέντι Παλαίμονι καὶ τῶν Ἰσθμίων <u>ἐπ᾽ αὐτῷ</u> τὸν ἀγῶνα ἄγουσι.

After the boy was brought to the Isthmus of Corinth <u>by a dolphin,</u> as they say, and among other honors that were granted to Melikertes renamed Palaimon, the Isthmian Games were founded <u>in compensation for his death</u>.
—Pausanias 1.44.8

Here again we find the ritual syntax we have seen in other narratives of heroizations. The games were established not only in honor of Melikertes, but also as a compensation for his death (*epi* with the dative case), after the dolphin plays the role of receiver of Melikertes' body.

Later in book 2, Pausanias visits the Isthmus, and there he finds a memento for Melikertes-Palaimon:

προιοῦσι δὲ ἡ <u>πίτυς</u> ἄχρι γε ἐμοῦ πεφύκει παρὰ τὸν αἰγιαλὸν καὶ Μελικέρτου <u>βωμὸς</u> ἦν. ἐς τοῦτον τὸν τόπον ἐκκομισθῆναι τὸν παῖδα ὑπὸ <u>δελφῖνος</u> λέγουσι.

The pine still grew by the shore in my time, and there was an altar of
Melikertes. They say that the boy was brought to this place by a dolphin.
—Pausanias 2.1.3

The altar has been built on the beach at the very spot where the dolphin
brought the body. Next to the altar is a tall pine tree, a tree that is sacred at
Isthmia and also used for the winners' crowns. After Sisyphos finds the dead
child, he gives him a funeral (*thaptein*) in the Isthmus and establishes the
Isthmian Games in his honor (2.1.3–4). Again, Pausanias uses the usual ritual
syntax for the foundation of the games (*epi* with the dative case).

Within the sacred precinct is a temple dedicated to the child hero:

τοῦ περιβόλου δέ ἐστιν ἐντὸς Παλαίμονος ἐν ἀριστερᾷ ναός, ἀγάλματα
δὲ ἐν αὐτῷ Ποσειδῶν καὶ Λευκοθέα καὶ αὐτὸς ὁ Παλαίμων. ἔστι δὲ καὶ
ἄλλο Ἄδυτον καλούμενον, κάθοδος δὲ ἐς αὐτὸ ὑπόγεως, ἔνθα δὴ τὸν
Παλαίμονα κεκρύφθαι φασίν. ὃς δ' ἂν ἐνταῦθα ἢ Κορινθίων ἢ ξένος
ἐπίορκα ὀμόσῃ, οὐδεμία ἐστίν οἱ μηχανὴ διαφυγεῖν τοῦ ὅρκου.

Statues of Poseidon, Leukothea, and Palaimon adorn the *naos*. There is also
something called the *adyton*, and there is an underground descent to it;
there, they say that Palaimon is hidden. Anyone, either Corinthian or foreign, who falsely swears an oath there has no way to escape his oath.
—Pausanias 2.2.1

Pausanias had described the altar on the beach as that of Melikertes, but
when he reaches the sacred precinct, he refers to the hero by his other name,
Palaimon. The meaning of *kekryphthai* is mysterious: in what sense is
Palaimon "hiding" in the *adyton*? It is tempting to understand the verb as "to
be buried" and to take it simply as an indication that Palaimon's body is resting there. The term is also reminiscent, however, of the story of Medea "concealing" (*katakryptein*) her children in the temple of Hera and their
subsequent death. As Brelich argues in the case of Medea's children, the concept of segregation in the context of a ritual of initiation is often understood
as a form of concealment.[31] Do those who descend in the *adyton* notionally
hide and undergo some kind of initiation? What sort of oath would one pro-
nounce in the *adyton*? Another *adyton*, described in Pausanias's account of
the oracle of Trophonios, may help answer these questions.

Those who wish to consult the hero Trophonios at his shrine in Lebadeia
undergo a series of tests: sacrifices have to be performed and interpreted as
favorable by seers. There is a final sacrifice of a ram on the night on which
one is to descend in the oracle. If that last sacrifice is propitious, the person
is allowed to consult Trophonios. The heroic shrine is signaled by a circular

base of white marble protected with a bronze barrier; a double door allows
entry within the enclosure, where stands a human-made chasm in the shape
of a bread-oven that leads to the oracle. There is no way to go down, but a
portable ladder is brought for those about to descend (9.39.5–10). Down in
the chasm is a hole, through which those who consult the oracle have to go
feet first, holding barley-honey cakes in their hands. It is hard to get their
knees into the hole, adds Pausanias, but once they get through, the rest of the
body is drawn in, as if carried forth by a river. Then:

τὸ δὲ ἐντεῦθεν τοῖς ἐντὸς τοῦ <u>ἀδύτου</u> γενομένοις οὐχ εἷς οὐδὲ ὁ
αὐτὸς τρόπος ἐστὶν ὅτῳ διδάσκονται τὰ μέλλοντα, ἀλλά πού τις καὶ
<u>εἶδε</u> καὶ ἄλλος <u>ἤκουσεν</u>.

And the future is disclosed to those who descend inside the <u>adyton</u>, not in
one single manner, but to some of them <u>through sight,</u> and to others
<u>through</u> <u>hearing</u>.
—Pausanias 9.39.11

Trophonios's *adyton* is where one can learn one's future, which is disclosed
in different ways to different people. The way out of the *adyton* is the same as
the way in: feet first through the same mouth. Priests wait for the man who
consulted Trophonios and place him on the seat of Memory, where they ask
him what he learned. Then, they hand him over to his friends, as he is still in
a state of shock: he is frightened and does not recognize his surroundings.
Later, he comes back to his senses and learns to laugh again. Everybody who
goes down has to dedicate a tablet on which is written what they saw or heard
from the oracle (9.39.11–14).

Athletes going down into the *adyton* of Melikertes presumably did not
learn anything about their future, yet from Pausanias's account we can get a
sense of the kind of experience such heroic shrines can generate. The oath
sworn in the *adyton* by the athletes must have been a haunting experience.
Pausanias makes it clear that swearing a false oath to Palaimon has dreadful
consequences, perhaps in the same way as those who consult Trophonios
under false pretense find a terrible fate, such as the bodyguard of Demetrios
who went down hoping to find gold and silver and whose body was later
found, thrown up from the ground (9.39.12). Another detail of interest in
Pausanias's account is the emphasis on both hearing and seeing as ways of
understanding the oracle's advice, something we will see in Ailios Aristeides'
description of the cult of Melikertes.

Ailios Aristeides (A.D. 117–81) mentions the cult of Melikertes at the end of
his hymn to Poseidon. He wonders whether the story of Melikertes and Ino
should be described as a tale (*logos*) or a myth (*mythos*) and is troubled by

the idea that the goddess Leukothea might have undergone the sufferings ascribed to the mortal Ino (46.32–34). Thus Leukothea never threw herself into the sea, and neither was the child Melikertes snatched away: he was actually entrusted to Poseidon, as a gift and source of joy (46.35 = Keil 2.373). Leukothea must have been a goddess from the beginning, and since, for Aristeides, there is no evil among the gods, he rejects the violent details of the narrative (46.36).

Aristeides also describes the cult of Melikertes as he mentions a painting—perhaps the same one described by Philostratos, which we will examine below—that he saw at the Isthmus:

Παλαίμονα δὲ καὶ εἰπεῖν καλὸν καὶ τοὔνομα αὐτοῦ ὀνομάσαι καὶ ὅρκον ποιήσασθαι καὶ τῆς τελετῆς τῆς ἐπ᾽ αὐτῷ καὶ τοῦ ὀργιασμοῦ μετασχεῖν—τοσοῦτός τις ἵμερος πρόσεστι τῷ παιδί—καὶ ἰδεῖν γε καὶ ἐν γράμματι, . . . ὅπου δὲ καὶ ἐπ᾽ αὐτῶν τῶν νώτων τῆς θαλάττης, ὅπου δὲ καὶ ἐν ταῖς χερσὶν τῆς μητρὸς τὸ θάλος τοῦ παιδὸς καὶ τὴν ὥραν καὶ τὸ ἄνθος. ταῦτα γὰρ θεάματα θεαμάτων ἥδιστα καὶ ἰδεῖν γε καὶ ἀκοῦσαι.

It is good to talk about Palaimon and say his name and swear his oath, as well as to take part in the initiation ritual [teletē] and the celebration of secret rites [orgiasmos] in his honor, and also—so great is the desire [himeros] attached to the boy—to see in the picture the bloom and freshness and flower of the boy when he is on the back of the sea, and when he is in his mother's arms. For these are the sweetest of sights to see and to hear.
—Ailios Aristeides, Isthmikos 46.40 (Keil 2.375)

Ailios Aristeides uses the traditional ritual syntax epi with the dative case, which indicates that the rites are performed in compensation for the death of Melikertes. The reference to the special role that the shrine of Palaimon plays in the swearing of the oath recalls Pausanias's description of the adyton, while the mention of an initiation ritual (teletē) recalls Plutarch's description of the festival. Although Aristeides simply dismissed the story of Ino and Melikertes throwing themselves into the sea, the picture he describes seems to show precisely this scene: the mother holding her child in the sea, and the child being carried forth by the sea, although Aristeides does not mention any dolphin.

Aristeides speaks of Melikertes as an object of desire and describes him in terms of beauty (thalos), spring (hōra), and youth (anthos), which all belong to the metaphorical world of flowers and spring and draw attention to Palaimon's youth. Aristeides also expresses in one sentence a dichotomy we will see present in all the visual sources: before the jump, when Melikertes is with his mother, he is consistently described as an infant; yet *after* the jump, when he is depicted alone, the boy is older. As he is heroized as Palaimon, his metamorphosis from baby to youth takes place, and the body brought to the Isthmus by the dolphin is that of a boy.

While Ailios Aristeides claims that these sights are the sweetest of all, he disapproves of other images showing scenes of a more violent type. Aristeides' ambivalence toward the traditional story of the death of Melikertes is fascinating. He is upset enough by the "impiety" of the images created by ancient artists that he avoids describing them, and he marvels at how other people can tolerate their presence in the shrine. This suggests a remarkable change in attitudes toward religious figures (and foreshadows the kind of reactions that we will later find in Christian sources): what originally made Melikertes-Palaimon into a cult figure is precisely the violence and meaninglessness of his premature death. By Aristeides' time, this violence is no longer considered appropriate for the narrative. Aristeides does not distinguish substantially between god and hero in this passage, and he does not want his gods to be in any way touched by the realm of mortals (46.41 = Keil 2.375). Yet, while he resists the violent (and mortal) elements of the narrative of the death of Melikertes, Aristeides is sensitive to the poetry of the story of Melikertes' body being brought ashore by a dolphin—something already present in the earlier sources—and describes the dead body of the boy as an object of desire.

Just as death makes unfulfilled desire perpetually beautiful and ageless in C. P. Cavafy's poem "Desires" (see epigraph), Melikertes' violent and premature death is what makes his youth and beauty so enticing. In both cases—Melikertes' body or Cavafy's unfulfilled desires—it is death that ultimately confers beauty, immortality, and meaning. Palaimon on the dolphin resembles the characteristic heroic "beautiful corpse" ("le beau mort") described by Vernant.[32] Just as Homeric warriors exhibit all the signs of *hēbē* after their death, so does Melikertes through death achieve eternal beauty and desirability and thereby become an appropriate subject for both laments and love songs. This is something we have also seen at work in depiction of Opheltes-Arkhemoros, who is similarly portrayed as a baby before (or during) his encounter with the serpent and as an adolescent after heroization.

Baby and child heroes can be objects of desire for both humans and gods. We have seen how Poseidon is famously attracted to young Pelops after he is revived through the boiling cauldron and how Baby Adonis seduced not only Aphrodite, but Persephone and Zeus as well (see chap. 4). The erotic dimension of the sacred narrative concerning Melikertes is strikingly manifest in

Ailios Aristeides' account of his trip to the child's *hērōon*. We will come back to this aspect of the narrative of the boy's heroization.

Lucian's *Dialogues of the Sea-Gods* (second century A.D.) briefly alludes to Melikertes-Palaimon:

εὖ γε, ὦ <u>Δελφῖνες</u>, ὅτι ἀεὶ φιλάνθρωποί ἐστε, καὶ πάλαι μὲν τὸ τῆς Ἰνοῦς <u>παιδίον</u> ἐπὶ τὸν Ἰσθμὸν <u>ἐκομίσατε</u> ὑποδεξάμενοι ἀπὸ τῶν Σκειρωνίδων μετὰ τῆς μητρὸς ἐμπεσόν.

Indeed, <u>dolphins,</u> you have always been man's friends, and already long ago you <u>brought home</u> the <u>little child</u> of Ino to the Isthmus, having received him when he fell from the Skeironian [rock] with his mother.
—Lucian, *Dialogues of the Sea-Gods* 8.1

Poseidon addresses the dolphins and notes their friendly behavior toward humans. They rescued the body of Ino's child, which Lucian describes as *paidion* (little child), and brought him to the Isthmus. Here again we find the key word *komizein* (to bring home).[33] The child's heroization is also linked to the rock from which Melikertes fell, here described as Skeironian (as in Pausanias's account above), a detail to which we will come back later.

We have already looked at the passage in Philostratos's *Heroikos* (third century A.D.) that likens the cult of Melikertes to that in honor of the children of Medea:

τὰ μὲν γὰρ Κορινθίων <u>ἐπὶ Μελικέρτῃ</u> (τούτους γὰρ δὴ τοὺς ἀπὸ Σισύφου εἶπον), καὶ ὁπόσα οἱ αὐτοὶ δρῶσιν ἐπὶ τοῖς τῆς Μηδείας παισίν, οὓς ὑπὲρ τῆς Γλαύκης ἀπέκτειναν, <u>θρήνῳ</u> εἴκασται <u>τελεστικῷ</u> τε καὶ <u>ἐνθέῳ</u>. τοὺς μὲν γὰρ <u>μειλίσσονται</u>. τὸν δὲ <u>ὑμνοῦσιν</u>.

The rites of the Corinthians <u>for Melikertes</u> (for these are the ones I called the descendants of Sisyphos), and what the same people do in honor of Medea's children, whom they killed for the sake of Glauke, resemble a <u>lament</u> that is both <u>initiatory</u> and <u>inspired,</u> for they <u>propitiate</u> the children and <u>sing hymns</u> to Melikertes.
—Philostratos, *Heroikos* 207 Kayser = 53.4 (Lannoy)

As we noted in chapter 1, Philostratos likens the rites for the children of Medea, who were killed on account of Glauke's death, to those for Melikertes, which were established by Sisyphos. Philostratos describes both cults as a mixture of different kinds of rituals, at once heroic and initiatory. Here again, we find the emphasis on singing laments and hymns in honor of the hero.[34]

We also find a description of a painting describing the events at the Isthmus in Philostratos's *Eikones*.[35] The painting described by Philostratos shows several discrete events simultaneously:

This people sacrificing at the Isthmus, that would be the people of Corinth, and the king of the people here is, I think, Sisyphos himself; this is the sacred precinct [*temenos*] of Poseidon, which resounds gently with the sea, for the leaves of the pine trees sing in this way, and this, my boy, is what it means: Ino, after she threw herself into the sea, became Leukothea and one of the circle of the Nereids; as for her son, the earth will benefit from the baby [*brephos*] Palaimon. Already he puts into port on the well-disposed dolphin, and the dolphin carrying the sleeping child spreads his back, slipping through the calm sea noiselessly, so that the child may not be wakened from his sleep. And as he approaches, an adyton breaks forth out of the earth split apart by Poseidon, who, it seems to me, announces the child's sailing-in to Sisyphos here, and also that he should sacrifice [*thyein*] to the child. And Sisyphos sacrifices this black bull here, having dragged him away from the herd of Poseidon. The logos of the sacrifice and the attire worn by those sacrificing as well as the offerings [*ta enagismata*], my boy, and the slaying [*to sphattein*] must be kept for the mystery rites [*orgia*] of Palaimon. For the *logos* is holy and altogether secret, since Sisyphos the wise himself deified it. That Sisyphos is wise is indeed shown by the thoughtfulness of his appearance. As for the face of Poseidon, if he were about to break the Gyrean rocks or the Thessalian mountains, he would certainly have been depicted as terrible and such as someone striking a blow, but since he is receiving him as a guest so that he might keep him in his land, he smiles at the child coming into harbor, and orders the Isthmus to unfold its breast and become a home [*oikos*] for Melikertes. The Isthmus, my boy, is painted in the form of a *daimōn* sprawling himself on the land, and he has been appointed by nature to lie between the Aegean and the Adriatic as if he were yoking the two seas together. There is a young man on the right, Lekhaios probably, and girls on the right, who are the two seas, beautiful and suitably calm, lying beside the land representing the Isthmus.

—Philostratos, *Eikones* 2.16

In this text, the people of Corinth perform a sacrifice alongside their king, Sisyphos. Along with the sacrifice, the image also depicts the aetiological myth behind the sacrifice. The reference to the pine trees' music is intriguing in a description of a picture, although it is a common feature of *loci amoeni*.[36] And it is the music made by the pine trees that signifies the story behind the sacrifice: the story of Ino throwing herself into the sea and being renamed Leukothea, and that of her baby son Melikertes-Palaimon. Leukothea becomes part of the band of Nereids, while the earth will "benefit" from her baby. One is inevitably reminded of the role that heroes play in fertility rituals, as well as the custom not to cremate babies, but simply to bury them in the earth.[37]

Although the dolphin is actually carrying a corpse, the painting described by Philostratos emphasizes the beauty and pleasure of the self-abandonment of Melikertes lying on the dolphin's back. The dolphin and the baby approach the shore at the Isthmus, and the dolphin takes care not to disturb the boy's sleep. There is no hint of violence or ugliness in this lovely image of the boy hero.

When it comes to the ritual itself, Philostratos describes Sisyphos sacrificing a black bull. The rest of the rites, however, are not to be disclosed: the "*logos* of the sacrifice," the costume of the people performing the sacrifice, the offerings, and the way of killing the animal are all secret. The "*logos* of the sacrifice" (*ho tēs thysias logos*) is in itself a mysterious phrase: does it refer to the language used during the sacrifice, the order in which it is performed, the beliefs of the participants, or the story behind it? If Philostratos uses the word *semnos* as an equivalent of *hieros,* this *hieros logos* could very well be an aetiological myth intended to explain the ritual. This also fits well with the passage from Ailios Aristeides (discussed above), who describes the ritual in honor of Palaimon in terms of swearing his oath and talking about him and saying his name. As for the offerings, the word *enagismata* unmistakably refers to sacrifices typically offered to heroes. The manner of killing the animal (*to sphattein*) is also the verb commonly used of the heroic way of sacrificing the bull.[38]

Poseidon is also depicted, and his visage expresses his care to make Melikertes welcome at the Isthmus: he smiles at the boy and orders the Isthmus to spread out and become a home for Melikertes. The Greek word *oikos* refers both to ordinary houses and to gods' or heroes' abodes. We find an example of such a use of the word at the end of Herodotos's *Histories* 9.116, where the Persian Artauktes obtains the *oikos* of the Greek hero Protesilaos from Xerxes. Xerxes does not realize that the *oikos* in question is not simply a house, but actually a hero shrine.[39] In the context of Philostratos's description, Melikertes' *oikos* is indeed a house in the religious sense of the term, that is, the shrine that he will inhabit at the Isthmus.

There is a remarkable conflation of cause and effect in the painting described by Philostratos: Sisyphos and his people in the painting are already performing a sacrifice (of a secret nature) that is the consequence of Melikertes' coming and of Poseidon's instructions. The story of the *adyton* made to appear by Poseidon is also interesting in light of Pausanias's description (2.2.1) of the real-life *adyton* at Isthmia. The structure must indeed have played an essential role in the rituals performed at Isthmia.

In his *Protreptikos,* the Christian writer Clement of Alexandria (c. A.D. 160–215) calls for putting an end to all Panhellenic Games, which he dismisses as "gatherings around tombs" (*epitymbios panēgyris*). He describes the Isthmian Games briefly:

Ἰσθμοῖ δὲ <u>σκύβαλον</u> προσέπτυσεν <u>ἐλεεινὸν</u> ἡ θάλαττα καὶ Μελικέρτην ὀδύρεται τὰ Ἴσθμια.

The sea cast out the <u>pitiful remains</u> at the Isthmus, and Melikertes is mourned at the Isthmian Games.
—Clement of Alexandria, *Protreptikos* 2.29

There is no sense here of the aesthetic aspect of the narrative of the death of Melikertes. Where the Greek sources depict a charming scene of a boy carried by a dolphin, the Christian writer sees only filth (*skybalon*). We know with certainty that he considers Melikertes to be a child because in the next sentence Clement describes the Nemean Games as being in honor of "another child" (*allo paidion*) Arkhemoros. A little later, Clement comments on the similar nature of all the Panhellenic Games:

<u>μυστήρια</u> ἦσαν ἄρα, ὡς ἔοικεν, <u>οἱ ἀγῶνες ἐπὶ νεκροῖς</u> διαθλούμενοι, ὥσπερ καὶ τὰ λόγια, καὶ δεδήμευνται ἄμφω. . . . <u>αἶσχος</u> δὲ ἤδη <u>κοσμικὸν</u> οἵ τε ἀγῶνες καὶ οἱ φαλλοὶ οἱ Διονύσῳ ἐπιτελούμενοι, κακῶς ἐπινενεμημένοι τὸν βίον.

It seems that <u>the games</u> held <u>in honor of the dead</u> are in fact <u>mysteries,</u> just like oracles, and both are public. . . . This is now a <u>cosmic shame,</u> both the games and the phalluses made for Dionysos, spreading over life in an evil manner.
—Clement of Alexandria, *Protreptikos* 2.29

Clement likens the games to mysteries and oracles and emphasizes the function of the games as mysteries. While no other sources use the word *mystēria,* and although Clement is not an impartial observer since he clearly seeks to discredit pagan cults, we have seen that earlier authors also stress the initiatory aspect of the games (cf. Plutarch and Philostratos above).[40]

Nonnos of Panopolis (fifth century A.D.) also recounts the story of the madness of Athamas. In this version, Athamas shoots Learkhos with an arrow and then decapitates him, under the delusion that his son is a deer.[41] Athamas then looks for his wife and comes upon Melikertes and puts him in a boiling cauldron. Despite the baby's cries, none of the servants come to his help, but his mother arrives and takes him out of the cauldron, half-burned, and escapes to the sea (*Dionysiaka* 10.67–70). Nonnos emphasizes the murders and says nothing of Melikertes' fate after his jump into the sea. The cauldron is here again a masculine instrument of death, and Ino does what she can to protect Melikertes from his father.

FIGURE 38. Terracotta votive plaque, late sixth century B.C. Berlin Staatliche Museum F780. Photograph by I. Luckert, courtesy Antikensammlung, Staatliche Museen zu Berlin—Preussischer Kulturbesitz, Berlin.

FIGURE 39. Line drawing by Z. Lafis.

Let us now turn to visual representations of Melikertes-Palaimon and Ino. There are few extant representations of Melikertes, but they are revealing. They span a period from the late sixth century B.C. to the second century A.D.[42]

The earliest representations of Melikertes-Palaimon are two late sixth-century votive terracotta plaques from Penteskouphia. They were found in a small sanctuary near Corinth, and both the iconography of these incised and painted pieces and the location of the find make the identification of Melikertes-Palaimon reasonably certain. One of these plaques shows a youth riding a sea monster (figs. 38–39). The boy sits in profile and holds onto the sea monster with his left leg and arm. He carries a trident in his right hand and some unidentifiable object (a seashell?) in his left. On the left side is a fish (just caught? or indicating the sea setting?) with its head upside down. The image is difficult to read, and it is impossible to determine a precise context.

Another votive plaque from Penteskouphia, from 550 to 500 B.C., shows a figure riding on a dolphin's back (figs. 40–41). The panel's top is missing, but the relative size of the dolphin and the figure riding it indicate that a young boy is depicted here. The boy's left hand is visible on the upper-left corner, and again he holds what looks like a seashell.

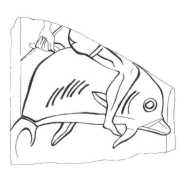

FIGURE 40. Terracotta votive plaque, late sixth century B.C. Berlin Staatliche Museum F779. Photograph by I. Luckert, courtesy Antikensammlung, Staatliche Museen zu Berlin— Preussischer Kulturbesitz, Berlin.

FIGURE 41. Line drawing by Z. Lafis.

It is also interesting to compare these early images of Melikertes with representations of the Nereids, who are also often represented sitting on sea creatures such as the *kētos* (sea monster) similar to the one that Melikertes rides on the Penteskouphia plaque. Nereids often hold objects such as caskets and drinking cups, appropriate ritual gifts for a funeral such as that of Achilles in the *Odyssey* or of Melikertes in Pindar. One late sixth-century B.C. Attic red-figure vase shows dancing Nereids on opposite sides of the neck (fig. 42). The Nereid holds a fish in each hand and looks like she is running or dancing; she may be part of a chorus such as the one that appears to Sisyphos and orders him to establish the games for Melikertes according to the scholia to Pindar. Barringer shows how the Nereids play a crucial role in accompanying major transitions, such as death and marriage. Melikertes shares the visual language of the Nereids, who are part of the same marine world and are, in fact, central to the establishment of his cult in the literary sources.[43]

A Boeotian stamnos-pyxis of about 430–420 B.C. from Thebes depicts another Nereid, sitting on a dolphin (fig. 43). This vase depicts Thetis and the Nereids bringing his new arms to Achilles. We also know of this episode through book 18 of Homer's *Iliad*, in which Thetis alone brings the new arms made by Hephaistos to her son. Both Nereids and dolphins are liminal beings who can act as intermediaries between gods and mortals and who can receive human beings at their deaths. Here again we find affinities between depictions of the

Nereids in the sea and the votive plaques from Penteskouphia portraying Melikertes sitting on marine creatures.

Although Baby Melikertes does not appear on any extant vase-paintings, one Apulian bell krater from 340 to 330 B.C. in a private collection depicts the madness of Athamas.[44] The Geneva krater by the Dareios Painter consists of two fragments. On the first one, Athamas (inscribed ATHA before the fragment breaks off) can be seen in the lower-right corner. He looks distraught, and his floating garment indicates that he is in the middle of some action. To his left is the head and right arm of a man. The man supplicates Athamas and is identified as a messenger or *paidagōgos*.[45] Amphitrite sits in the center of the upper register, holding a barely visible crown in her right hand and a scepter in the other. An animal runs away on the left, and the tail of a sea monster (*kētos*) is visible on the right side. Amphitrite looks toward the right over the sea monster, perhaps toward the figure, whose foot is barely perceptible, who sits on the *kētos*, and toward Poseidon on the other side of the vase.

The second fragment depicts Poseidon. To his right is a column, topped with a vase. To the left, part of the *kētos*'s head appears: it is covered with a

FIGURE 42. Neck of an Attic red-figure amphora, 520–515 B.C. Louvre G 3. Musée du Louvre, Paris. Photograph by H. Lewandowski, © Réunion des Musées Nationaux / Art Resource, NY.

FIGURE 43. Boeotian black-figure stamnos-pyxis in the Cabeiran style, c. 430–420 B.C. Paris, Musée du Louvre CA 4502. Line drawing by Z. Lafis.

crest, and an ear is visible. Poseidon looks toward the left over the *kētos,* toward Amphitrite on the other side.

These two fragments are unfortunately insufficient to establish with any certainty what else was depicted on the vase, but the appearance of Athamas, looking disheveled and distressed, leads scholars to identify the scene as that of the madness sent by Hera and his slaying of his children. Bruneau argues that the presence of the sea divinities make the presence of Ino with Melikertes in her arms very likely.[46]

One late source, Kallistratos (third or fourth century A.D.), describes a painting of the madness of Athamas, purportedly set up on the Scythian shores for a painting contest. The painting shows Athamas naked, splattered with blood, and holding a sword. Ino runs away in terror, nursing her baby in her arms. She runs toward the Skeironian rock, while dolphins, Amphitrite, and Nereids swim in the water at the foot of the rock. This lost painting includes many of the same details that occur on coins depicting Ino and Melikertes, and the figure of Athamas recalls the fragmentary Geneva krater. Although Athamas is not shown on the votive plaques or coins associated with Ino and Melikertes, his role is obviously an important one, and, from a cultic point of view, his behavior leads to the most important element of the story: Ino's jump into the sea and the subsequent deification and heroization (Kallistratos, *Descriptions* 14).

Melikertes-Palaimon is consistently represented as a baby or young boy on Corinthian coins from the Roman period. Established as a Roman colony in 44 B.C. (about a hundred years after it was destroyed by Mummius and his army), Corinth had the right of coinage and produced many coins that pre-served local and traditional Greek myths.[47] The coins also preserve local mon-uments such as statues and, as we will see, the temple in honor of Melikertes at the Isthmus.

Ino and Melikertes often appear together. A typical example shows Ino as she runs toward the left (fig. 44). She holds Baby Melikertes with her left arm, as her veil floats behind her.

Other coins from the same period and area focus on the same theme of Ino holding the child Melikertes. On one coin, Ino runs toward the left, hold-ing Melikertes in her left arm (fig. 45). There is much more movement in this example. Ino runs toward the left, holding her baby in front of her.

Another coin (inscribed CLI COR, meaning "Colonia Laus Iulia Corinthia") shows Ino running, her veil floating in the air behind her on the right, with her baby on her left arm (fig. 46). In the lower-left corner, a dolphin—per-haps the dolphin that brings Melikertes to the Isthmus—swims at Ino's feet.[48]

Another coin depicts a remarkably similar motif (fig. 47). Ino holds Melikertes on her left arm, as her veil floats behind her on the right. In the lower-left corner, in the same position where the dolphin was shown in the preceding coin, a figure, perhaps a Nereid or a Triton, extends its arms toward Ino and the baby, as if to receive the mother and son into the sea.

Ino's veil is often given a prominent place on coins from the same period. As we have seen in the Homeric passage discussed at the beginning of this chapter, Ino's veil plays an essential role in the *Odyssey*. The veil also plays an important part on many of the coins depicting Ino, although in very differ-ent circumstances. On this coin (fig. 48), Ino, this time alone, holds her immortal veil almost like a sail as she runs toward the right, while a sea horse stands by her feet in the lower-right corner. The veil that becomes Odysseus's salvation appears on coins as a sign of fear and flight (fig. 49).

A Hellenistic silver plate combines many of the elements we have seen depicted on coins of Ino and Melikertes (fig. 50).[49] Ino sits on the back of a Triton while she nurses Melikertes, in a depiction that is reminiscent of Ailios Aristeides' depiction of the boy in his mother's arms as well as Kallistratos's description of the nursing baby on the lost painting of the madness of Athamas.

The recurrence on coins of the motif of Ino holding Melikertes indicates that it may have been based on some work of art, perhaps a statue standing within a *temenos*.[50] As we saw, all the coins of Melikertes and Ino date from the first and second century, thus late, yet they emphasize details—a mother's fear, flight, and the sea (in the form of various sea creatures)—that are already emphasized in the early literary sources.

FIGURE 44. Bronze coin from Corinth (Antoninus Pius, A.D. 138–61). Numismatik Lanz, Auction 105. 661. Photograph by Luebke & Wiedemann, Stuttgart; courtesy of H. Lanz, Munich.

FIGURE 45. Bronze coin from Corinth (Hadrian, A.D. 117–38). Numismatik Lanz, Auction 105, 591. Photograph by Luebke & Wiedemann, Stuttgart; courtesy of H. Lanz, Munich.

FIGURE 46. Bronze coin from Corinth (Septimius Severus, A.D. 193–211). Figure Numismatik Lanz, Auction 105, 857. Photograph by Luebke & Wiedemann, Stuttgart; courtesy of H. Lanz, Munich.

FIGURE 47. Coin from Corinth (Antoninus Pius, A.D. 138–61). From Imhoof-Blumer and Gardner, *Numismatic Commentary on Pausanias*, table B 24.

FIGURE 48. Bronze coin from Corinth (Lucius Verus, A.D. 161–69). Line drawing by Z. Lafis.

FIGURE 49. Bronze coin from Corinth (Marcus Aurelius, A.D. 161–80). Numismatik Lanz, Auction 105, 699. Photograph by Luebke & Wiedemann, Stuttgart; courtesy of H. Lanz, Munich.

FIGURE 50. Hellenistic silver plate. Athens, Benaki Museum 11.446. Line drawing by Z. Lafis.

Melikertes alone, without Ino, is also often depicted on coins, always riding on a dolphin's back. There are many variations on this theme on coins from the region of the Isthmus, and Melikertes is shown sitting, standing, or lying on the dolphin's back. One such coin from Corinth, honoring Lucius Verus and dating between A.D. 161 and 169, shows a young boy straddling a dolphin so plump it could be mistaken for a small whale (fig. 51).

There are many variants on the theme of Melikertes and the dolphin. On a coin of the late first century A.D., the boy and dolphin face right, and the boy is standing (fig. 52).[51] In an interesting variant, the boy sitting on the dolphin is placed on an altar as if the group were a sculpture (fig. 53).[52]

Altars are found on other coins alluding to the Isthmian Games. A coin from Corinth from the end of the second century A.D. shows an athlete next to an altar (fig. 54). Another coin shows a similar scene with Poseidon standing on the right (fig. 55); he holds a trident in his left hand, while he extends

FIGURE 51. Bronze coin from Corinth (Lucius Verus, A.D. 161–69). Numismatik Lanz, Auction 105, 752. Photograph by Luebke & Wiedemann, Stuttgart; courtesy of H. Lanz, Munich.

FIGURE 52. Bronze coin from Corinth (Antoninus Pius, A.D. 138–61). Numismatik Lanz, Auction 105, 680. Photograph by Luebke & Wiedemann, Stuttgart; courtesy of H. Lanz, Munich.

FIGURE 53. Bronze coin from Corinth (Commodus, A.D. 177–92). Numismatik Lanz, Auction 105, 822. Photograph by Luebke & Wiedemann, Stuttgart; courtesy of H. Lanz, Munich.

FIGURE 54. Bronze coin from Corinth (Marcus Aurelius, A.D. 161–80). Numismatik Lanz, Auction 105, 698. Photograph by Luebke & Wiedemann, Stuttgart; courtesy of H. Lanz, Munich.

his right hand toward an altar. A pine tree, on the left, provides shade. Both the pine tree and the altar have strong ritual connotations: the former is associated with mourning, and the latter with sacrifice.[53]

Another favorite motif of the Corinth mint is Melikertes lying on the dolphin (fig. 56). This is reminiscent of Philostratos's description of the boy asleep on the dolphin's back as they make their way across the sea to the Isthmus. Another coin uses the same motif, along with a victory crown (fig. 57).

Another key element in the narrative's visual tradition is the pine tree (fig. 58). We have seen the pine tree on coins showing Melikertes and the dolphin on the altar and the ones depicting Poseidon performing a sacrifice. Here we

FIGURE 55. Bronze coin (Marcus Aurelius, A.D. 161–80). Line drawing by Z. Lafis.

FIGURE 56. Bronze coin (Marcus Aurelius, A.D. 161–80). Numismatik Lanz, Auction 105, 700. Photograph by Luebke & Wiedemann, Stuttgart; courtesy of H. Lanz, Munich.

FIGURE 57. Bronze coin from Corinth (Marcus Aurelius, A.D. 161–80). Numismatik Lanz, Auction 105, 702. Photograph by Luebke & Wiedemann, Stuttgart; courtesy of H. Lanz, Munich.

FIGURE 58. Bronze coin from Corinth (Septimius Severus, A.D. 193–211). Numismatik Lanz, Auction 105, 880. Photograph by Luebke & Wiedemann, Stuttgart; courtesy of H. Lanz, Munich.

see an athlete carrying a torch and a palm branch on the left, with a palm tree behind the dolphin and child on the right side.

Another similar coin plays with the same elements (fig. 59).[54] The pine tree occupies a central position and links, as it were, the athlete on the left and the dolphin and boy on the right. As we have seen, pine trees are associated with Melikertes at the Isthmus. Philostratos tells that the pine trees themselves sing

FIGURE 59. Bronze coin from Corinth (Marcus Aurelius, A.D. 161–80). Line drawing by Z. Lafis.

FIGURE 60. Bronze coin from Corinth (Lucius Verus, A.D. 161–69). Numismatik Lanz, Auction 105, 754. Photograph by Luebke & Wiedemann, Stuttgart; courtesy of H. Lanz, Munich.

the story of Melikertes-Palaimon on the painting he describes in his *Eikones*, and indeed pine trees often frame the images on coins (*Eikones* 2.16; cf. discussion above). In figure 59, the pine tree links the games with the figure of the dead boy.

Some coins show the same image of Melikertes and the dolphin placed inside a shrine. These coins have in fact been used by archaeologists to reconstruct the Palaimonion at Isthmia, the heroic shrine named for Palaimon, already described by Pausanias (2.2.1).[55] A coin from the second century A.D. depicts a round temple with an open colonnade (fig. 60). A statue of Melikertes riding the dolphin is in the center of the temple. A door is seen in the base of the building, perhaps leading to the *adyton*. Pine trees here frame the scene on each side of the temple.

Other coins from the same period offer variations on the same theme (fig. 61). Sometimes the temple appears with a sacrificial animal (fig. 62). A similar motif shows both a sacrificial animal and worshiper (fig. 63).

Baby Melikertes does not appear on any extant vase-painting, although he may have been represented on the Geneva krater discussed above. All the later representations of Melikertes-Palaimon depict him as a baby. As in the case of Opheltes, we find a tendency to represent the mortal child (i.e., before death) as a baby (typically with his mother), and the hero (usually with the dolphin) as a boy.[56]

FIGURE 61. Bronze coin from Corinth (Lucius Verus, A.D. 161–69). Numismatik Lanz, Auction 105, 755. Photograph by Luebke & Wiedemann, Stuttgart; courtesy of H. Lanz, Munich.

FIGURE 62. Bronze coin from Corinth (Caracalla, A.D. 198–217). Numismatik Lanz, Auction 105, 939. Photograph by Luebke & Wiedemann, Stuttgart; courtesy of H. Lanz, Munich.

FIGURE 63. Bronze coin from Corinth (Geta, A.D. 209–11). Numismatik Lanz, Auction 105, 980. Photograph by Luebke & Wiedemann, Stuttgart; courtesy of H. Lanz, Munich.

We saw that Pausanias describes the temple of Palaimon and the somewhat mysterious *adyton*, which he places in the sanctuary of Poseidon "to the left" (2.2.1). The relationship of the *adyton* to the temple is not clear from Pausanias's words, and it is possible that the *adyton* might have been a different structure altogether.[57] When he excavated the area and found the temple and sanctuary of Poseidon, Broneer expected to uncover the temple of Palaimon as described by Pausanias.[58] The only traces left of any building, however, are from the Roman period, yet the celebrations of rites in honor of the hero in connection with the Isthmian Games can be inferred from the literary sources, from Pindar on.[59] Broneer suggests that the Roman temple of Palaimon represented a later development of an original Palaimonion, which "owed its location to the existence of an earlier cult place, however insignificant it may have been" (fig. 64).[60]

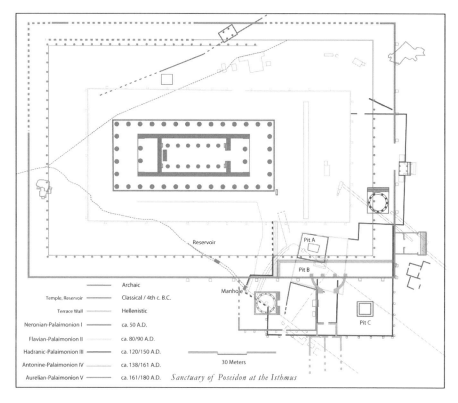

Archaic
Temple, Reservoir — Classical / 4th c. B.C.
Terrace Wall — Hellenistic
Neronian-Palaimonion I — ca. 50 A.D.
Flavian-Palaimonion II — ca. 80/90 A.D.
Hadranic-Palaimonion III — ca. 120/150 A.D.
Antonine-Palaimonion IV — ca. 138/161 A.D.
Aurelian-Palaimonion V — ca. 161/180 A.D.    *Sanctuary of Poseidon at the Isthmus*

30 Meters

FIGURE 64. Sanctuary of Melikertes-Palaimon. Phases from the first to mid-third centuries A.D. Courtesy of University of Chicago Excavations at Isthmia.

The earliest remains in the Roman Palaimonion is a pit from the mid-first century A.D. filled with animal bones, pottery, and lamps. Around A.D. 80, a second pit replaced the first, and lamps of highly unusual shape unknown anywhere else in Greece make their appearance.[61] The Palaimonion was rebuilt later and a third sacrificial pit added in the eastern part of a new precinct that occupied a large area at the southeast side of the main *temenos*. There are remains of a semicircular building, which could have been part of the main entrance to the Palaimonion complex.[62]

In the time of Hadrian the first temple to Palaimon, represented on Corinthian contemporary coins, was erected in a precinct that stretched along the east side of Poseidon's *temenos* (fig. 65).[63] The final Roman rebuilding of

FIGURE 65. Bronze coin from Corinth (Hadrian, A.D. 117–38). Numismatik Lanz, Auction 105, 599. Photograph by Luebke & Wiedemann, Stuttgart; courtesy of H. Lanz, Munich.

the Palaimonion, when a colonnaded square was planned for the main *temenos*, included moving the temple of Palaimon to the western area of the southern precinct. The most recent sacrificial pit remained in use in the eastern part of the precinct after the construction of the second temple. In each case, only the concrete core of the podium remains. It is possible to reconstruct the second temple from representations on Corinthian coins, which show a small *tholos*, consisting of Corinthian columns supporting a conical roof (fig. 66).

Inside, in the center, according to many of the coins, was a statue of Palaimon lying on a dolphin's back. Using the images on the coins, the second temple can be reconstructed as having eleven columns; an opening on the façade indicates a door leading to a passageway under the temple, perhaps the entrance to the *adyton* described by Pausanias (fig. 67).[64]

The second circular temple was the latest addition to the Palaimonion, but unfortunately the few remains do not give enough information to date it exactly. The earliest representation of it appears on coins of Lucius Verus (A.D. 161–69; see figs. 60–61). The development of the south precinct with the third sacrificial pit took place before that period and should be understood as contemporary with the construction of the first temple, which is represented on coins of Hadrian.[65]

The cult of the child hero was flourishing in the Roman period when the *temenos* of Palaimon was rebuilt and included a sacrificial pit for holocausts as well as the *tholos* with a statue of Melikertes lying on the dolphin. Most of the lamps found in Isthmia date from the Roman imperial period, and the great number of so-called Palaimonion lamps begin toward the end of the first century A.D., indicating that the cult was thriving then. The peculiarly shaped lamps are round and have no handle; some of them were found in the sacrificial pits and must have been votive offerings, while others were used for illuminating the area around the Palaimonion. Broneer argues that the number of lamps and the reconstruction and renovations taking place at that time indicate that the cult of Palaimon "eclipsed" that of Poseidon in that period.[66]

FIGURE 66. Reconstruction of the Palaimonion. From Broneer, *Isthmia*, vol. 2, frontispiece.

FIGURE 67. Sanctuary of Melikertes-Palaimon. Three-dimensional reconstruction of Phase V, ca. A.D. 161/167 (viewed from the east). Courtesy of University of Chicago Excavations at Isthmia.

One inscription once in Isthmia, but now in Verona, mentions the Palaimonion (*IG* 4.203). The inscription of uncertain date is dedicated by P. Licinius Priscus Iuventianus, a high priest for life at Isthmia.[67] It gives valuable information on the construction and organization of the Palaimonion. Licinius describes the construction and repairs of various buildings undertaken while he was priest: the inscription mentions new lodgings for the athletes coming to Isthmia, the Palaimonion with its decorations, the *enagistērion,* the sacred entrance, the altars of the ancestral gods, the athletes' examination room, and many other temples and sacred precincts (either built or restored). The *enagistērion* could be another name for the *adyton* described by Pausanias.[68]

Although direct information on the cult of Melikertes is scant, it is possible to reconstruct some of its elements by using the different sources at our disposal. Melikertes, with or without his mother Ino-Leukothea, was at the center of many cults spread all across the Mediterranean world. When it comes to the cult of Melikertes at the Isthmus in pre-Roman times, literary sources provide most, if not all, of the information. Throughout the literary sources is an emphasis on lament, darkness, and mourning, but also on the beauty of the boy riding the dolphin and the joy that he inspires in his worshipers.

The cult of the baby hero Melikertes-Palaimon is unusual insofar as it is found in different places. No other child hero finds himself worshiped over such an extended geographic area. The manner of death of Ino and Melikertes makes it easy for various cities to claim that they found their bodies; thus we find Palaimon in Tenedos, according to Lykophron (*Alexandra* 229) and Callimachus (*Aitia* IV fr. 91 Pfeiffer), as well as in Asia Minor.

Ino is worshiped as a heroine in Megara and all over the Greek mainland and Asia Minor; one myth relates how Ino-Leukothea instituted athletic games for boys in Miletus (Konon *FGrH* 26.33).[69] A Roman inscription from Syria also mentions a cauldron associated with the cult of Ino of Segeira. The inscription from 'Ain al-Burj asks for the safety of the emperor Trajan and is dedicated to the goddess Leukothea by a certain Menneas, a relative of Neteir who has been "consecrated through the cauldron":

ὑπὲρ σωτηρίας αὐτοκράτορος
Τραιανοῦ Νέρουα Σεβαστοῦ
υἱο[ῦ] Σεβαστο[ῦ] Γερμανικοῦ
Δακικο[ῦ] Μεννέας Βεελιαβου
τοῦ Βεελιαβου πατρὸς Νε-

τειρου, τοῦ ἀποθεωθέντος
ἐν τῷ λέβητι δι᾽ οὗ (ἐ)ορταιν ἄγ[ο]ν-
ται, ἐπίσκοπος πάντων τῶν ἐν-
θάδε γεγενότων ἔργων κατ᾽ εὐ-
σεβείας ἀνέθηκεν θεᾷ Λευκο-
θέᾳ Σεγειρῶν

For the safety of the emperor
Traianus Augustus,
Germanicus Dacicus,
son of Nerva Augustus,
Menneas, son of Beeliab,
son of Beeliab, the father of
Neteir, who was deified
in the cauldron with which the festival
is celebrated, the guardian of all
the tasks performed here dedicates [this] to the
goddess Leukothea of Segeira, on account of his piety.
—*IG* 3.1075 (= *OGIS* 611 = *SEG* 7.241)[70]

The inscription dates between A.D. 102 and 116, and the town of Segeira has not been identified. Commentators disagree on the significance of the inscription. Bonnet argues that Neteir must have undergone some initiatory rite in the cauldron, a rite "whose forms we do not understand."[71] Sartre, like Bonnet, rejects the hypothesis that the inscription refers to some kind of human sacrifice, but he disagrees with her interpretation and suggests that the strong verb *apotheoein* (to deify) must refer to the death and subsequent deification of the child: he notes that a regular initiation would hardly be commemorated in a dedication that otherwise is not concerned with the event and that the death of Neteir must be linked to the cauldron in some way: Neteir could have drowned or been boiled to death either accidentally or during some kind of failed ritual.[72] Sartre argues that by duplicating the death of Melikertes, the death of Neteir was perceived as an *apotheōsis*. Melikertes is in fact not named in this inscription, although he does appear in at least one other inscription from the same area alongside Leukothea's name. The inscription is dedicated to the vineyard of the goddess Leukothea and Melikertes by a certain Asklas, who consecrates an altar at his own expenses, on account of his piety.[73]

While a cult of Leukothea and Melikertes may have existed in 'Ain al-Burj, Sartre's explanation for Neteir's apotheosis seems far-fetched. Another, simpler, explanation might be that the cauldron mentioned in the inscription was used in funeral rituals.[74] Heroization of human beings, especially children, was a common occurrence in the Hellenistic and Roman world, and there is no reason to think that Neteir's apotheosis was necessarily a unique event.[75] The cauldron is certainly reminiscent of the myth of Baby Melikertes, and a cauldron such as the one that Ino-Leukothea uses to try to save Baby Melikertes would be a perfect medium for heroization or deification of a dead human being.

To summarize the archaeological evidence, the most important cult location is at the Isthmus, where Melikertes' body is supposed to have been found and buried. Like the cult of Opheltes-Arkhemoros at Nemea, the cult of Melikertes at Isthmia focuses on lament, mourning, and funeral games. The narrative of Melikertes and the dolphin is prevalent in both the literary and visual sources, and it seems to be at the center of the ritual too. According to the coins, a statue of the boy lying on the dolphin was placed in the Roman sanctuary of Melikertes. The Penteskouphia panels show that a narrative of the boy riding on the dolphin was present at Corinth from the mid-sixth century B.C. on, while Pindar confirms that the Isthmian Games were first celebrated as funeral games for the dead child Melikertes. Roman coins show that the link between the athletic games and the baby hero was still strong in the first and second century A.D.

By way of a conclusion, I return to the literary sources and the erotic aspect of the narrative concerning Melikertes-Palaimon that we saw reflected in Ailios Aristeides' description of the hero as an object of desire. While this dimension might not be immediately obvious in the earlier sources, let us go back to the fragment by Pindar that describes the ritual in honor of Melikertes and look more carefully at the vocabulary he uses. When the Nereids ask Sisyphos to honor Melikertes with a *tēlephanton geras,* I suggest that they are asking him to keep the story of the death of Melikertes alive, and Ailios Aristeides is in fact reacting precisely to this *tēlephanton geras,* which is the sacred narrative itself.

The words *tēlephantos* and *tēlephanēs* were used in the descriptions of the ritual in honor of Melikertes and of the tomb of Achilles. We find the same word in a passage clearly associated with love, death, and poetry. According to a quotation in Strabo, Sappho, maddened by love, jumped into the sea from a white rock:

> οὗ δὴ λέγεται πρώτη Σαπφώ,
> (ὥς φησιν ὁ Μένανδρος)
> τὸν ὑπέρκομπον θηρῶσα Φάων',

οἰστρῶντι πόθῳ ῥῖψαι πέτρας
ἀπὸ τηλεφανοῦς ἄλμα κατ᾽ εὐχὴν
σήν, δέσποτ᾽ ἄναξ.

"Where Sappho is said to have been the first,"
as Menander says,
"When she was chasing the haughty Phaon
to throw herself with a leap from the far-seen
rock, driven mad with desire, calling upon
you, lord and king [Apollo Leukatas], in prayer."
—Strabo 10.2.9

Wilamowitz argues that the White Rock in Strabo's passage must refer to a similar motif in Sappho's poetry, although it does not survive in the extant works.[76] This passage is fascinating because Sappho's jump mirrors that of Ino-Leukothea and also because we find here again a form of *tēlephanēs*, the word used by Pindar in fragment 6.5 about the honors due to Melikertes.

The White Rock has parallels in Anacreon (*PMG* 376) and Euripides (*Cyclops* 163–68), and as Nagy shows, in all instances it is associated with the intoxication of love and wine.[77] According to a mythographer, Aphrodite, driven mad by her love for the dead Adonis, herself jumps off the White Rock of Leukas.[78] The White Rock indeed stands at the center of a nexus of erotic and lyric motifs, and in Sappho's jump, death, love, and poetry are conflated. Jumping into the sea from the White Rock is also thematically linked to hero-ization.[79] The very name of the rock from which Ino and Melikertes jump into the sea evokes another White Rock located on the island Skyros. Both Pausanias (1.44.7) and Lucian (*Dialogues of the Sea-Gods* 8.1) refer to the other name of the Molourian rock near Megara as Skeironian, or related to the fig-ure of Skiron; similarly, Kallistratos describes the Skeironian rock shown on a painting depicting the madness of Athamas. There is an island, Skyros, which, in fact, derives its name from its white rocks, from which Theseus falls to his death.[80] Ino's and Melikertes' jump from the Skeironian rock, then, evokes images of falling from the other White Rock. And what happens to Sappho's body after she jumps from the White Rock? The tradition does not say, but in all likelihood, it was rescued, like that of another poet, Hesiod, by a dolphin (or a Nereid, similarly associated with death and poetry) and brought to the shore to become an object of love and worship.[81]

By way of the White Rock, I return to the story of Baby Melikertes. The hero Melikertes-Palaimon is commemorated not only through the games and rituals in his honor at the Isthmus, but he is also celebrated through songs and images that retell the story of his death and heroization. The focus of the hero cult at Isthmia is not simply the dead hero, but very much the narrative of his heroization, and both the literary and visual sources find their inspiration in the cult.

Before I conclude this chapter, I go back to the dolphin theme on a short detour through Roman literature. The image of a boy sitting on a dolphin has universal appeal and is found again and again in different traditions. One letter from Pliny, for example, tells a story that could be illustrated by a similar image:

> Incidi in materiam veram sed simillimam fictae, dignamque isto laetissimo altissimo planeque poetico ingenio; incidi autem, dum super cenam varia miracula hinc inde referuntur. magna auctori fides: tametsi quid poetae cum fide? is tamen auctor, cui bene vel historiam scripturus credidisses.
>
> Est in Africa Hipponensis colonia mari proxima. adiacet navigabile stagnum; ex hoc in modum fluminis aestuarium emergit, quod vice alterna, prout aestus aut repressit aut impulit, nunc infertur mari, nunc redditur stagno. omnis hic aetas piscandi navigandi atque etiam natandi studio tenetur, maxime pueri, quos otium lususque sollicitat. his gloria et virtus altissime provehi: victor ille, qui longissime ut litus ita simul natantes reliquit. hoc certamine puer quidam audentior ceteris in ulteriora tendebat. delphinus occurrit, et nunc praecedere puerum nunc sequi nunc circumire, postremo subire deponere iterum subire, trepidantemque perferre primum in altum, mox flectit ad litus, redditque terrae et aequalibus.
>
> Serpit per coloniam fama; concurrere omnes, ipsum puerum tamquam miraculum adspicere, interrogare audire narrare.

I have come across a true story that is very similar to fiction and would be a worthy subject for that most delightful and great poetical talent of yours. I heard it over dinner while various marvelous stories were being told on all sides. I have it on good authority—though what poet would care about that? Nevertheless, this source is one that even a historian would trust.

The Roman colony of Hippo is on the coast of Africa. A navigable lake is nearby with an estuary like a river coming out of it, which at times flows into the sea or back into the lake depending on the tides. People of all ages spend time here eager for fishing, boating, and swimming, especially boys, who have free time to play, and for whom the greatest feat is to swim out into deep water. The winner is the one who has left both the shore and the other swimmers farthest behind. In one of those contests, a particularly audacious boy went farther out than the others. A dolphin met him and swam now in front of the boy, now behind him, then went around him, and finally dove under to take him on its back, then put him down, then take him on again, and first carried the terrified boy out to sea, afterward turned to the shore, and brought him back to the shore and his friends.

The rumor spread through town; everybody ran to the boy as if he were a prodigy to stare at him, question and listen and repeat the story.
—Pliny, *Letter* 9.33

The letter goes on to describe more wonderful anecdotes about the dolphin, who becomes such a tourist attraction that the town's inhabitants have no other resort than to have the dolphin "quietly destroyed" (*occulte interfici*).

This story of Pliny is somewhat reminiscent of the tale of Melikertes and the dolphin. The people of Hippo are as eager to relive the story of the boy and the dolphin as Ailios Aristeides is eager to experience the sacred narrative of Melikertes. Pliny seems to be experimenting with genres and presents the story as a combination of an ethnological and historical report. In both cases, experiencing the story through retelling involves all senses: as Aristeides "sees" and "hears" the narrative of Melikertes, the people of Hippo want to relive the tale through seeing (*adspicere*) and hearing (*audire*) the story of the dolphin.

Pliny tells us he got the story on good authority, and indeed we find it in the works of his uncle, Pliny the Elder, who gives much factual information about dolphins, including their love of music and their weakness for children. Pliny tells of several dolphins who fall madly in love with young boys. This happened during the life of Alexander the Great, as well as in the reign of Augustus, and again and again dolphins become inflamed with desire (*incenso amore*) to such a degree that many of them commit suicide on the beach when the object of their affection dies (Pliny, *Natural History* 9.25–26). There are so many examples that even Pliny did not have the patience to detail them all.

These accounts, however, lack a context, which is what I have tried to establish for the myth of Melikertes.[82] The death of Melikertes in the sea, the dolphin's rescue of his body, and the subsequent heroization of the boy at Isthmia are all neatly expressed in the statue of the boy and dolphin placed in the temple at Isthmia. As the tale of the boy and the dolphin spreads in the town described by Pliny the Younger, the story of Melikertes and the dolphin spreads through representations in literature and art. The sacred narrative of his death and heroization is indeed *tēlephantos.*

The story of the boy sitting or sleeping on the dolphin is at the center of the sacred narrative concerning the hero Melikertes and the foundation of the Isthmian Games. A Roman coin that depicts the statue of the boy within the temple can be understood as a visual narrative (fig. 68). The story of the boy hero and the dolphin is framed, as it were, by its religious context. Death has undergone metamorphosis into beauty and become poetry. The aesthetics of

FIGURE 68. Bronze coin from Corinth (Lucius Verus, A.D. 161–69). Line drawing by Z. Lafis.

ritual is reflected in both literary and visual representations of the death of Melikertes. The image of the boy and dolphin on the coin is framed by the sacred space of the shrine and pine trees, just as the myth itself is framed by the sacred context that makes it into a narrative of initiation into mysteries, a narrative that, to quote Ailios Aristeides one more time, is "the sweetest of sights to see and to hear" (*Isthmikos* 46.40 Keil 2.375).

The narratives concerning child heroes embody the many dangers threatening infants and young children: children die because of human negligence, anger, madness, divine intervention. Heroic narratives stress the dangers posed to children by those who are the closest to them: their community, their relatives, their parents. Although the myths start out as dreadful tales of violence and death, narratives of heroization ultimately emphasize the youth and beauty of the victims, who become recipients of cult and objects of admiration and desire.

Both the visual and the written sources agree on essential details of narrative of child heroes. The link between the written word and the painted record is controversial, but the assumption that guides this book is that vase-paintings are not "illustrations" of the literary sources and that they offer us their own articulations of the myths. Each myth comes in multiform narratives, yet we always find the same key elements emphasized in both types of evidence. The visual variants also develop their own metaphorical language to express important components of the myths, such as the altar symbolizing sacred space and transgression and the fallen hydria signifying fear.

Other than violent death, there are no prerequisites to become a child hero. Sons and daughters of kings, as well as anonymous children, are heroized and receive cult. In the myths, the brutal deaths of children often bring about dreadful results for those who survive them. Famine, plagues, infertility, and infant deaths befall the communities who neglect to honor the young victims in an appropriate manner. Thus, the citizens of Corinth and Khalkis establish cults for their child heroes only after they experience plague and illness in consequences of their transgression. In other cases, these ills are averted by swift preemptive action: the citizens of Kaphyai and the Seven against Thebes establish rites in honor of the children immediately after their deaths, just as Sisyphos founds the Isthmian Games directly after finding the body of Melikertes-Palaimon. In both cases, whether there is a delay, the myths make explicit the need to atone for the children's deaths with regularly held festivals, often of an athletic nature.

Mothers, nurses, and fathers play a central, and often ambivalent, role: protectors as well as destroyers, saviors as well as murderers of children, they

181

often cause their wards' deaths and establish rituals for them. Fathers (e.g., Herakles, Tantalos, Athamas) are cast as their children's killers, while mothers play a less predictable role: their attempts to protect their offspring frequently fail and bring about the opposite result. Some myths translate mothers' desire for their offspring's safety as a desire for their immortality. Thus, hoping to make them immortal, Medea endangers her children by concealing them in the sanctuary of Hera. This paradigm resembles myths of mothers, such as Metaneira and Astarte, who entrust their infants to goddesses with high expectations and tragic consequences. In other myths, immortalization is not an explicit issue, but caring for children is fraught with danger, as in the case of Hypsipyle or Medea, who cause the deaths of their charges because of a moment of inattention or a mistaken assumption. With Ino, we see a mother who chooses death for herself and her child to save him from his father's murderous rage, so that Ino also is transformed into a heroine or a goddess, according to different local traditions.

The evidence for the rituals tends to be late and fragmentary, but literary sources consistently describe them as mixtures. Rites in honor of child heroes include traits typical of initiation rites, marking the passage into adulthood (separation, haircutting) and also aspects of mourning rituals (special clothes, athletic contests). We see this in the case of the cult for Medea's children, in which seven girls and seven boys wearing special clothing are segregated for a year in the sanctuary of Hera Akraia. This mixture of initiation and mourning practices is also imbedded in the Panhellenic athletic competitions at Olympia, Nemea, and Isthmia, which are founded in honor of dead child heroes and play an important role in the formation of Greek youth. While the connections between Greek athletics and heroism are made explicit in the association of such figures as Achilles and Herakles with the Panhellenic festivals,[1] the more modest narratives of child heroes are in fact at the heart of the myths and rituals at Olympia, Nemea, and Isthmia.

As dead children become immortal in song and ritual, brutality and gruesomeness yield to mourning and commemoration. Cults of child heroes not only fulfill vital religious functions for the ancient Greeks, but narratives of the hero's death and heroization expressed in both the poetic and visual representations were also sources of pleasure. Violence and transgression are given aesthetic and ritual meaning through storytelling and cult. Remembrance is a key element that functions as both atonement for and celebration of interrupted lives. Vernant describes epic as not only a literary genre, but also as "one of the institutions the Greeks developed to give an answer to the problem of death in order to acculturate death and integrate it into social thought and life."[2] This definition could just as well describe the institution of hero cult, which makes sense of the meaninglessness of death by effectively keeping the hero alive through poetry as well as through cult rituals.

In ancient Greece, baby and child heroes exist in parallel with the adult heroes celebrated in epic and tragic poetry, and the narratives of the child heroes' deaths function in myth and ritual in much the same way as do the deaths of their grown-up counterparts. Yet one way in which child heroes differ from adult heroes is their extraordinary reach: while heroes typically are worshiped locally, the child heroes at Nemea and Isthmia become Panhellenic figures at the center of some of the most important ancient religious festivals. The humbler narratives of child heroes also stress unique and unexpected elements: we find here no tales of martial valor or daring deeds; child heroes and their stories give voice to parents', and especially mothers', more domestic and mundane fears, as they strive to make sense of the most meaningless of deaths.

Through mourning and storytelling, athletic competitions and festivals, the children are remembered, and violence and dread give way to poetry.

---

## INTRODUCTION

1. For the beginnings of hero cult, see Coldstream, "Hero-Cults in the Age of Homer"; Snodgrass, "Les origines du culte des héros"; and idem, "Archaeology of the Hero." For a survey of ritual practices associated with heroes, see Burkert, *Greek Religion,* 203–13. Antonaccio, *Archaeology of Ancestors,* surveys the archaeological evidence. See also Morris, "Tomb Cult"; and Whitley, "Early States and Hero Cults."

2. Fontenrose, "Hero as Athlete," for example, surveys a pattern of heroizing dead athletes who either became violent or were mistreated and eventually murdered by fellow citizens. The athlete's death subsequently causes plagues or famines, and invariably the oracle orders a cult to be established in the dead man's honor to compensate for his death. See also Visser, "Worship Your Enemy." For a miraculous death that transforms a mortal into a hero, see Sophocles' *Oedipus at Colonus,* especially the messenger's speech in 1586–1666.

3. Parker, *Athenian Religion,* 37–39.

4. For more on this and the link between ancient texts and images, see chap. 1.

5. Rohde, *Psyche,* 115–17.

6. Usener, *Götternamen,* 149–52.

7. "Les Grecs n'ont jamais douté que leur Héros avaient été des hommes"; Foucart, *Le culte des héros,* 67.

8. Farnell, *Greek Hero Cults.*

9. Rohde, *Psyche,* 117.

10. Farnell, *Greek Hero Cults,* 32–47.

11. Pfister, *Der Reliquienkult im Altertum,* 313–17, 495–97.

12. Brelich, *Gli eroi greci,* 121; and idem, *Paides e parthenoi,* 388, 428, 443 (Kharila), 355–65 (children of Medea).

13. For heroes in Attica, see Kron, *Die zehn attischen Phylenheroen;* and Kearns, *Heroes of Attica;* for heroine cults, see Larson, *Greek Heroine Cults;* and Lyons, *Gender and Immortality.* Cf. Richard Buxton's review of Lyons's book in the *Times Literary Supplement,* January 9, 1998, "How to Be a Heroine," which describes the reaction to Princess Diana's death as a "heroization."

14. Larson, *Greek Heroine Cults,* 89.

15. Schol. Pollux, *Onomasticon* 2.1 (Bethe 80); cf. Solon fr. 27. See Demand, *Birth, Death, and Motherhood,* 141–44, for references to children in the Hippocratic corpus. See also Golden, *Children and Childhood.*

16. See S. Edmunds, *Homeric Nēpios.* See also Vermeule, *Aspects of Death,* 112–15, 237 n. 36.

17. For age classes in the context of athletic competition, see Golden, *Sports and Society*, 104–16.

18. Garland, *Greek Way of Life*, 14–15.

19. Brelich, *Paides e parthenoi*. See Jeanmaire, *Couroi et courètes;* see also Muellner, "Glaucus redivivus," on initiation in myth and ritual.

## CHAPTER 1: THE CHILDREN OF MEDEA

1. For discussion of mothers as killers of their daughters, see Loraux, *Mothers in Mourning*.

2. See Brelich, "I figli di Medeia."

3. As we will see below, the number of the children varies according to the sources. Different authors give different details and even different names. Although most of the sources describe the children as male, some traditions, such as Parmeniskos and Kinaithon of Lakedaimon, identify one or several of Medea's children as female: Kinaithon of Lakedaimon, a sixth-century B.C. composer of genealogies, identifies Medea's children by Jason as a son, Medeios, and a daughter, Eriopis (Pausanias 2.3.9 = fr. 2 Bernabé). For more on Parmeniskos, see below.

4. The concealing incidentally also recalls certain burial practices: children were usually buried close to the surface, while babies were placed in amphorae: see Vidal-Naquet, *Black Hunter*, 139–40, 154 n. 31; and Bérard, *L'hérôon à la porte de l'ouest*, 52. The discovery of a well deposit in the Athenian agora containing bones of 450 infants remains to be explained. It is unclear whether the children were killed or died natural deaths. See Little, "Babies in Well G5:3"; and Rotroff, "Artifacts from Well G5:3."

5. Nagy, *Best of the Achaeans*, 116.

6. Ibid., 118–19 (for *timē* as a compensation for death), 184 (for immortality gained through the permanence of the religious institution).

7. On the ambiguities of the character of Medea in Pindar's *Pythian* 4, see Segal, *Pindar's Mythmaking*, 157–62, 173.

8. See below for the similarities in the cults for the children of Medea and for Melikertes. Cf. chap. 6 for discussion of the *Medea* passage in the context of the myth of Ino and Melikertes.

9. See Pausanias 2.2.2 for secret tombs of Sisyphos and Neleus at the Isthmus; Pausanias often describes how difficult it is to learn the location of such tombs, for example, the location of the tomb of Oedipus (1.28.7). See also L. Edmunds, *Theatrical Space and Historical Place*, 95–100, for other examples of secret heroic graves.

10. Delcourt, *Stérilités mystérieuses*, 10–16. In some contexts, *loimos* does not quite fit the paradigm of sterility. There is a *loimos* at the beginning of Sophocles' *Oedipus Tyrannos*, where illness strikes both the earth and women who become sterile (*tokoisi te agonois gynaikōn;* 26–27). The *loimos* sent by Apollo at the beginning of the *Iliad* is described as the result of the god's *mēnis* (anger), and the only way to put an end to the illness is by appeasing (*hilassamenoi;* 1.100, 444) Apollo.

11. Brelich, "I figli di Medeia," 247–48.

12. The period of segregation is not a sacrifice per se of course, but, as J. Barringer points out to me, the number recalls the story of the seven young men and women who had to be sent annually as a sacrifice to the Minotaur by the Athenians. The number seven is indeed central to a number of myths dealing with children and adolescents.

13. There is disagreement among scholars about the dates of Kreophylos, who is dated to post-431 B.C. and ante-200 B.C. by Jacoby in *FGrH*. Some argue that he was the ancient epic poet of Ephesus (cf. Séchan, *Études sur la tragédie grecque,* 266; and Will, *Korinthiaka,* 106); others claim he was a chronicler living after Euripides (Jacoby on *FGrH* 417). In any case, as Brelich notes in "I figli di Medeia," 222, the scholiast probably reports a pre-Euripidean version.

14. Burkert, "Greek Tragedy and Sacrificial Ritual," 118 n. 71, argues that Medea was the original (even if inadvertent, as in Eumelos's version) killer of the children and that the myth was altered because it "seemed strange that the Corinthians should atone for Medea's crime." See also McDermott, *Euripides' Medea,* 10–20. Cf. Page, *Medea.* See also Easterling, "Infanticide in Euripides' *Medea.*"

15. Brelich, "I figli di Medeia," 221–22.

16. See discussion of *alastos* and *alastōr* in Slatkin, *Power of Thetis,* 95–96; see also Loraux, *Mothers in Mourning,* 99–103.

17. For example, Pausanias 6.6.7–11 tells the story of the hero of Temesa, who indiscriminately kills the citizens of the town until they build him a temple and offer him, each year, the prettiest girl in town. See Breed, "Odysseus Back Home," 156–59, for discussion of this story and the use of the motif of the angry revenant in the *Odyssey.*

18. For more on the history of the ritual terminology of *enagizein* in hero cult, see Ekroth, "Sacrificial Rituals of Greek Hero-Cults"; see also idem, "Pausanias and the Sacrificial Rituals."

19. Brelich, "I figli di Medeia," 247–48, compares the Kaphyaian narrative to another myth, the story of Erigone, in which punishment also strikes targets who are very much like the original victim. The myth tells of Dionysos as he first comes to Athens; he is received by Ikarios, and the god thanks him by giving him a vine branch and teaching him to make wine. Later on, Ikarios, eager to share the god's gift, offers some wine to shepherds. They get very drunk, and under the influence of the alcohol, they kill Ikarios. When they come out of their drunken stupor they realize what they have done and quickly bury the body. But Ikarios's daughter, Erigone, with the help of her dog, finds her father's dead body and subsequently hangs herself from a tree (Apollodoros, *Library* 3.14.7). In one tradition, a strange madness then falls upon Athenian girls who hang themselves (Hyginus, *Astronomica* 2.4). The Delphic oracle orders the Athenians to punish the shepherds and institute a festival for Erigone in which young girls and, later on, masks were swung from trees. This festival, the *Aiora,* was held annually on the third day of the Anthesteria, the festival celebrating the opening of the new wine. See Burkert, *Homo Necans,* 241 n. 11.

20. The story explaining the institution of the cult of Persuasion (*Peithō*) at Sikyon, for example, parallels the Corinthian myth and ritual, not only with the numbers of children involved (see above), but also with the presence of a *deima.* As Apollo and Artemis are on their way to Sikyon to obtain purification for the killing of the Python,

they are struck by *deima*, "there at the place they now call Fear [*phobos*]"; Pausanias 2.7.7). Terrified by the *deima*, the two gods turn away and go to Crete. Simultaneously, the Sikyonians are struck with a sickness (*nosos*) and consult the oracle. See also Will, *Korinthiaka*, 93.

21. See, for example, the saffron robes in the *Arkteia* at Brauron (Aristophanes, *Lysistrata* 641–67 and scholia) and the haircutting ritual in honor of Hippolytos at Troezen (Pausanias 2.32.1) or in honor of the Hyperborean maidens at Delos (Herodotos 4.34; Callimachus, *Hymn to Delos* 296–99; Pausanias 1.43.4). See Brelich, *Paides e parthenoi*, 31, 34, 115, 464; Calame, *Choruses of Young Women*, 106–7; Barringer, *Hunt in Ancient Greece*, 144–46.

22. See Hornblower and Spawforth, *Oxford Classical Dictionary*, 1171, for discussion of the different Philostrati and the works attributed to them.

23. See Maclean and Aitken, *Flavius Philostratus;* Betz, "Heroenverehrung und Christusglaube"; Anderson, *Philostratus*, 247–48; and Mantero, *Ricerche sull' Heroikos di Filostrato*, 1–18.

24. Translation adapted from Maclean and Aitken's *Flavius Philostratus*, 153–55.

25. See chap. 6 for more on this passage and the cult of Melikertes; see also Pache, "Singing Heroes."

26. Simon, "Die Typen der Medeadarstellung," 221. See also Shapiro, *Myth into Art*, 176–82, on vases representing Medea and her children.

27. Trendall, *Red Figure Vases*, fig. 28 = *LIMC* Medeia 35.

28. Sourvinou-Inwood, "Medea at a Shifting Distance," 271.

29. Séchan, *Études sur la tragédie grecque*, 404.

30. See Schmidt, *LIMC* Medeia 37. See also Shapiro, *Personifications in Greek Art;* and Séchan, *Études sur la tragédie grecque*, 404–5.

31. See Séchan, *Études sur la tragédie grecque*, 401, fig. 118 = *LIMC* Kreousa II 16. A variant of this scene is a krater in the Louvre by the Dolon Painter (CA 2193 = Trendall and Webster, *Illustrations of Greek Drama*, 3.3, 35 = Séchan, *Études sur la tragédie grecque*, pl. 7 = *LIMC* Kreousa II 1) that shows Glauke receiving the gifts from a female servant. Neither Medea nor the children are present, but a *paidagōgos* standing on the right side hints at their presence.

32. Séchan, *Études sur la tragédie grecque*, 401.

33. Séchan, *Études sur la tragédie grecque*, 119 = *LIMC* Medeia 30.

34. The "typische Gewandschürzung der Opferschlächterin"; *LIMC* Medeia 30.

35. Burkert, "Greek Tragedy and Sacrificial Ritual," 118. Cf. Euripides, *Medea* 1053–55.

36. Trendall and Webster, *Illustrations of Greek Drama*, 97.

37. Princeton, University Museum 83-13 = Trendall and Cambitoglou, *Red-Figured Vases of Apulia*, 1.78, 41a, table 12 = *LIMC* Herakles 1409 = *LIMC* Herakleidai 9.

38. Trendall, "Medea at Eleusis," 9; and Schmidt, "Medea und Herakles," 169.

39. Hippotes is mentioned elsewhere as the son of Kreon: in one tradition, Jason marries the daughter of Hippotes instead of the daughter of Kreon (schol. Euripides, *Medea* 19); Diodorus Siculus 4.55 mentions Hippotes and the Athenian court; and finally, in Hyginus, *Fabula* 27, Medea's son Medos impersonates Hippotes, with ensuing mistaken identity, etc.

40. See Shapiro, *Myth into Art*, 181.

41. "Er ist gleichsam eine männliche Erinys"; Simon, "Die Typen der Medeadarstellung," 213.

42. Shapiro, *Personifications in Greek Art*, 168–70.

43. Simon, "Die Typen der Medeadarstellung," 213.

44. Sourvinou-Inwood, "Medea at a Shifting Distance," 272. See also Schmidt's commentary on *LIMC* Medeia 397.

45. Cf. Schmidt, *LIMC* Medeia 11.

46. Goldhill, "Naïve and Knowing Eye," 212–14.

47. Cf. *LIMC* Medeia 19, 21, 23 for second- and third-century A.D. reliefs showing a strong Medea, sword in hand, with her children at her feet, supplicating her.

48. Cf. Gaggadis-Robin, *Jason et Médée*, 151–53.

49. See Taplin, *Comic Angels*, 22, for difference between iconography and Euripides' tragedy.

50. Sourvinou-Inwood, "Medea at a Shifting Distance," 284.

51. Ibid., 287.

52. Ibid., 289.

53. Ibid., 285.

54. Or is she simply wearing the kind of costume that actors would wear, *pace* Sourvinou-Inwood. Cf. M. Miller, "Priam, King of Troy," for the orientalization of mythical figures in iconography.

55. Giuliani, "Rhesus between Dream and Death," 74 n. 14: "The question of the genesis of a motif must be fundamentally distinguished from that of its meaning: the long-sleeved garments must be considered as a sign in their iconographic context, and as such they have quite a different function from that of signifying 'theatre.'" See Taplin, *Comic Angels*, 21–22, about the history of the controversy about the link between vases and theater, starting with Carl Robert. See also Green, "On Seeing and Depicting the Theatre." Taplin, *Comic Angels*, 23 n. 4 and 25, argues that the Munich volute krater (see fig. 8) illustrates not Euripides but Neophron's *Medea*. He explains differences by reference to nonliterary factors.

56. Giuliani, "Rhesus between Dream and Death," 85: "The painter's interest is focused not upon one literary text or another, but upon the mythological material." Taplin, *Comic Angels*, 27, claims that "the vases confirm that Athenian tragedy was part of life in fourth-century Megale Hellas, and that it helped people to cope with mortality and the human condition." That may well be true, but why restrict his point to Athenian tragedy? While it is clear that Athenian tragedy was an influence in Southern Italy, certainly other versions (of the *Medea* and of other plays) were not centered on Athens and may have reflected different local traditions. The important point is that the same narratives (the children of Medea, the children of Herakles, etc.) were used.

57. For an analysis of scenes of killing at the altar on Attic vases, see Durand and Lissarrague, "Mourir à l'autel," 84, which likens shed human blood to virtual sacrifice: "Men's blood is virtually sacrificial blood" ("le sang des hommes est virtuellement un sang sacrificiel même"). See also Blome, "Das Schreckliche im Bild," 84–86, for the role played by the altar on depictions of the death of Medea's children.

58. Williams, "Pre-Roman Cults," 46–49; and Payne, *Perachora*, 1.19–20, locate the temple in Corinth; Dunn locates it at Perachora; "Euripides and the Rites of Hera Akraia," 110.

59. Including the scholiast to Euripides' *Medea* 1379, who seems to confuse Hera Akraia with Hera Bounaia.

60. Scranton, *Corinth*, 1/2.162 n. 40.

61. In 1907, between the archaic temple of Apollo and the archaic rock-cut fountain of Glauke in Corinth, archaeologists discovered the ruins of an early Roman temple— from the late Augustan or early Tiberian period—which they called Temple C. At one point in the western wall of the enclosure it becomes one with the eastern wall of the fountain of Glauke, with a gaping hole opening into the reservoir, perhaps a door or some kind of an opening. Scranton argues that there is no apparent reason why the wall of the *temenos* should be placed so close to the fountain house unless communication between the two was desired. Pausanias does not mention this *temenos* at all, and the connection between its precinct and the fountain of Glauke remains obscure. Scranton argues that the cult practiced in the temple must have had some relationship to the fountain and the myth of Glauke. There seems to be no possible connection between a new Roman cult and the fountain, unless Temple C was actually the successor of an archaic Greek temple associated with the fountain, a temple that would have been destroyed alongside the Greek city and in such a way that it could not be rebuilt on its original site (Scranton, *Corinth*, 1/2.149–51; the Romans seem to have used the area of the fountain as a quarry). With this hypothesis in mind, and from his examination of the site around the fountain, Scranton concludes that an earlier, archaic sanctuary was built directly on top of the fountain with direct access to the water and that the link made between the physical location of the fountain of Glauke and the Roman temple indicates a cultic link between the two structures. Thus, Scranton argues that the story of the death of Glauke in the fountain is central to the ritual taking place in the temple. He suggests that the rituals performed in the temple included a mimetic dance and a mimetic leap by Glauke into the fountain, which accounts for the peculiarities of the cult buildings. Such a theory, of course, is impossible to verify and, as tempting as it is to locate the rituals in honor of Hera Akraia in Corinth following Pausanias's account, there is no physical evidence for placing the cult there. See Scranton, *Corinth*, 1/2.151–58, 160, 162. Scranton's hypothesis has not found much support in subsequent scholarship. See Menadier, "Sixth-Century Temple," 202.

62. One sacrificial ritual we know about only through late sources also links the children and Perachora: "They say that after she killed her children in Corinth, Medea hid the knife there. The Corinthians, in accordance with the oracle given to them, sacrifice [*enagizein*] a black goat, which lacks a knife [*makhaira*]: digging with its foot, the goat finds [*aneurein*] the knife" (Eusebius, *Against Marcellus* 1.3; see Burkert, "Greek Tragedy and Sacrificial Ritual," who cites the passage from Klostermann, *Eusebius of Caesarea*, fr. 125). Cf. Theodoridis, *Photii patriarchae lexicon*, s.v. *aigos tropon* (the way of the goat), where the story is used to explain a Corinthian maxim, "the goat gives the knife," which is applied to people who bring about their own destruction. See Burkert, "Greek Tragedy and Sacrificial Ritual," 117–19; Picard, "L'héraeon de

Pérachora," 220–21; Menadier, "Sixth-Century Temple," especially chaps. 5–9, who argues that the grave of the children is at Perachora and that the *mnēma* commemorating the events at Corinth is not necessarily connected with a ritual. On the sacrificial knife (*machaira*), see Martin, *Healing, Sacrifice, and Battle,* 85–93.

63. For example, in the Arkteia at Brauron or the Arrhephoria in Athens (Aristophanes, *Lysistrata* 641–67 with scholia). See Brelich, *Paides e parthenoi;* and Burkert, *Homo Necans,* 150–54.

64. Brelich, "I figli di Medeia," 213.

65. Ibid., 229.

66. Graf, "Medea, the Enchantress from Afar," 40–41, analyzes the ritual in terms of formal elements and suggests that it follows an initiatory pattern, with Medea playing the role of initiatrix, which, he argues, is usually reserved for goddesses. Johnston, "Medea and the Cult of Hera Akraia," 60–61, focuses on the ritual in terms of its mythical function, which is to appease the dangerous wrath of Hera. Johnston also builds upon a suggestion by Will, *Korinthiaka,* 114–18, that there were originally two cults: *enagismata* and *thrēnoi* for the murdered baby heroes, and the annual dedication of fourteen Corinthian children to the kourotrophic deity Hera/Medea. The second cult attempts to protect young mothers and their newborn babies from a reproductive demon, similar to the reproductive demons Lamia or Mormo (Johnston, "Medea and the Cult of Hera Akraia," 63; for Lamia, cf. ibid., 58 n. 48). According to this hypothesis, the two stories become entwined, and the conflated myth explains the amalgam of rituals performed in honor of the child heroes of Corinth.

67. Cf. Homeric *Hymn to Demeter* 239, 249, where Demeter puts (*krypteske* and *kryptei*) the child Demophon in the fire. See also *Odyssey* 5.488, where Odysseus burying himself under a pile of leaves is compared to burying (*enekrypse*) a log in an ash heap. In Xenophon's *Kyropaideia* 3.3.3, the word is specifically used of burying bodies in the ground.

68. On Spartan *krypteia,* see Plutarch, *Lykourgos* 28, and schol. Plato, *Laws* 633b. See also Brelich, *Paides e parthenoi,* 113–96 (Spartan *krypteia*), 356–65 (the children of Medea); and idem, "I figli di Medeia," 225–26. Similarly, Jeanmaire, *Couroi et courètes,* 298–301, understands the myth of the children of Medea as an *aition* for a ritual of initiation.

69. Will claims that *katakryptein* implies a ritual of inhumation. He argues that, in both the scholiast's and Eumelos's versions, the agricultural nature of ancient myth is preserved: the story begins with Medea saving the Corinthians from a famine; later, she buries her babies in the ground, thereby linking her actions with other fertility rituals (*Korinthiaka,* 89). Picard understands it as a ritual of incineration and links it with the famous passage in the Homeric *Hymn to Demeter* ("L'héraeon de Pérachora," 225). Brelich notes that even if the verb *kryptein* is indeed linked with a fire ritual in the *Hymn to Demeter,* there is no basis for understanding this rite as an incineration; it is more likely that the term *katakryptein* is to be understood literally as "to hide" or "to conceal"; Johnston understands the *katakryptein* as belonging to the paradigm of the reproductive demon, who steals young children and needs to be appeased ("Medea and the Cult of Hera Akraia," 64–65).

70. On Demeter, see Homeric *Hymn to Demeter* 231–74; on Thetis, see Apollonios Rhodios, *Argonautika* 4.869–79. Cf. Isis in Plutarch, *Isis and Osiris* 357c. In these three cases, the process of immortalizing the baby is interrupted by an ignorant human who mistakes the operation for an attempt to destroy the child; in Medea's case, the circumstances of the failure are unknown. The women involved, unlike Medea, are also goddesses, and, except for Thetis, they are trying to immortalize the human babies of other women. See also chap. 3 for more on this motif of failed immortalization.

71. The number of seven boys and seven girls, which is found in Parmeniskos's version of the children's death to describe the number of victims as well as the number of participants in the ritual, is a traditional number found elsewhere in Greek myth and ritual. Theseus's companions on his trip to Crete, for example, and the children of Niobe also come in groups of seven girls and seven boys.

72. Brelich, "I figli di Medeia," 227.

73. Brelich notes that the cure to an original pollution is to be found in the perpetuation of a primordial mythical event (ibid., 248).

## CHAPTER 2: THE CHILDREN OF HERAKLES

1. As in the case of the children of Medea, the numbers of children vary, and they tend to be described as male. Aristotle incidentally mentions Herakles in his discussion of human reproduction (*History of Animals* 7.6.45). According to him, Herakles had difficulty fathering daughters and had only one girl out of seventy-three children.

2. Bernabé, *Poetarum epicorum Graecorum*, 1.40 (= Davies 31).

3. Gantz, *Early Greek Myth*, 380, notes that Pindar does not mention Herakles in connection with the children's death. One wonders if the word could be used to describe statues. Pindar uses the word *khalkoarēs* one other time to describe Memnon in *Isthmian* 5.42.

4. Thummer, *Pindar*, 2.79.

5. Burkert, *Greek Religion*, 210.

6. See chap. 1, n. 18, for bibliography on *enagizein* as a ritual term reserved for hero cult. Ritualized fighting and athletic competitions, as we will see in later chapters, is well attested in ancient Greece as a way of compensating the dead for their death and of atoning for the guilt of the living. See Meuli, *Der griechische Agon;* and Burkert, *Homo Necans.*

7. See discussion of Medea concealing her children in the sanctuary of Hera Akraia in chap. 1; see also the case of Demophon in chap. 3, Pelops in chap. 4, and the children of Ino and Athamas in chap. 6.

8. Gantz, *Early Greek Myth*, 382. Hyginus (second century A.D.), like Euripides, whom he perhaps follows, places the murder just after the labors and has Lykos trying to kill Megara and her sons while Herakles is still in Hades (*Fabulae* 31, 32, 72, 241). Hyginus specifies the names of Herakles' two sons: Therimachus and Ophites. The name Ophites does not appear anywhere else in the extant Greek sources, but interestingly Hyginus uses the same word to describe Baby Opheltes-Arkhemoros in *Fabula* 74.

9. Halm-Tisserant, *Cannibalisme et immortalité*, 184, argues that Euripides chooses these three modes of murder better to underline the "network of confusions between sacrifice, hunting, and war" ("réseau d'interférences entre sacrifice, chasse et guerre"). Cf. the similar pattern found in Nonnos of Panopolis's version of the death of the children of Athamas and Ino in chap. 6.

10. We will come back below to narratives of children dying from fear with the story of Isis and the children of Astarte.

11. Trendall, *Paestan Pottery*, 115, no. 33, table 7, and 1952, no. 39 = *LIMC* Herakles 1684 = *LIMC* Alkmene 18.

12. It is also interesting that the painter chooses to depict the personification of madness as Mania rather than as the Euripidean Lyssa. See Shapiro, *Personifications in Greek Art*, 168.

13. Schmidt, "Medea und Herakles," 170.

14. Cf. Statius 3.187 and Nonnos of Panopolis 10.61 for descriptions of Athamas exhibiting a similar joyful reaction after the murder of his son.

15. Aelian notes in *Varia Historia* 12.36 that the ancients disagree about the number, while Aulus Gellius describes the phenomenon as "a strange and almost ridiculous variation" ("mira et prope adeo ridicula diversitas") (*Attic Nights* 20.7).

16. Stern, *Erotika Pathemata*, 94.

17. Cf. Dunn, "Pausanias on the Tomb of Medea's Children," 348–49; and discussion of the *mnēma* for the children of Medea in chap. 1.

18. Pausanias describes the base of the statue of Zeus at Olympia: "Theban children" are being snatched by Sphinxes, while Apollo and Artemis shoot down the children of Niobe (5.11.2). Copies of parts of these sculptures have been identified; see Carpenter, *Art and Myth*, 43.

19. Demand, *Thebes in the Fifth Century*, 52, 145 nn. 7–8.


## CHAPTER 3: LINOS AND DEMOPHON

1. Chantraine, *Dictionnaire étymologique de la langue grecque*, s.v. *linos*.

2. Farnell, *Greek Hero Cults*, 27.

3. Kirk, *Iliad*, 5.225, argues that it is odd to have a *linos*-song in this particular passage, since the *linos* is always referred to as a dirge, and this is a happy occasion. He adds: "If Linos was actually a dying vegetation god, perhaps the song was proper to the autumn." Cf. Farnell, *Greek Hero Cults*, 30. Herodotos 2.79 links the Greek Linos with the Egyptian Maneros (see more on this below). See Pindar fr. 128c6 (Maehler).

4. Farnell, *Greek Hero Cults*, 30.

5. On Konon, see Henrichs, "Three Approaches to Greek Mythography," 244–47.

6. See Larson, *Greek Heroine Cults*, 133–35, on the "substitute avenger." Whether Poine or the plague avenge the baby's or the mother's death, Larson argues, it seems that neither the former nor the latter have the strength to avenge themselves. See also Fontenrose, "Hero as Athlete."

7. Delcourt, *Stérilités mystérieuses*, 16, argues that the word *loimos* refers to sterility, both animal and vegetal, rather than to plague or sickness. As we will see in the other

versions of the story of Linos, it is very likely that the bane in question strikes young mothers and their newborn infants.

8. See Ovid's *Ibis* 573–76, where Krotopos punishes Psamathe by burying her alive.

9. Is Statius actually punning on the monster's name when he says that Psamathe exposed her child because she was afraid of her father's *poena* (*ac poenae metuens;* 1.578)?

10. For more on Lamia and other baby-snatching monsters, see Johnston, "Medea and the Cult of Hera Akraia"; and idem, *Restless Dead,* 161–99.

11. Pfeiffer, *Callimachus,* 1.36, argues that the word must refer to Krotopos as the killer of his own daughter.

12. Burkert, *Homo Necans,* 107–8, notes that the days of the Lamb correspond to the dog days of Sirius, which are also very close to the time of the Olympic Games. He also argues that the dogs killed in the ritual in honor of Linos can be understood as wolflike animals barred from the kingdom of people and therefore from the agora of Apollo, who, in Argos, is called *Lykeios* (wolflike). On Lykeia, see also Burkert, *Greek Religion;* and Vidal-Naquet, *Black Hunter.*

13. See Delcourt, *Stérilités mystérieuses,* 16.

14. Pfeiffer, *Callimachus,* 1.36, quoting A. Hecker.

15. Alexiou, *Ritual Lament in Greek Tradition,* 57.

16. See Frazer's *Apollodorus* 2.311, on "Putting Children on the Fire."

17. For more on the "bloom" of child heroes, see especially chap. 6.

18. Nagy, *Best of the Achaeans,* 181–82.

19. Schol. Homeric *Hymn to Demeter* 254, cited by Richardson, *Homeric Hymn to Demeter,* 242. Richardson argues that the poet suppresses the death, which was part of the traditional version, because it is *aprepēs* (unseemly).

20. *Georgics* 1.19 with Servius's commentary, as well as Servius on 1.163. See Clinton, *Myth and Cult,* 100–102.

21. There is no direct connection between the Mysteria (the initiation into the mysteries of Eleusis) and the Eleusinia (the athletic games themselves). The exact location of the Eleusinia remains mysterious. The games presumably did not take place inside the sanctuary, like the Mysteria, since only initiates could enter it. Cf. Clinton, "IG 1² 5," 2. Moreover, the Mysteria and the Eleusinia were not celebrated on the same date and perhaps not even the same month. See Deubner, *Attische Feste,* 91 (Eleusinia), 69 (*ballētys*). The prize consisted of barley (Drachmann 3.302).

22. The minimum age at Olympia was twelve, but age was determined by the *Hellanodikai,* who decided to which categories participants belonged. See Lee, "Ancient Olympic Games," 129–30, 133 about the *Hellanodikai* (judges of the Greeks). See also Golden, *Sports and Society;* and Scanlon, *Eros and Greek Athletics.*

23. Kern, *Die Religion der Griechen,* 2.208–10, argues that the games originated in the *ballētys,* but there is no reason to equate the two. Clinton, "IG 1² 5," 5 n. 17, argues that "there is nothing to indicate that the contest described in the *Hymn* was the Eleusinia. If these lines are an *aition* of a festival, it is more likely that it was the festival called *ballētys.*" Clinton further argues that the Eleusinia was a type of harvest festival, held annually, with the athletic competition held only every two years, in the

second and fourth years of every Olympiad; on harvest festival, see 3 n. 10; on dates, see 9–11.

24. Schol. Homeric *Hymn to Demeter* ad 254, cited by Richardson, *Homeric Hymn to Demeter,* 245, 247.

25. See ibid., 246, for sources on ritual battles.

26. Ibid., 12; and Clinton, "IG 1² 5," 3.

27. Richardson, *Homeric Hymn to Demeter,* 12. From the first century on, the Homeric *Hymn to Demeter* was included among the works attributed to Orpheus and was probably also performed in the context of Orphic ritual; see fr. 49.100–101 (Kern); Richardson, *Homeric Hymn to Demeter,* 12.

28. Muellner, "Glaucus redivivus," 21–22. For the Cretan ritual, see Willetts, *Cretan Cults and Festivals,* 43–53, 116–17. For the excavation of a shrine honoring Glaukos at Knossos, see Callaghan, "KRS 1976."

29. Sotades cup, Athenian whiteware, fifth century B.C., British Museum D5. This cup is part of the same group of cups among which is the depiction of a snake and man sometimes linked to the episode of the death of Opheltes. See chap. 5 for more on the Sotades cups.

30. Muellner, "Glaucus redivivus," 27.

31. See Nagy, *Pindar's Homer,* 32–33, on the verb *myein* "which means 'I have my mouth closed' or 'I have my eyes closed' in everyday situations, but 'I say in a special way' or 'I see in a special way' in marked situations of ritual," and the related noun *mystēs* (one who is initiated) and *mystērion* (that into which one is initiated). As Muellner, "Glaucus redivivus," 7–8, notes, the story of Glaukos seems to play on the various meanings of *my-* words: open and closed eyes and mouths are a recurrent concern, and Glaukos's spitting into the seer's mouth can be understood as a failure to keep his mouth shut or, in other words, to remain a *mystēs.*

32. Muellner, "Glaucus redivivus," 16; Willetts, *Cretan Cults and Festivals,* 43–53; Burkert, *Greek Religion,* 212–13.

33. Jeanmaire, *Couroi et courètes,* 453–55, considers the story of Zeus and Ganymedes an *aition* for this ritual, while Muellner, "Glaucus redivivus," 18–21 and n. 18, prefers to regard both myths as belonging to a similar "semantic context." Burkert, *Greek Religion,* 261, notes the similarity between the story of Ganymedes and Glaukos without commenting on the resemblance. See also Willetts, *Cretan Cults and Festivals,* 117; Sergent, *Homosexuality in Greek Myth;* and Koehl, "Chieftain Cup."

34. Muellner, "Glaucus redivivus," 19–20. See Ephorus cited by Strabo 10.483–84; see also, Willetts, *Cretan Cults and Festivals,* 60–67.

35. Richardson, *Homeric Hymn to Demeter,* 70, notes that it is possible that "both passages might reflect an earlier epic model," but he argues on internal grounds that Apollodoros probably based his narrative on the Homeric *Hymn to Demeter.* Mackie, "Achilles in Fire," argues on thematic grounds that both versions go back to an earlier epic model.

36. Swallows are often linked with lament, as, for example, in the myth of Prokne and Philomela, who are transformed into a nightingale and a swallow, after the latter is raped by the former's husband and Prokne serves her son Itys as a meal to him. See

Loraux, *Mothers in Mourning,* 56–57; and Alexiou, *Ritual Lament in Greek Tradition,* 97.

37. Griffiths, *Plutarch's de Iside et Osiride,* 334, notes that there is no city of that name and that it seems to be a gloss added by a scribe.

38. Ibid., 327 and n. 6; and Froidefond, *Plutarque,* 267.

39. Griffiths argues that the child who dies because of her mourning cry, the youngest one, is the same child that she had attempted to make immortal; see *Plutarch's de Iside et Osiride,* 17.

40. Demophon, in fact, appears nowhere on Eleusinian art or inscriptions. See Clinton, *Myth and Cult,* 30, 100–102.

41. Except, interestingly enough, as children, as in the myth of Baby Dionysos/Zagreus, whom the Titans trick with toys and then prepare as a meal. See Clement of Alexandria, *Protreptikos* 2.18 (Kern 34).

## CHAPTER 4: PELOPS AT OLYMPIA

1. Pelops is already familiar to the Greeks for his deeds as an adult in Homer: see *Iliad* 2.104, where he is described as the first human owner of the scepter eventually handed down to Agamemnon. See Phlegon *FGrH* 257 F 1 on the various myths concerning the establishment of the Olympian Games. For the victory of Pelops, see also Pindar, *Olympian* 1.67–88; for Herakles, see Pindar, *Olympian* 10.24–77. For the various myths concerning Olympia, see Nagy, *Pindar's Homer,* 119–20 with notes. As Nagy argues, "the variations in these myths reflect the political vicissitudes of the festivals themselves, in that different versions may represent the traditions of different groups, places, and times" (119 n. 13). The Olympic Games were the earliest Panhellenic festival, held every four years, in August or September, starting in 776 B.C. according to the victors' lists. The original competition was the footrace (*stadion*), while other events, such as chariot and horse races were added later on. See Golden, *Sports and Society;* and S. Miller, "Organisation et fonctionnement," with bibliography.

2. As Nagy argues, the death of Pelops as a child can be understood as the motivation for the very athletic competition in which he later competes as an adult, a competition that subsequently provides an *aition* for the games as a whole: "In fact the two layers of myths are integrated into a sequence, just like the two layers of athletic events" (*Pindar's Homer,* 127–28).

3. See ibid., 116–35, for Nagy's examination of Pindar's *Olympian* 1 and the Olympic Games. This chapter is very much indebted to Nagy's analysis.

4. See Calame, *Choruses of Young Women,* 244–49; see also Nagy, *Pindar's Homer,* 129.

5. "Pulchritudine Pelops infans post primam lavationem ita nitet, ut a Neptuno amore incenso rapiatur"; Kassel, *Quomodo quibus locis,* 24 and n. 82.7.

6. Halm-Tisserant, *Cannibalisme et immortalité,* 137, interprets Poseidon's desire for Pelops as a sign that the latter is old enough to be an *erōmenos,* but clearly infants in myth can be the objects of divine desire. See also chap. 6 for Melikertes and the desire that he evokes in his worshipers.

7. Slater, "Pelops at Olympia," 490–91; Burkert, *Greek Religion*, 205. See also Nock, "Cult of Heroes."

8. See Slater, "Pelops at Olympia," 493 (for the Boeotian origin of the word *haimakouria*), 494 (for meaning of *memiktai*). Later literary sources differ on the location or even the existence of the tomb of Pelops, but most agree that it is not at Olympia. The scholia to Pindar record various hypotheses: some say that there was no *mnēma*, but only a sanctuary (*hieron*) for Pelops (149a Drachmann); others note that Pindar calls the site *amphipolos* because it was in the middle of the city, where the inhabitants buried Pelops as was their habit (149b); another version explains that the tomb (*taphos*) was circled by the contestants since it was located in the stadium itself (149c, e). In this tradition, of course, the tomb of Pelops contains the body of a young man, rather than a baby.

9. Apollodoros also mentions the prophecy alluded to by Lykophron and later recounted by Pausanias about the bones of Pelops. In the *Epitome*, Odysseus captures the Trojan seer Helenos, who tells him that the Greeks have to do three things in order to seize Troy. The first of these is the need to fetch the bones of Pelops (*Epitome* 5.10), which the Greeks do.

10. Scodel, "Hesiod redivivus," 304. Scodel further argues that the word *hēbēs* has shades of both rejuvenation and vitality, that it "is less a defined period in life than a state; it is etymologically connected with Lithuanian *jega*, 'force,' 'vital energy'" (307).

11. Garland, *Greek Way of Death*, 77–78.

12. Halm-Tisserant, *Cannibalisme et immortalité*, 7.

13. See Cook, *Zeus*, 2.212, fig. 149, no. 5.

14. For iconography of Pelops as an adult, see Shapiro, *Myth into Art*, which discusses Pindar's *Olympian 1* and the iconographic tradition of the chariot race; similarly, Lacroix, "La légende de Pélops," discusses only the adult Pelops. For more on the iconography of children and cauldron, see Laurens, "L'enfant entre l'épée."

15. See Burkert, *Homo Necans*, 93–103.

16. See Mallwitz, "Cult and Competition Locations," 79–81, for discussion.

17. Contra Mallwitz who argues that even if the early fourth-century B.C. Pelopeion (the earliest extant remains) had an archaic predecessor, Dörpfeld's prehistoric *hērōon* never existed. If there was a cult in honor of Pelops prior to the archaic period, it had to take place at another location; see Mallwitz, *Olympia und seine Bauten*, 134–37; idem, "Cult and Competition Locations," 86–87. See also Antonaccio, *Archaeology of Ancestors*, 170–76, for a summary of Dörpfeld's hypothesis in *Alt-Olympia* and objections by Herrmann and Mallwitz. Cf. Herrmann, "Pelops in Olympia." See also Morgan, *Athletes and Oracles*, 27–105, for early finds at Olympia.

18. As Golden puts it: "The current consensus is that the sanctuary's beginnings cannot be pushed back beyond the geometric period, that it was Zeus's from the start, that there is no early evidence for Pelops's cult" (*Sports and Society*, 14).

19. Kyrieleis, "Les fouilles allemandes à Olympie," 60: "Our own excavations . . . showed that Dörpfeld's observations were theoretically perfectly correct" ("nos propres fouilles . . . révélèrent que les observations de Dörpfeld étaient dans leur principe parfaitement exactes"). See also S. Miller, "Shrine of Opheltes," for his suggestion that the shrine at Nemea was a copy of the no longer extant prior Pelopeion at Olympia,

which would have been the focal point for two race traces, one for men and one for horses.

20. See Hadzisteliou-Price, "Hero Cult in the 'Age of Homer,'" 223.

21. As Burkert notes in his *Homo Necans,* the ritual also combines the same three figures encountered in the myth: Pelops, Zeus, and Demeter, and thus he concludes "the cannibalistic myth of Pelops that so shocked Pindar clearly refers to the Olympic festival" (100); for more on Pelops and Olympia, see 93–103. Nagy, *Pindar's Homer,* 127, agrees with Burkert about the link between Pelops and Olympia, but instead of seeing the myth as an *aition* for the games, he sees it as an *aition* for one specific event, the footrace (*stadion*), which is subsequently transformed with the advent of the chariot race and a new *aition* to justify it.

22. For more on this pattern of children in cauldrons, cannibalism, and resuscitation, see Halm-Tisserant, *Cannibalisme et immortalité.*

23. Burkert, *Homo Necans,* 84–93, for sources and bibliography.

24. See ibid., 89–91.

25. See ibid., 84–93; see also Nagy, *Pindar's Homer,* 125–26. For age classes at Olympia, see Golden, *Sports and Society,* 104–16.

26. See also Burkert, *Homo Necans,* 86 with n. 15 for sources.

27. Ibid., 87.

## CHAPTER 5: OPHELTES-ARKHEMOROS

1. Other, less well-known versions are reported in the scholia to Pindar's *Nemeans.* The games were founded in honor of Adrastos's brother, Pronax, or long before the Seven ever came to Nemea. A variant of the Herakles myth has Herakles come to Nemea *after* the Seven founded the games in honor of Opheltes and consecrated them to Nemean Zeus. See Maehler, *Die Lieder des Bakchylides,* 1.143–45; and Doffey, "Les mythes de fondation," for discussions of the variants of the myth.

2. The Nemean Games, first attested in 573 B.C. when they were either reestablished or restored, are the most recent of the four Panhellenic Games. The Parian Marble (*IG* 12/5.444 = *FGrH* 239.22) states that the games were founded by Adrastos and his companions in the equivalent of 1251 B.C., but in historical times the games are not attested until 573 B.C. See Gebhard, "Beginnings of Panhellenic Games," for dates of Panhellenic festivals. The games were held biennially, in alternation with the Isthmian ones, in July of the second and fourth year of every Olympiad. The city of Kleonai was responsible for administering the games until about 460 B.C., when Argos took over. The program, like the one at Olympia, excluded musical contests. See S. Miller, *Nemea,* 4–7, for lists of the different gymnastic, equestrian, and nonathletic events. Judges, who wore mourning clothes, divided the contestants into three categories: *paides* (12–16), *ageneioi* (16–20), and *andres* (20 and over). As at Olympia, Delphi, and Isthmia, winners were rewarded by wreaths, in this case of wild celery. *Selinon,* which probably denotes wild celery, though some translate it parsley, is clearly a plant associated with death and mourning for the ancient Greeks. See Plutarch's *Timoleon* 26 for the expression "to need celery" when one is close to death; see also schol. Pindar,

*Olympian* 13.45; Garland, *Greek Way of Death,* 26, 116, on celery and death; Blech, *Studien zum Kranz bei den Griechen,* 94–95 (on celery), 131–37 (on the Isthmian and Nemean crown of celery). On the translation of *selinon* or *apium* as wild celery, see Andrews, "Celery and Parsley as Foods."

3. The phrase does not appear elsewhere in ancient literature, although the combination *thymon apopneein* is attested several times. It is used to describe the death of another serpent, the Python, in the Homeric *Hymn to Apollo* 3.362. Homeric poetry attests the phrase twice to describe dying warriors in the *Iliad* (4.524; 13.654). Tyrtaeus uses it once (quoted by Lykourgos 1.107); and Pindar uses a variant, *euanthe' apepneusas halikian,* in *Isthmian* 7.34.

4. It is particularly interesting to compare versions of the death of Opheltes and the story of Baby Herakles and the serpents, since they function as mirror images of each other. The same basic elements are found in both stories: an infant is left unattended (for the night or on account of some errand), sometimes falls asleep, and is attacked by a monstrous beast. We will come back to the element of sleep and its dangers below. For the story of Baby Herakles strangling the serpents sent by Hera, see Pindar, *Nemean* 1.33–47; Theokritos 24; Diodorus Siculus 4.10.1; Apollodoros 2.4.8; Pausanias 1.24.2; Plautus, *Amphitryo* 1123–25; Vergil, *Aeneid* 8.288–28; and Hyginus, *Fabulae* 30. According to Apollodoros, Herakles was eight months old at the time of the incident; according to Theokritos, ten months old. See below for more on the echoes between Baby Herakles and the serpent.

5. Severyns, *Bacchylide,* 131 thinks that epinician 9 was composed sometime after Bacchylides' exile in 466 B.C.; see also Maehler, *Die Lieder des Bakchylides,* 1.6–9.

6. The lion of Nemea is born out of the union of Ekhidna and Orthros and is raised in the plain of Nemea by Hera. Herakles himself alludes to his labor in Pindar's *Isthmian* 6.48.

7. See schol. Vergil, *Georgics* 3.19. Some argue that the connection between the two events is made in Callimachus's *Victoria Berenices,* but it cannot be pushed back earlier than the third century B.C.; see the discussion of the Lille papyrus of Callimachus below. See also Maehler, *Die Lieder des Bakchylides,* 1.143–45, for analysis of variants of the myths.

8. Nagy, *Pindar's Homer,* 137–38.

9. *Hēmitheoi* is attested once in the Homeric corpus at *Iliad* 12.23 at a point when the epic describes the wall built by the Achaeans and its subsequent destruction. As the narrative flashes forward into the future and switches to consider the story and its protagonists from the perspective of the audience, it no longer uses the usual Homeric word for hero, *hērōs/hērōes.* Nagy sees this shift in diction as a sign that the narrative is sensitive to various traditional perspectives and that whereas *hērōs/hērōes* is the "appropriate word in epic, *hēmitheoi* is more appropriate to a style of expression that looks beyond epic" (*Best of the Achaeans,* 159–61). West, by contrast, thinks that the word refers to "parentage (cf. *hēmionos* and our 'half-brother'), not to semi-divine status" (*Hesiod,* 191).

10. See Nagy, *Pindar's Homer,* 119–21, about *epi* with dative, especially nn. 21–23.

11. Ibid., 121; cf. Roller, "Funeral Games for Historical Persons," 2–3, for examples of inscriptions using the idiom concerning historical figures.

12. See chap. 2 for the games in honor of the children of Herakles, and chap. 3 for the games in honor of Baby Demophon. See Meuli's study of the Greek *agōn: Der griechische Agon.*

13. See Nagy, *Pindar's Homer*, 208–12, for a discussion of the word *sēma.*

14. For R. A. Neil's conjecture, see Kenyon, *Poems of Bacchylides*, 72–73 n. 13; and Jebb, *Bacchylides.* Both Snell, *Bacchylidis*, and Maehler, *Die Lieder des Bakchylides*, accept the conjecture.

15. A reading that is supported by Euripides' *Hypsipyle.* See below.

16. In Homeric poetry, the verb is used in conjunction with the word *hypnos (Iliad* 10.159 and *Odyssey* 10.548). Simonides uses the same verb without *hypnos* (fr. 543 *PMG*). Jebb, *Bacchylides*, 303, thinks that Simonides' use of the verb without the addition of *hypnos* makes it "probable" that his nephew would use the verb *aōteuein* in the sense of *aōteein.* See also Cairns, "*Aōtos, Anthos,* and the Death of Archemorus," who argues that *aōteuein* originally must have referred to flowers rather than sleep.

17. Richardson, *Homeric Hymn to Demeter*, 140, argues for a thematic connection between picking flowers and being carried away: "Girls were traditionally carried off while picking flowers."

18. While Richardson, *Homeric Hymn to Demeter*, 140–42, does not make the link between picking flowers and death explicit, he does note that some of the flowers mentioned in the Homeric *Hymn to Demeter* later acquire a special significance in relation to Demeter, Persephone, and their cult.

19. At the same time the poem functions as a compensation for the athlete's ordeal; Nagy argues that the genre of the victory ode, the *epinikion*, is itself a compensation for the victory and that "the epinician performance is the final realization, the final constitutive event, of the ritual process of athletics" (*Pindar's Homer*, 142 and n. 38).

20. Wecklein, *Aeschyli fabulae*, 532, 545, 591. See also Radt, *Tragicorum graecorum fragmenta*, 3.233–34, 261–62, 352.

21. Punzi, "Osservazione sull' episodio nemeo," restores a purely Lemnian stage of the myth, using the second hypothesis to Pindar's *Nemeans;* Lactantius *ad Thebaid* 4.740; and Hyginus 273–74. By contrast, a purely Argive version would focus exclusively on the Seven and omit Hypsipyle and her sons; see Séchan, *Études sur la tragédie grecque*, 341 n. 4, for discussion of this hypothesis.

22. Nauck, *Tragicorum graecorum fragmenta*, 594-Imhoof-Blumer and Gardner, *Numismatic Commentary on Pausanias*, 99.

23. Grenfell and Hunt, *Oxyrhynchus Papyri*, 6.852. Bond's *Hypsipyle* includes a useful introduction and commentary, while Cockle's *Hypsipyle* reexamines the papyri and suggests some new joins. While she doubtlessly was an important character in Aeschylus's *Hypsipyle*, it is unknown whether Hypsipyle played the role of Opheltes' nurse in any source before Euripides.

24. Bond puts the play in 407 B.C.; see *Hypsipyle*, 144, for his discussion of the evidence for dating the *Hypsipyle.*

25. Dover, *Aristophanes: Frogs*, 351; West, *Ancient Greek Music*, 123, 125; Wegner, *Das Musikleben der Griechen*, 62–63 and pl. 28A.

26. See Richardson, *Homeric Hymn to Demeter*, 143; *Odyssey* 11.539, 573; 24.13; Aristophanes, *Frogs* 373–75 and 449–53 (where the verb *paizein* is found twice in close connection with the flowery fields of the underworld, although in this context, the word also means "to dance"); Plutarch fr. 178; Orphic fragments 32f6, 222.3, 293 (Kern). For an example of a flowery meadow that offers protection to a baby, cf. the story of Iamos in Pindar's *Olympian* 6.43. See also Motte, *Prairies et jardins*.

27. For examples of other traditions associating snakes with springs, see Frazer, *Pausanias's Description of Greece*, 5.44–45, on Pausanias 9.10.5.

28. There is here an obvious parallel to draw between the Nemean serpent and the serpent from Delphi, the Python, killed by Apollo.

29. For more details on the fragments and the dating of the cartonnage, see Parsons, "Callimachus," 4–5. The text also contains lines of commentary on the poem itself. These scholia are indented by three letters and refer to the lines immediately above them. They usually consist of a short gloss or paraphrase.

30. Lloyd-Jones and Parsons, *Supplementum Hellenisticum*, 100–102.

31. Parsons, "Callimachus," 54, thinks that Callimachus either invented or somehow discovered the story.

32. Cf. Plutarch, *Quaestionum convivialum* 676F–677B; Broneer, "Isthmian Victory Crown"; Blech, *Studien zum Kranz bei den Griechen*, 131–37.

33. See Nagy, *Pindar's Homer*, 117, for two myths associating Pelops with the foundation of the Olympic Games.

34. Parsons, "Callimachus," 41, argues that Callimachus took both the story of Herakles' founding the games and of Athena's prophecy from Bacchylides 13.54–57: "Some day, I prophesy, / that there will be strenuous toil here / for the Greeks competing / for garlands in the pankration." Callimachus, in fact, is the earliest extant Greek author explicitly to link Herakles' first labor with the foundation of the Nemean Games. According to his scheme, the Seven against Thebes were refounding ancient games that had already been established by Herakles prior to their own time. The funeral character of the Nemean Games is nevertheless the first and foremost characteristic of the contest and the one that Callimachus initially mentions. In terms of ritual, athletes run beside Opheltes' grave, and it is his death and funeral that are commemorated in the institution of the games. Doffey, "Les mythes de fondation," 187, argues that the story of Herakles and the lion, traditionally seen as an antecedent to the Seven's first competing in the games, eventually comes to be confused with it, until there is no clear distinction made between the antecedent event and the later foundation of the games.

35. See Waern, "Greek Lullabies."

36. Vermeule, *Aspects of Death*, 145–54.

37. Adapted from Rosenmeyer's translation in "Simonides' Danae Fragment Reconsidered."

38. Ibid., 19.

39. For flowers in the Greek song tradition, see Alexiou, *Ritual Lament in Greek Tradition*, 291, s.v. flower(s) and garden.

40. The most famous exception is the double cult of Herakles, who is worshiped as both a hero and a god; see Herodotos 2.42–44 on the double cult of Herakles at

Thasios; and Pausanias 2.10.1 on the double cult at Sikyon. Most heroes, however, are local cult figures who can be described with the adjective *divine* but are understood as heroic, that is, formerly mortal, figures. See also chap. 6 for a child hero who is also described as divine.

41. See Hughes, "Hero Cult."

42. Pausanias uses the same phrase to describe the shrine of Ino-Leukothea at Megara and the Pelopeion at Olympia (5.13.1). See S. Miller, "Shrine of Opheltes," for the possible influence of Olympia on the Nemean shrine.

43. Beazley, *Attic Red-figure Vase-Painters*, 763, 3; addenda 1.286 = *LIMC* 11. See also Burn, "Honey Pots," 101. The cup is part of a group of nine vases found in a single tomb in 1890 in Athens. Six of the vessels fall into natural pairs: two phialai (in London and Boston), two mastoi (in London), and two cups (in Brussels). Of the three remaining cups (in London), two form a pair: one depicts the story of Glaukos, the young son of Minos who drowned in a vat of honey, with Polyeidos, the seer who revived him (see discussion of Glaukos in chap. 3, and also Muellner, "Glaucus redivivus"), while another shows a scene with two women picking apples from a tree, with one of the women identified as Melissa. The third cup showing the man and snake is the only one of the nine vessels that has no extant partner.

44. Beazley, *Attic Red-figure Vase-Painters*, 763, 1.

45. Burn, "Honey Pots," 100, 102.

46. Ibid., 98, 99.

47. Ibid., 97. See Vergil, *Georgics* 4.321–25.

48. While Burn makes an excellent case for the scene being a depiction of Aristaios right after the moment that Eurydike is bitten by a snake, many of her arguments against the identification with the Opheltes episode are not convincing. The story of Aristaios and Eurydike is not extant in literature before Vergil's *Georgics,* and some argue that the story was Vergil's invention, while others see it as a traditional myth. While it is likely that the story is an old one, it is of course impossible to determine with any certainty whether the story precedes Vergil's version (Burn, "Honey Pots," 100).

49. Kearns, *Heroes of Attica*, 163.

50. Burn, "Honey Pots," 103.

51. Hoffmann, *Sotades*, 139–40.

52. Trendall and Webster, *Illustrations of Greek Drama,* 90–91 = *LIMC* Arkhemoros 2.

53. Trendall and Cambitoglou, *Red-Figured Vases of Apulia,* 1.416, 12 = *LIMC* Arkhemoros 8.

54. Simon, "Archemoros," 37.

55. Trendall and Webster, *Illustrations of Greek Drama,* 981.

56. Trendall and Cambitoglou, *Red-Figured Vases of Apulia,* 2.496, 42 = *LIMC* Arkhemoros 10.

57. Simon, "Archemoros," 37.

58. Schmidt, "Medea und Herakles," 170.

59. Trendall and Cambitoglou, *Red-Figured Vases of Apulia,* 2.913–14, 36, table 350 = *LIMC* Arkhemoros 9.

60. The scene is identified as the death of Astyanax or a generic scene of mourning. See Séchan, *Études sur la tragédie grecque*, 359.

61. The scene depicted in the top register is difficult to link with the one on the bottom. Séchan thinks that it might be some kind of allusion to the games that will be founded in honor of Opheltes (ibid., 360).

62. Naples, Museo Nazionale 8987 = *LIMC* Arkhemoros 3.

63. Simon, "Archemoros," 45.

64. Ibid.

65. Helbig, *Guide to the Public Collections*, 2.164.

66. Simon, "Archemoros," 43–44.

67. *LIMC* Hypsipyle I 14 (supplement), with bibliography.

68. Several stories could account for a fight between Amphiaraos and Lykourgos. Some see it occurring as a result of Amphiaraos killing Pronax, Lykourgos's father, but this is not attested in ancient sources. Only one extant ancient source, Statius's *Thebaid* (5.660–753), relates the story of a fight between Lykourgos and Amphiaraos. In Statius's account, Lykourgos, enraged by the death of his son, throws himself on Hypsipyle with his drawn sword. Amphiaraos stands in his way with his shield and angrily urges him to restrain himself. Hippomedon and Kapaneus rush to Amphiaraos's aid, and a crowd of farmers help the king. Adrastos stands between the two men, and Amphiaraos defuses the situation with a speech calling for truce. The scene on the archaic shield band is somewhat different: no Hypsipyle appears, and Amphiaraos plays a more aggressive role. Simon thinks the discrepancies between the shield and Statius's version can be explained in terms of the influence of the fifth-century B.C. tragedies relating the story of the death of Opheltes. This transformation is especially noticeable in the way in which Amphiaraos is depicted: in archaic times, Amphiaraos is typically shown as an angry and violent character; during the classical era, his role as a seer is emphasized and he evolves into a wiser and more peaceful character, especially under the influence of tragedy. Pausanias (5.17.8) gives a good example of the earlier Amphiaraos, as he is shown on the chest of Kypselos. Amphiaraos is depicted as he takes his leave from his wife, Eriphyle. He already has one foot in the chariot and his sword is drawn; he is turned toward Eriphyle, overcome by his anger and barely able to restrain himself from striking her. This is the aggressive Amphiaraos shown on the Olympia bronze shield band. See Simon, "Archemoros," 32 and n. 8.

69. Meuli, *Der griechische Agon*. On the rites instituted at Eleusis for Demophon, see Homeric *Hymn to Demeter* 265–67.

70. Simon, "Archemoros," 45.

71. S. Miller, *Nemea;* cf. Miller's excavation reports in *Hesperia* 49 (1980): 194–98; 50 (1981): 60–65; 53 (1984): 173–74; idem, "Shrine of Opheltes." The final publication of the Hero Shrine of Opheltes, including recent excavations by Jorge Bravo, is forthcoming. See Bravo, "Preliminary Report on Excavations."

72. S. Miller, *Nemea*, 110.

73. Ibid., 108.

74. See chap. 4, n. 19, for S. Miller's suggestion that the Nemean shrine may have copied an earlier shrine of Pelops at Olympia.

75. The krater contained a greasy dark brown substance that could have been composed of the bean mixture that was traditionally used in vessels set in the foundation trenches of ritual buildings. See S. Miller, *Nemea*, 27–28, 104–7.

76. Ibid., 26–30.

77. Ibid., 28. See also idem, "Excavations at Nemea," 64–65.

78. S. Miller, *Nemea*, 29. See also, Felsch, "Apollon und Artemis," with bibliography.

79. S. Miller, *Nemea*, 26–27.

## CHAPTER 6: MELIKERTES-PALAIMON

1. In the background of Ino's and Melikertes' leap into the sea is another myth of an attempt to kill children: Ino, because she is jealous of her husband Athamas's children from his first wife, Nephele, plans for the children's destruction. She sows the earth with parched wheat, and when the crop fails, she sends messengers to Delphi for advice from the oracle. She bribes the messengers so that they bring back the answer that Phrixos, Athamas's son, must be sacrificed to put an end to the earth's barrenness. Phrixos's mother, Nephele, intervenes and saves Phrixos along with his sister Helle by sending a golden ram that rescues the children by taking them up in the sky. The golden ram flies eastward, and Helle falls into the sea between Sigeum and the Chersonese, hence the Hellespont. Phrixos arrives safely in Colchis on the ram's back. There he sacrifices the ram and gives the Golden Fleece to Aietes. Cf. Apollodoros, *Library* 1.9; and Pindar, *Pythian* 4. 159–62. While this myth is often included in the story of Melikertes, as we shall see, it remains peripheral; even though the story of Phrixos is only tangential to that of Melikertes, it does create an interesting link between Boeotia and Colchis, and thus between Ino and Medea.

2. The Parian Marble attributes the foundation of the Isthmian Games to Theseus and dates it to 1259 B.C. An Athenian law from Solon's time awarded one hundred drachmas to all Athenian winners, and by 582 B.C., the Isthmian Games were officially recognized as the second Panhellenic festival after Olympia. The games, like those at Nemea that were founded a few years later, were held biennially in the spring (April or May) on the second and fourth year of every Olympiad and included the usual athletic events with an emphasis on horse and chariot races. Musical contests are attested from the third century B.C. on. The games were organized by the city of Corinth until 392 B.C., when the region came under the power of Argos until the peace of Antalkidas in 387 B.C.; the Sikyonians temporarily took over the administration of the games in 146 B.C. until Corinth was rebuilt. Originally, the crown awarded at the games was of pine, later changed to celery, then pine again (Pindar's poetry refers only to the celery crown). The Athenians had a place of honor because of their association with Theseus, while the Eleans were altogether excluded from the games. See Plutarch, *Theseus* 25; Pausanias 5.2.1–3; 6.16.2. Although Theseus is connected with the foundation of the games in some myths, it is clear that the story of Baby Melikertes played an important part in the Isthmian Games from early on. In the scholia to Pindar's *Isthmian*, one of the versions has Theseus coming to the Isthmus after the games had been established for Melikertes by Sisyphos, but interrupted because of robbers;

Theseus cleans up the area and refounds the games. As we will see below, the story involving Theseus reflects an Athenian version of the myth.

3. Pfister, *Der Reliquienkult im Altertum*, 214, mentions Melikertes as a representative example of a hero whose body is washed ashore, a typical event following heroic drowning. He also notices the parallels between Melikertes at Isthmia and Opheltes at Nemea (316 n. 1032). Farnell, "Ino-Leukothea," 41, and *Greek Hero Cults*, 39–47, sees in Melikertes "the child-son of the earth-mother who dies in the heat of the year" and links him with Opheltes at Nemea and Sosipolis of Elis, whom he also considers to belong to the category of "vegetation-powers." Fontenrose, "Sorrows of Ino and of Procne," 125, links the story of Ino and Melikertes with that of Prokne and the child Itys and detects in it a similar pattern of "triangle tales" that goes back to a story-type he interprets as a remnant from a polygamous society. Burkert, *Homo Necans*, 196–204, examines the myth of the "return of the Dolphin" from a formalistic point of view and argues that the myth is a "gruesome" and "gloomy" aetiological legend. Sartre, "Du fait divers," and Bonnet, "Le culte de Leucothéa et de Mélicerte," look at the cult of Leukothea and Melikertes outside Greece. Lyons, *Gender and Immortality*, 122–24, briefly discusses Ino and Melikertes; and Larson, *Greek Heroine Cults*, 16, mentions the myth as a typical example of heroic death (cf. Nagy, *Best of the Achaeans*, 203), but both experts are interested in heroine cults and do not expand on the role of Melikertes. Halm-Tisserant, *Cannibalisme et immortalité*, 173, examines the story of Melikertes and places the narrative at the center of "a triptych devoted to the theme of human sacrifice, framed by the episodes of Phrixos's pseudo-immolation and Dionysos's dismemberment" ("un tryptique consacré au thème du sacrifice humain, encadrée par les épisodes de la pseudo-immolation de Phrixos et du démembrement de Dionysos"). Hawthorne, "Myth of Palaimon," and Piérart, "Le culte de Palaimon," argue that the cult was not established until the Augustan age—a hypothesis that clearly goes against the evidence, as I will argue below. Koester, "Melikertes at Isthmia," focuses on the cult of Melikertes in the Roman period.

4. See discussion of the archaeological evidence below. See Gebhard, "Beginnings of Panhellenic Games," for a survey of archaeological evidence at Isthmia and dating of the first games.

5. Cf. Alcman fr. 50b (Davies), in which Ino is described "ruling the sea" (*salassomedoisa*). See Nagy, "Theognis and Megara," 78–81, for the relationship between the Homeric Ino-Leukothea and the Megaran tradition.

6. See Nagy, "Theognis and Megara," 79; cf. Nagler, "Dread Goddess Endowed with Speech," 80. See also Hadzisteliou-Price, "Hero Cult and Homer."

7. On Sisyphos as founder of the Isthmian Games, see Aristotle fr. 637 (Rose); Pausanias 2.1.3; schol. Apollonios Rhodios 3.1240.

8. For *tēlephanton geras* as a Panhellenic festival in honor of Melikertes, see Gebhard and Dickie, "Melikertes-Palaimon."

9. Thus *prophasis* (meaning both "first manifestation of a sickness" and "pretext") and *apophainein* (meaning both "to make appear" and "to declare"). See Chantraine, *Dictionnaire étymologique de la langue grecque*, s.v. *phēmi*.

10. See Nagy, "Library of Pergamon," 207, about Hipparkhos "bringing" the words of Homer home to Athens.

11. Cf. also *Odyssey* 24.85–92 (funeral games for Achilles) and Pindar *Isthmian* 8.56–61. See Barringer, *Divine Escorts.*

12. Alexiou, *Ritual Lament in Greek Tradition,* 55–58.

13. Nagy, *Best of the Achaeans,* 115–17.

14. See below for discussion of the different types of crowns awarded to winners at Isthmia.

15. Schol. *Olympian* 3.27 (Drachmann 2.112) gives a list of the garlands associated with the different games. The scholia here mention only the celery crown and ignore the tradition of the crown made out of pine. The adjective *xēros* (withered, dry), used to describe *selinon,* fits with the sterility theme we find in many hero cult narratives. The Isthmian celery garlands are mentioned once again in *Olympian* 13.45, and the scholiast adds that *selinon* is sacred to the dead (Drachmann 1.366). The connection between celery and the dead is a recurrent one in Greek thought, and crowns of wild celery are offered at both Nemea and Isthmia, since both festivals are *epitaphioi* (lit., over a tomb) and in honor of dead children. See also Plutarch, *Timoleon* 26, for the expression "to need celery" when one is close to death; see also schol. Pindar, *Olympian* 13.45; Garland, *Greek Way of Death,* 26, 116 (on celery and death); Blech, *Studien zum Kranz bei den Griechen,* 94–95 (on celery), 131–37 (on the celery crown from Isthmia and Nemea).

16. The hypothesis to the second play was found at Oxyrhynchus and shows that the events depicted included the story of Ino tampering with the grain seeds, the fake oracle, Dionysos's attempt to drive Phrixos and Helle mad, and their rescue by their mother, Nephele, by means of a golden ram. The story of the death of Learkhos and Melikertes, which would have been part of the *Ino,* was probably not included in either of the *Phrixos* drama. See Gantz, *Early Greek Myth,* 179.

17. Cf. Rose, *Hygini Fabulae,* on *Fabula* 1.6, where he notices the resemblance with popular tales, such as Perrault's *le Petit Poucet.*

18. See Lyons, *Gender and Immortality,* who describes Ino "as problematic a figure of motherhood as possible" (123).

19. Lyons notes that the claim of a unique precedent "makes the myth presented stand out in relief" (ibid., 38).

20. Gantz, *Early Greek Myth,* 177.

21. See Brown, *Late Carthaginian Child Sacrifice,* 55, for archaeological evidence of the Carthaginian practice. Cf. Burkert, *Greek Religion,* 37, for discussion of evidence of Greek human sacrifice. See also Hughes, *Human Sacrifice in Ancient Greece;* and Bonnechère, *Le sacrifice humain en grèce ancienne.* Despite the superficial resemblance of their names, there is no link between the Tyrian Melqart and the Isthmian hero Melikertes. See West, *East Face of Helicon,* 58.

22. For a different interpretation, cf. Gebhard, "Child in the Fire," who argues that the story of the death of Melikertes fits a pattern of myths dealing with child sacrifices performed in times of crisis to save a city.

23. Scullard, *Festivals and Ceremonies,* 150, dismisses Ovid's identification of the goddess Mater Matuta with Ino as poetic invention. Yet Ovid is not the only Latin author to connect the Roman and the Greek goddesses: we find the same identification made explicit in Cicero and Hyginus, as well as in Lactantius. For Cicero's iden-

tification of Ino = Mater Matuta, see *Tusculan Disputations* 1.12.28, and Pease on Cicero, *Natura deorum* 3.19.48. See also Plutarch, *Roman Questions* 267d.

24. The scholia to Vergil derive Portunus's name from the word for harbor: schol. Vergil, *Aeneid* 5.241 glosses Portunus's name (*Portunus deus marinus qui portubus praeest*) and tells the myth of Ino and Melikertes jumping in the sea; schol. Vergil, *Georgics* 1.437 glosses *Inoo Melicertae: Patronymicon est a matre. . . . Sane Ino et Melicerta postquam sunt in numina commutati, Graece Palaemon et Leucothea sunt nominati, Latine Portunus et Mater Matuta.* Portunus is often represented holding a key, and his festival, the *Portunalia,* took place on August 17.

25. On *teletē* as a term used for rituals of an initiatory nature, see Burkert, *Ancient Mystery Cults*, 9–11.

26. Here I disagree with Lyons's analysis that the cauldron "could be called the ulti- mate projection of maternal ambivalence" (*Gender and Immortality*, 124). See Laurens "L'enfant entre l'épée"; and Uhsadel-Gülke, "Knochen und Kessel." Even when Medea uses the cauldron to kill Pelias, she is able to do this only because he is deceived into thinking she will use the cauldron to rejuvenate him.

27. Gantz, *Early Greek Myth*, 178; cf. *Phrixos B* fr. 827 (Snell and Kannicht) for the grain bins; P. Oxyrhynchus 2455 fr. 17 = hypothesis 32 in Austin, *Nova fragmenta Euripidea.*

28. See Rose, *Hygini Fabulae.*

29. Melikertes and Learkhos are also mentioned briefly in Pausanias's Boeotian Book, when he describes Orkhomenos. Athamas lives there after the death or disap- pearance of all his male children. In this version of the events, Ino is not mentioned, and Athamas apparently kills both of his sons himself (9.34.7).

30. For Nemea and Olympia, see S. Miller, "Shrine of Opheltes." For the probable influence of Olympia and Nemea on Isthmia, see Gebhard and Dickie, "Melikertes- Palaimon," 165.

31. Brelich, "I figli di Medeia," 225–26.

32. Vernant, *Mortals and Immortals*, 50–74.

33. Another dialogue attributed to Lucian, the *Nero*, mentions Melikertes-Palaimon. The dialogue tells of how Nero falls in love with a grandiose scheme when he sees the Isthmus and decides to dig a passage: "Coming in front of the tent, he sang a hymn to Amphitrite and Poseidon, and a little song for Melikertes and Leukothea" (Lucian, *Nero* 3). Right after he sings his songs, Nero falls to the ground amid applause and clapping and starts digging with a golden fork offered by the governor of Greece. The *Nero* also claims that the Isthmian Games contained no tragic or comic contest, which is a problem for the emperor, who wants to win a tragic victory (*Nero* 9). This claim is contradicted by a passage in Philostratos's *Life of Apollonios of Tyana* that describes Nero entering an already existing contest for lyre players and heralds at the Isthmian Games (4.24). Be that as it may, music and singing seem to have played a very impor- tant part at the Isthmus, whether in the context of the games themselves or of the cult of Melikertes.

34. For more on the mixture of heroic and initiatory rituals, see Pache, "Singing Heroes."

35. Cf. Hornblower and Spawforth, *Oxford Classical Dictionary*, 1171, for discussion of the different Philostrati and the works attributed to them. The *Eikones* is attributed to two different Philostrati, grandfather and grandson.

36. Theokritos, *Idyll* 1.1–2; see Hunter, *Theocritus,* commentary on lines 1.1–3 + 3.38; Plato, *Greek Anthology* 16.13.

37. See Garland, *Greek Way of Death,* 78–80, 82, for an exception to the rule that infants are never cremated. See also chap. 1, n. 4.

38. For the vocabulary of heroic cult, see Ekroth, "Sacrificial Rituals of Greek Hero-Cults." For the vocabulary of *orgia* and *hieros logos,* see Burkert, *Ancient Mystery Cults,* 32–34. See also idem, *Homo Necans,* 197–98, for discussion of the sacrifice to Palaimon. He argues that the ritual follows a path that "leads from grief to vitality, from death to the order of life, from Palaimon's sacrificial pit to the altar of Poseidon."

39. See Nagy, *Pindar's Homer,* 268–69, for discussion of this passage. See also L. Edmunds, "Cults and the Legend of Oedipus," 223 n. 8, about *oikos* and related words in *Oedipus at Colonus;* and Henrichs, "Despoina Kybele," 278 n. 71, about welcoming a god or hero in his new house.

40. Cf. Burkert, *Homo Necans,* 197–98, who does not, however, consider the initiation pattern of the ritual. Cf. Farnell, *Greek Hero Cults,* 35–47. For more on the vocabulary of mysteries, see Burkert, *Ancient Mystery Cults.*

41. "The double infanticide thus juxtaposes the themes of hunting crime, committed under the influence of *mania,* and sacrificial murder, borrowed from narratives of cannibalistic feasts" ("le double infanticide juxtapose donc les thèmes du crime cynégétique, accompli sous l'empire de la *mania,* et du meurtre sacrificiel, emprunté aux récits du festin cannibale"); Halm-Tisserant, *Cannibalisme et immortalité,* 184.

42. On vases, a character named Palaimon is represented as an older man with a beard, holding a horn of plenty, and often in the company of Herakles. This has no parallels in the literary tradition, and an analysis of these images is beyond the scope of this study.

43. See Barringer, *Divine Escorts;* see also Vermeule, *Aspects of Death,* 160.

44. Geneva krater, private collection: Trendall and Cambitoglou, *Red-Figured Vases of Apulia,* 2.504, 84; cf. Aellen, Cambitoglou, and Chamay, *Le peintre de Darius et son milieu,* 168–70.

45. Aellen, Cambitoglou, and Chamay, *Le peintre de Darius et son milieu,* 168.

46. Bruneau in *LIMC* Ino 14.

47. Besides Melikertes, Opheltes, Bellerophon, Poseidon, Athena, Aphrodite, Asklepios, Dionysos, and Tykhe, the goddess of the city, regularly appear on coins produced in this period. See Edwards, *Corinth,* 6.1–9.

48. Imhoof-Blumer and Gardner, *Numismatic Commentary on Pausanias,* table B 23.

49. See *LIMC* Ino 24.

50. Imhoof-Blumer and Gardner, *Numismatic Commentary on Pausanias,* 13.

51. See ibid., table B 15 and 17, for more examples. Cf. Zeuner, "Dolphins on Coins," pls. 8–9, for more on dolphins and coins from the earlier period.

52. See Imhoof-Blumer and Gardner, *Numismatic Commentary on Pausanias,* table B 16 = *LIMC* Melikertes 24.

53. See above, schol. Pindar, *Isthmians.*

54. Imhoof-Blumer and Gardner, *Numismatic Commentary on Pausanias,* table B 5 = *LIMC* Melikertes 40.

55. See also Broneer, *Isthmia,* 2.106–11, pl. 42. Cf. Imhoof-Blumer and Gardner, *Numismatic Commentary on Pausanias,* place B, 1, 11, 12, 13; Walbank, "Aspects of Corinthian Coinage," 346–47, fig. 20.12.

56. Cf. Gebhard, "Rites for Melikertes-Palaimon," who argues that the two figures become two different entities: the lying figure is the dead hero Melikertes, while the sitting and standing position belongs to the god Palaimon. To me, the story of the dolphin makes sense only insofar as the dolphin is carrying the body of the dead boy Melikertes, and therefore all these images depict the hero. Although some authors refer to Palaimon as a god, it is clear that Palaimon is a new name given to Melikertes after heroization and not necessarily a different figure. It is not uncommon for Greek authors to describe heroes as *theos* (divine); the two categories are somewhat fluid, especially after heroization.

57. For the *adyton* as a separate holy place, see Gebhard, "Beginnings of Panhellenic Games," who argues on the basis of Pausanias's language that the structure is different from that of the temple. See Pausanias 2.2.1; cf. 1.1.4; 2.35.9; 5.24.6.

58. Broneer, *Isthmia,* 2.99–112.

59. The absence of archaeological evidence to date leads some to the conclusion that the cult of Melikertes did not exist before the Augustan period. See Hawthorne, "Myth of Palaimon"; see also Piérart, "Le culte de Palaimon." The literary sources, however, clearly show that Melikertes-Palaimon was known as a hero and recipient of cult from Pindar on, even though the place of offerings has not been located. See Gebhard and Dickie, "Melikertes-Palaimon," 159–65; Gebhard, "Rites for Melikertes-Palaimon."

60. Broneer, *Isthmia,* 2.100. Gebhard suggests that a Greek precinct existed at the southeast of Poseidon's *temenos,* but excavation in 1989 revealed no evidence of cult activity; see "Early Sanctuary of Poseidon," 476.

61. For the so-called Palaimonion lamps, see Broneer, *Isthmia,* vol. 3; Koester, "Melikertes at Isthmia," 359–60; Gebhard, Hemans, and Hayes, "University of Chicago Excavations," 445–46, figs. 17.41–42. The lamps were introduced before c. A.D. 80 but were not in common use until the end of the century.

62. Broneer, *Isthmia,* 2.100–106; Gebhard, Hemans, and Haynes, "University of Chicago Excavations," 428–44. See also Gebhard, "Rites for Melikertes-Palaimon."

63. See Gebhard, "Evolution of a Pan-Hellenic Sanctuary," 80–93, with figs. 5 (coin) and 7 (restored view); Gebhard, Hemans, and Hayes, "University of Chicago Excavations," 438–41.

64. For the *adyton* as separate structure, see n. 57. For the temple, see Broneer, *Isthmia,* 2.106–11, pl. 42. Cf. Imhoof-Blumer and Gardner, *Numismatic Commentary on Pausanias,* place B, 1, 11, 12, 13; Walbank, "Aspects of Corinthian Coinage," 346–47, fig. 20.12.

65. For details of the archaeological evidence, see Gebhard, "Evolution of a Pan-Hellenic Sanctuary," 89–93; Gebhard, Hemans, and Hayes, "University of Chicago Excavations," 438–41.

66. Broneer, *Isthmia*, 3.

67. For the date of the inscription, not earlier than Hadrian or Antonines, cf. Boeckh, *Corpus inscriptionum graecarum* #1104; and Geagan, "Isthmian Dossier."

68. Frazer, *Pausanias's Description of Greece*, 3.15, suggests this possibility in his commentary on Pausanias. On *enagistēria*, see Ekroth, "Altars in Greek Hero-Cults."

69. See Farnell, "Ino-Leukothea," 37. See also Larson, *Greek Heroine Cults*, 123–25, for more on the various cults of Ino-Leukothea; Lyons, *Gender and Immortality*, 48–50.

70. Inscription also published in Sartre, "Du fait divers," 57; and Cumont, *Catalogue des sculptures*, 166–68, no. 141.

71. "Dont nous ne saisissons pas les modalités"; Bonnet, "Le culte de Leucothéa et de Mélicerte," 64.

72. Sartre, "Du fait divers," 64.

73. Ibid., 52. The text is somewhat problematic: *ampelōn theas Leukotheas kai Melikertēs*. Either *Melikertēs* is a mistake for the more usual genitive *Melikertou*, or it is a nominative case parallel with *ampelōn*, in which case the sense would be unclear.

74. See Uhsadel-Gülke, "Knochen und Kessel," 50–51; and Burkert, *Homo Necans*, 178 n. 42, on the 'Ain al-Burj inscription: "The lebes, as a funerary urn, signifies both death and deification."

75. See Hughes, "Hero Cult."

76. See Wilamowitz-Moellendorff, *Sappho und Simonides*, 33–37.

77. On the associations between *Kolōnos* and the White Rock and the cosmic implications of plunging off the White Rock into the sea, see Nagy, "Phaethon," 145–47 *(Kolōnos);* Nagy later revisited the same topic in *Greek Mythology and Poetics*.

78. Ptolemaios Chennos in Westermann, *Mythographoi*, 197–99. See Nagy, "Phaethon," 142–43, with n. 23.

79. See Pfister, *Der Reliquienkult im Altertum*, 211–16; Nagy, *Greek Mythology and Poetics*, 223–62; and Larson, *Greek Heroine Cults*, 17, 125.

80. *Skyros*, the name of the island, is derived from *skiros*, the word for chalk (glossed as "gypsum" or *gē leukē* in the *Souda*); see Nagy, "Phaethon," 144–45.

81. See Thucydides 3.96.1 for the murder of Hesiod; Plutarch 162c for the story of a dolphin bringing the body of Hesiod to the Isthmus; see also Pausanias 9.31.5 (contradictory stories about the death of Hesiod) and 9.38.3 (grave of Hesiod at Orkhomenos). See also Burkert, *Homo Necans*, 203–4.

82. As modern versions of similar stories often do. See, for example, Zeuner, "Dolphins on Coins," 99, who mentions the dolphin tales of Pliny and adds: "This is no more than can be seen in Miami to-day." In the same vein, Higham, "Nature Note," cites an article entitled "Opo and Hippo," in the *Journal of the Royal Numismatic Society of New Zealand*, which includes "a photograph of Mr. Allan Wells of Wellington, N.Z. riding on Opo in 1955." Opo the dolphin became so popular that "her death caused genuine and widespread sorrow, though objections were raised in certain quarters at a cross being set upon her grave." In June 2002, several web sites on the internet fea-

tured an enticingly titled article, "Sexually Frustrated Dolphin Sparks Alert," describing the darker side of mammal fatal attraction. A dolphin, nicknamed George, attempted to mate with divers off Weymouth, Dorset. U.S. marine mammal expert Ric O'Barry is quoted as saying: "When dolphins get sexually excited, they try to isolate a swimmer, normally female. They do this by circling around the individual and gradually move them away from the beach, boat or crowd of people" (http://www.cnn.com/2002/WORLD/europe/06/04/uk.dolphin/).

## CONCLUSION

1. For the women of Elis lamenting Achilles at the beginning of the Olympic Games, see Pausanias 6.23.3.

2. Vernant, *Mortals and Immortals*, 86.

# BIBLIOGRAPHY

## ABBREVIATIONS

*FGrH*   F. Jacoby, ed., *Die Fragmente der griechischen Historiker* (Leiden: Brill, 1923–58)
*IG*   *Inscriptiones graecae* (Berlin: de Gruyter, 1873–)
*LIMC*   *Lexicon iconographicum mythologiae classicae* (Zurich: Artemis, 1981–97)
*OGIS*   W. Dittenberger, ed., *Orientis graeci inscriptiones selectae* (2 vols.; Leipzig: Hirzel, 1903–5)
*PMG*   D. L. Page, ed., *Poetae melici graeci* (Oxford: Clarendon, 1962)
*SEG*   Supplementum epigraphicum graecum (Amsterdam: Gieben, 1923–)


## SOURCES

Aellen, C., A. Cambitoglou, and J. Chamay. *Le peintre de Darius et son milieu.* Geneva: Association Hellas et Roma, 1986.
Alexiou, M. *The Ritual Lament in Greek Tradition.* Rev. ed. Lanham, Md.: Rowman & Littlefield, 2002.
Anderson, G. *Philostratus: Biography and Belles Lettres in the Third Century* A.D. London: Croom Helm, 1986.
Andrews, A. "Celery and Parsley as Foods in the Greco-Roman Period." *Classical Philology* 44 (1949): 91–99.
Antonaccio, C. M. *An Archaeology of Ancestors: Tomb Cult and Hero Cult in Early Greece.* Lanham, Md.: Rowman & Littlefield, 1995.
Austin, C. *Nova fragmenta Euripidea in papyris reperta.* Berlin: de Gruyter, 1968.
Barringer, J. *Divine Escorts: Nereids in Archaic and Classical Greek Art.* Ann Arbor: University of Michigan Press, 1995.
———. *The Hunt in Ancient Greece.* Baltimore: Johns Hopkins University Press, 2001.
Beazley, J. D. *Attic Red-figure Vase-Painters.* 2d ed. Oxford: Clarendon, 1963.
Bérard, C. *L'hérôon à la porte de l'ouest: Eretria,* vol. 3. Bern: Francke, 1970.
Bernabé, A. *Poetarum epicorum graecorum testimonia et fragmenta,* part 1. Leipzig: Teubner, 1987.
Bethe, E., ed. *Pollux: Onomasticon.* Leipzig: Teubner, 1900.
Betz, H. D. "Heroenverehrung und Christusglaube: Religions-geschichtliche Beobachtungen zu Philostrats *Heroicus.*" In *Griechische und Römische Religion,* vol. 2: *Geschichte-Tradition-Reflexion: Festschrift für Martin Hengel zum 70. Geburtstag.* Ed. H. Cancik, H. Lichtenberger, and P. Schäfer. Tübingen: Mohr (Siebeck), 1996.

Blech, M. *Studien zum Kranz bei den Griechen.* Berlin: de Gruyter, 1982.

Blome, P. "Das Schreckliche im Bild." In *Ansichten griechischer Rituale: Geburtstags-Symposium für Walter Burkert, Castelen bei Basel, 15. bis 18. Marz 1996.* Ed. F. Graf. Stuttgart/Leipzig: Teubner, 1998.

Boeckh, A., ed. *Corpus inscriptionum graecarum.* Berlin: Deutsche Akademie der Wissenschaften zu Berlin, 1825–77.

Bond, G. W. *Hypsipyle.* Oxford: Oxford University Press, 1963.

Bonnechère, P. *Le sacrifice humain en grèce ancienne.* Kernos Supplément 3. Athens: Centre international d'étude de la religion grecque antique, 1994.

Bonnet, C. "Le culte de Leucothéa et de Mélicerte en Grèce, au Proche-Orient et en Italie." *Studi e materiali di storia delle religioni* 52 (1986): 53–71.

Bravo, J. J., III. "A Preliminary Report on Excavations in the Hero Shrine at Nemea, 1997–2001." *American Journal of Archaeology* 106 (2002): 262.

Breed, B. "Odysseus Back Home and Back from the Dead." In *Nine Essays on Homer.* Ed. M. Carlisle and O. Levaniouk. Lanham, Md.: Rowman & Littlefield, 1999.

Brelich, A. *Gli eroi greci: Un problema storico-religioso.* Rome: Edizioni dell'Ateneo, 1958.

———. "I figli di Medeia." *Studi e materiali di storia delle religioni* 30 (1959): 213–54.

———. *Paides e parthenoi.* Rome: Edizioni dell'Ateneo, 1969.

Broneer, O. *Isthmia*, vol. 1: *Temple of Poseidon.* Princeton, N.J.: American School of Classical Studies at Athens, 1971.

———. *Isthmia*, vol. 2: *Topography and Architecture.* Princeton, N.J.: American School of Classical Studies at Athens, 1973.

———. *Isthmia*, vol. 3: *Terracotta Lamps.* Princeton, N.J.: American School of Classical Studies at Athens, 1977.

———. "The Isthmian Victory Crown." *American Journal of Archaeology* 66 (1962): 259–63.

Brown, S. *Late Carthaginian Child Sacrifice and Sacrificial Monuments in Their Mediterranean Context.* Sheffield, England: JSOT Press for the American Schools of Oriental Research, 1991.

Burkert, W. *Ancient Mystery Cults.* Cambridge: Harvard University Press, 1987.

———. *Greek Religion.* Trans. J. Raffan. Cambridge: Harvard University Press, 1985.

———. "Greek Tragedy and Sacrificial Ritual." *Greek, Roman, and Byzantine Studies* 7 (1966): 87–121.

———. *Homo Necans: The Anthropology of Ancient Greek Sacrificial Ritual and Myth.* Trans. P. Bing. Berkeley: University of California Press, 1983.

Burn, L. "Honey Pots: Three White-Ground Cups by the Sotades Painter." *Antike Kunst* 28 (1985): 93–105.

Cairns, D. "*Aōtos, Anthos,* and the Death of Archemorus in Bacchylides' Ninth Ode." *Papers of the Leeds International Latin Seminar* 10 (1998): 57–73.

Calame, C. *Choruses of Young Women in Ancient Greece: Their Morphology, Religious Role, and Social Functions.* Rev. ed. Trans. D. Collins and J. Orion. Lanham, Md.: Rowman & Littlefield, 2001.

Callaghan, P. J. "KRS 1976: Excavations at a Shrine of Glaukos, Knossos." *Annual of the British School at Athens* 73 (1978): 1–30.

Carpenter, T. H. *Art and Myth in Ancient Greece*. London: Thames & Hudson, 1991.

Chantraine, P. *Dictionnaire étymologique de la langue grecque*. Paris: Klincksieck, 1968–80.

Clinton, K. "IG 1²5, the Eleusinia and the Eleusinians." *American Journal of Philology* 100 (1979): 1–112.

———. *Myth and Cult: The Iconography of the Eleusinian Mysteries*. Stockholm: Svenska Institutet i Athen/Åströms, 1992.

Cockle, W. E. H. *Hypsipyle*. Rome: Edizioni dell'Ateneo, 1987.

Coldstream, J. N. "Hero-Cults in the Age of Homer." *Journal of Hellenic Studies* 96 (1976): 8–17.

Cook, A. B. *Zeus: A Study in Ancient Religion*. Cambridge: Cambridge University Press, 1914–40.

Cumont, F. *Catalogue des sculptures et inscriptions antiques (monuments lapidaires) des musées Royaux du Cinquantenaire*. 2d ed. Brussels: Vromant, 1913.

Davies, M. *Epicorum graecorum fragmenta*. Göttingen: Vandenhoeck & Ruprecht, 1988.

Delcourt, M. *Stérilités mystérieuses et naissances maléfiques dans l'antiquité classique*. Liège: Faculté de Philosophie et Lettres, 1938.

Demand, N. *Birth, Death, and Motherhood in Classical Greece*. Baltimore: Johns Hopkins University Press, 1994.

———. *Thebes in the Fifth Century: Heracles Resurgent*. London: Routledge & Kegan Paul, 1982.

Deubner, L. *Attische Feste*. 2d ed. Berlin: Akademie-Verlag, 1966.

Doffey, M.-C. "Les mythes de fondation des concours Néméens." *Bulletin de correspondance hellénique Supplément* 22 (1992): 185–93.

Dörpfeld, W. *Alt-Olympia: Untersuchungen und Ausgrabungen zur Geschichte des ältesten Heiligtums von Olympia und der älteren griechischen Kunst*. Berlin: Mittler, 1935.

Dover, K. *Aristophanes: Frogs*. Oxford: Clarendon, 1993.

Drachmann, A. B. *Scholia vetera in Pindari carmina*. Leipzig: Teubner, 1903–27.

Dunn, F. "Euripides and the Rites of Hera Akraia." *Greek, Roman, and Byzantine Studies* 35 (1994): 103–15.

———. "Pausanias on the Tomb of Medea's Children." *Mnemosyne* 48 (1995): 348–51.

Durand, J.-L., and F. Lissarrague. "Mourir à l'autel: Remarques sur l'imagerie du 'sacrifice humain' dans la céramique attique." *Archiv für Religionsgeschichte* 1 (1999): 83–106.

Easterling, P. E. "The Infanticide in Euripides' *Medea*." *Yale Classical Studies* 25 (1977): 177–91.

Edmunds, L. "The Cults and the Legend of Oedipus." *Harvard Studies in Classical Philology* 85 (1981): 221–38.

———. *Theatrical Space and Historical Place in Sophocles' Oedipus at Colonus*. Lanham, Md.: Rowman & Littlefield, 1996.

Edmunds, S. *Homeric Nēpios*. New York: Garland, 1990.

Edwards, K. *Corinth*, vol. 6: *Coins*. Cambridge: Harvard University Press, 1933.

Ekroth, G. "Altars in Greek Hero-Cults: A Review of the Archaeological Evidence." In *Ancient Greek Cult Practice from the Archaeological Evidence.* Ed. R. Hägg. Stockholm: Åströms, 1998.

———. "Pausanias and the Sacrificial Rituals of Greek Hero-Cults." In *Ancient Greek Hero Cult: Proceedings of the Fifth International Seminar on Ancient Greek Cult.* Ed. R. Hägg. Stockholm: Åströms, 1999.

———. "The Sacrificial Rituals of Greek Hero-Cults in the Archaic to the Early Hellenistic Periods." Ph.D. dissertation, Stockholm University, 1999.

Farnell, L. R. *Greek Hero Cults and Ideas of Immortality.* Oxford: Clarendon, 1921.

———. "Ino-Leukothea." *Journal of Hellenic Studies* 36 (1916): 36–44.

Felsch, R. C. S. "Apollon und Artemis: Kalapodi Bericht, 1973–1977." *Archäologischer Anzeiger* (1980): 92–94.

Fontenrose, J. "The Hero as Athlete." *Classical Antiquity* 1 (1968): 73–104.

———. "The Sorrows of Ino and of Procne." *Transactions and Proceedings of the American Philological Association* 79 (1948): 125–67.

Foucart, P. *Le culte des héros chez les grecs.* Paris: Imprimerie nationale, 1918.

Frazer, J. G. *Pausanias's Description of Greece.* 2d ed. 6 vols. London: Macmillan, 1913.

———, trans. *Apollodorus: Bibliotheca.* 2 vols. Loeb Classical Library. London: Heinemann, 1921.

Froidefond, C. *Plutarque, oeuvres morales, Isis et Osiris.* Paris: Belles Lettres, 1988.

Gaggadis-Robin, V. *Jason et Médée sur les sarcophages d'époque impériale.* Rome: École Française de Rome, 1994.

Gantz, T. *Early Greek Myth: A Guide to Literary and Artistic Sources.* Baltimore: Johns Hopkins University Press, 1993.

Garland, R. *The Greek Way of Death.* Ithaca, N.Y.: Cornell University Press, 1985.

———. *The Greek Way of Life: From Conception to Old Age.* Ithaca, N.Y.: Cornell University Press, 1990.

Geagan, D. J. "The Isthmian Dossier of P. Licinius Priscus Juventianus." *Hesperia* 58 (1989): 349–60.

Gebhard, E. R. "The Beginnings of Panhellenic Games at the Isthmus." In *Akten des Internationalen Symposions Olympia 1875–2000.* Ed. H. Kyrieleis. Mainz am Rhein: Zabern, 2002.

———. "Child in the Fire, Child in the Pot: The Making of a Hero." Paper read at the Seventh International Seminar on Ancient Greek Cult, 16–18 April 1999.

———. "The Early Sanctuary of Poseidon at Isthmia." *American Journal of Archaeology* 91 (1987): 475–76.

———. "The Evolution of a Pan-Hellenic Sanctuary: From Archaeology towards History at Isthmia." In *Greek Sanctuaries: New Approaches.* Ed. N. Marinatos and R. Hägg. London: Routledge, 1993.

———. "Rites for Melikertes-Palaimon in the Early Roman Corinthia." In *Urban Religion in Roman Corinth: Interdisciplinary Approaches.* Ed. D. N. Showalter. Forthcoming.

Gebhard, E. R., and M. Dickie. "Melikertes-Palaimon, Hero of the Isthmian Games." In *Ancient Greek Hero Cult: Proceedings of the Fifth International Seminar on Ancient Greek Cult.* Ed. R. Hägg. Stockholm: Åströms, 1999.

Gebhard, E. R., F. P. Hemans, and J. W. Hayes. "University of Chicago Excavations at Isthmia, 1989: III." *Hesperia* 67 (1998): 405–56, pls. 70–75.

Giuliani, L. "Rhesus between Dream and Death: On the Relation of Image to Literature in Apulian Vase-Painting." *Bulletin of the Institute of Classical Studies* 41 (1996): 71–91.

Golden, M. *Children and Childhood in Classical Athens*. Baltimore: Johns Hopkins University Press, 1990.

———. *Sports and Society in Ancient Greece*. Cambridge: Cambridge University Press, 1998.

Goldhill, S. "The Naïve and Knowing Eye: Ecphrasis and the Culture of Viewing in the Hellenistic World." In *Art and Text in Ancient Greek Culture*. Eds. S. Goldhill and R. Osborne. Cambridge: Cambridge University Press, 1994.

Graf, F. "Medea, the Enchantress from Afar: Remarks on a Well-Known Myth." In *Medea: Essays on Medea in Myth, Literature, Philosophy, and Art*. Ed. J. Clauss and S. I. Johnston. Princeton, N.J.: Princeton University Press, 1997.

Green, J. R. "On Seeing and Depicting the Theatre in Classical Athens." *Greek, Roman, and Byzantine Studies* 32 (1991): 15–50.

Grenfell, B. P., and A. S. Hunt. *The Oxyrhynchus Papyri*. London: Egypt Exploration Fund, 1898.

Griffiths, J. G. *Plutarch's de Iside et Osiride*. Cardiff: University of Wales Press, 1970.

Hadzisteliou-Price, T. "Hero Cult and Homer." *Historia* 22 (1973): 129–44.

———. "Hero-Cult in the 'Age of Homer' and Earlier." In *Arktouros: Hellenic Studies Presented to Bernard M. W. Knox*. Berlin: de Gruyter, 1979.

Halm-Tisserant, M. *Cannibalisme et immortalité: L'enfant dans le chaudron en Grèce ancienne*. Paris: Les Belles Lettres, 1993.

Hawthorne, J. "The Myth of Palaimon." *Transactions of the American Philological Association* 89 (1958): 92–98.

Helbig, W. *Guide to the Public Collections of Classical Antiquities in Rome*. Leipzig: Baedeker, 1895–96.

Henrichs, A. "Despoina Kybele: Ein Beitrag zur religiösen Namenkunde." *Harvard Studies in Classical Philology* 80 (1976): 253–86.

———. "Three Approaches to Greek Mythography." In *Interpretations of Greek Mythology*. Ed. J. Bremmer. London: Croom Helm, 1987.

Herrmann, H.-V. 1980. "Pelops in Olympia." In *Stēlē: Tomos eis mnēmēn Nikolaou Kontoleontos*. Athens: Sōmateio Hoi Philoi tou Nikolaou Kontoleontos, 1980.

Higham, T. F. "Nature Note: Dolphin-Riders. Ancient Stories Vindicated." *Greece and Rome* 7 (1960): 82–87.

Hoffmann, H. *Sotades: Symbols of Immortality on Greek Vases*. Oxford: Clarendon, 1997.

Hornblower, S., and A. Spawforth, eds. *The Oxford Classical Dictionary*. 3d ed. Oxford: Oxford University Press, 1996.

Hughes, D. D. "Hero Cult, Heroic Honors, Heroic Dead: Some Developments in the Hellenistic and Roman Periods." In *Ancient Greek Hero Cult: Proceedings of the Fifth International Seminar on Ancient Greek Cult*. Ed. R. Hägg. Stockholm: Åströms, 1999.

———. *Human Sacrifice in Ancient Greece*. London: Routledge, 1991.

Hunter, R. *Theocritus: A Selection*. Cambridge: Cambridge University Press, 1999.

Imhoof-Blumer, F., and P. Gardner. *A Numismatic Commentary on Pausanias*. London: Clay, 1887.

Jeanmaire, H. *Couroi et courètes: Essai sur l'éducation spartiate et sur les rites d'adolescence dans l'antiquité hellénique*. Repr. New York: Arno, 1975.

Jebb, R. *Bacchylides*. London: Frowde, 1904.

Johnston, S. I. "Medea and the Cult of Hera Akraia." In *Medea: Essays on Medea in Myth, Literature, Philosophy, and Art*. Ed. J. Clauss and S. I. Johnston. Princeton, N.J.: Princeton University Press, 1997.

————. *Restless Dead: Encounters between the Living and the Dead in Ancient Greece*. Berkeley: University of California Press, 1999.

Kassel, R. *Quomodo quibus locis apud veteres scriptores graecos infantes atque parvuli pueri inducantur describantur commemorentur*. In *Kleine Schriften*. Ed. H.-G. Nesselrath. Berlin: de Gruyter, 1991.

Kayser, C. L. *Flavii Philostrati opera*. Leipzig: Teubner, 1870–71.

Kearns, E. *The Heroes of Attica*. Bulletin of the Institute of Classical Studies Supplement 57. London: University of London, Institute of Classical Studies, 1989.

Keil, B., ed. *Aelii Aristidis Smyrnaei quae supersunt omnia*, vol. 2: *Orations xvii–liii continens*. Berlin: Weidmann, 1958.

Kenyon, F., ed. *The Poems of Bacchylides: From a Papyrus in the British Museum*. London: British Museum, 1897.

Kern, O. *Die Religion der Griechen*. 2d ed. 3 vols. Berlin: Weidmann, 1963.

Kirk, G. S., et al., eds. *The Iliad: A Commentary*. 6 vols. Cambridge: Cambridge University Press, 1985–93.

Klostermann, E., ed. *Eusebius of Caesarea: Werke*, vol. 4: *Gegen Marcell; Über die kirchliche Theologie; Die Fragmente Marcells*. Die griechischen christlichen Schriftsteller der ersten drei Jahrhunderte 14. Berlin, Akademie-Verlag, 1906.

Koehl, R. "The Chieftain Cup and a Minoan Rite of Passage." *Journal of Hellenic Studies* 109 (1986): 99–110.

Koester, H. "Melikertes at Isthmia: A Roman Mystery Cult." *Greeks, Romans, and Christians: Essays in Honor of Abraham J. Malherbe*. Ed. D. L. Balch, E. Ferguson, and W. A. Meeks. Minneapolis: Fortress, 1990.

Kron, U. *Die zehn attischen Phylenheroen*. Berlin: Mann, 1976.

Kyrieleis, H. "Les fouilles allemandes à Olympie." In *Olympie: Cycle de huit conférences organizées au musée du Louvre par le Service culturel du 18 janvier au 15 mars 1999*. Ed. A. Pasquier. Paris: La Documentation Française, 2001.

Lacroix, L. "La légende de Pélops et son iconographie." *Bulletin de correspondance hellénique* 100 (1976): 327–41.

Lannoy, L. de, ed. *Flavii Philostrati Heroicus*. Leipzig: Teubner, 1977.

Larson, J. *Greek Heroine Cults*. Madison: University of Wisconsin Press, 1995.

Laurens, A.-F. "L'enfant entre l'épée et le chaudron: Contribution à une lecture iconographique." *Dialogues d'histoire ancienne* 10 (1984): 203–51.

Lee, H. M. "The Ancient Olympic Games." *Classical Bulletin* 74 (1998): 129–41.

Little, L. M. "Babies in Well G5:3: Preliminary Results and Future Analysis." *American Journal of Archaeology* 103 (1999): 284.

Lloyd-Jones, H., and P. Parsons, eds. *Supplementum Hellenisticum*. Berlin: de Gruyter, 1983.

Loraux, N. *Mothers in Mourning.* Trans. C. Pache. Ithaca, N.Y.: Cornell University Press, 1998.

Lyons, D. *Gender and Immortality: Heroines in Ancient Greek Myth and Cult.* Princeton, N.J.: Princeton University Press, 1997.

Mackie, C. J. "Achilles in Fire." *Classical Quarterly* 48 (1998): 329–38.

Maclean, J. K. B., and E. B. Aitken, eds. *Flavius Philostratus: Heroikos.* Writings from the Greco-Roman World 1. Atlanta: Society of Biblical Literature, 2001.

———. *Heroikos: Identity and Religion.* Atlanta: Society of Biblical Literature, forthcoming.

Maehler, H. *Die Lieder des Bakchylides,* vol. 1: *Die Siegeslieder.* Leiden: Brill, 1997.

Mallwitz, A. "Cult and Competition Locations at Olympia." In *The Archaeology of the Olympics: The Olympics and Other Festivals in Antiquity.* Ed. W. Raschke. Madison: University of Wisconsin Press, 1988.

———. *Olympia und seine Bauten.* Munich: Prestel, 1972.

Mantero, T. *Ricerche sull' Heroikos di Filostrato.* Genova: Università di Genova, Istituto di Filologie Classica e Medioevale, 1966.

Martin, R. P. *Healing, Sacrifice, and Battle: Amechania and Related Concepts in Early Greek Poetry.* Innsbrucker Beiträge zur Sprachwissenschaft 41. Innsbruck: Institut für Sprachwissenschaft der Universität Innsbruck, 1983.

McDermott, E. *Euripides' Medea: The Incarnation of Disorder.* University Park: Pennsylvania State University Press, 1989.

Menadier, B. "The Sixth-Century Temple and the Cult of Hera Akraia." Ph.D. dissertation, University of Cincinnati, 1995.

Merkelbach, R., and M. L. West. *Fragmenta Hesiodea.* Oxford: Clarendon, 1967.

Meuli, K. *Der griechische Agon: Kampf und Kampfspiel im Totenbrauch, Totentanz, Totenklage und Totenlob.* Cologne: Historisches Seminar der deutschen Sporthochschule, 1968.

Miller, M. "Priam, King of Troy." In *The Ages of Homer.* Ed. J. B. Carter and S. P. Morris. Austin: University of Texas Press, 1995.

Miller, S. G. *Nemea: A Guide to the Site and Museum.* Berkeley: University of California Press, 1990.

———. "Organisation et fonctionnement des jeux Olympiques." In *Olympie: Cycle de huit conférences organizées au musée du Louvre par le Service culturel du 18 janvier au 15 mars 1999.* Ed. A. Pasquier. Paris: La Documentation Française, 2001.

———. "The Shrine of Opheltes and the Earliest Stadium of Nemea." In *Akten des Internationalen Symposions Olympia 1875–2000.* Ed. H. Kyrieleis. Mainz am Rhein: Zabern, 2002.

Morgan, C. *Athletes and Oracles: The Transformations of Olympia and Delphi in the Eighth Century* B.C. Cambridge: Cambridge University Press, 1990.

Morris, I. "Tomb Cult and the 'Greek Renaissance': The Past in the Present in the Eighth Century B.C." *Antiquity* 62 (1988): 750–61.

Motte, A. *Prairies et jardins de la Grèce antique: De la religion à la philosophie.* Brussels: Palais des Académies, 1973.

Muellner, L. "Glaucus redivivus." *Harvard Studies in Classical Philology* 98 (1998): 1–30.

Nagler, M. "Dread Goddess Endowed with Speech." *Archeological News* 6 (1977): 77–85.

Nagy, G. *The Best of the Achaeans: Concepts of the Hero in Archaic Greek Poetry.* Rev. ed. Baltimore: Johns Hopkins University Press, 1999.

———. *Greek Mythology and Poetics.* Ithaca, N.Y.: Cornell University Press, 1990.

———. "The Library of Pergamon as a Classical Model." In *Pergamon, Citadel of the Gods: Archaeological Record, Literary Description, and Religious Development.* Ed. H. Koester. Harrisburg, Pa.: Trinity, 1998.

———. "Phaethon, Sappho's Phaon, and the White Rock of Leukas." *Harvard Studies in Classical Philology* 77 (1973): 137–77.

———. *Pindar's Homer: The Lyric Possession of an Epic Past.* Baltimore: Johns Hopkins University Press, 1990.

———. "Theognis and Megara: A Poet's Vision of His City." In *Theognis of Megara: Poetry and the Polis.* Ed. T. J. Figueira and G. Nagy. Baltimore: Johns Hopkins University Press, 1985.

Nauck, A. *Tragicorum graecorum fragmenta.* Hildesheim: Olms, 1964.

Nock, A. D. "The Cult of Heroes." In *Essays on Religion and the Ancient World.* Ed. Z. Stewart. Oxford: Clarendon, 1944.

Pache, C. "Singing Heroes: The Poetics of Hero Cult in the *Heroikos*." In *Heroikos: Identity and Religion.* Ed. J. K. B. Maclean and E. B. Aitken. Atlanta: Society of Biblical Literature, forthcoming.

Page, D. L., ed. *Medea.* Oxford: Clarendon, repr. 1961.

Parker, R. *Athenian Religion: A History.* Oxford: Clarendon, 1996.

Parsons, P. J. "Callimachus: Victoria Berenices." *Zeitschrift für Papyrologie und Epigraphik* 25 (1977): 1–51.

Payne, H. *Perachora: Excavations of the British School of Archaeology at Athens,* vol. 1: *Architecture, Bronzes, Terracottas.* Oxford: Clarendon, 1940.

Pease, A. S., ed. *Cicero: De natura deorum.* Cambridge, Mass.: Harvard University Press, 1955.

Pfeiffer, R. *Callimachus.* Repr. Salem, N.H.: Ayer, 1988.

Pfister, F. *Der Reliquienkult im Altertum.* Giessen: Töpelmann, 1909–12.

Picard, C. "L'héraeon de Pérachora et les enfants de Médée." *Revue archéologique* 35 (1932): 218–29.

Piérart, M. "Le culte de Palaimon à Corinthe." *Kernos* 11 (1998): 85–109.

Punzi, Q. "Osservazione sull' episodio nemeo nel ciclo tebano." *Studi Italiani di Filologia Classica* 18 (1910).

Radt, S. *Tragicorum graecorum fragmenta,* vol. 3: *Aeschylus.* Göttingen: Vandenhoeck & Ruprecht, 1985.

Richardson, N. J. *The Homeric Hymn to Demeter.* Oxford: Clarendon, 1974.

Rohde, E. *Psyche: The Cult of Souls and Belief in Immortality among the Greeks.* Trans. W. B. Hillis. New York: Harcourt, Brace, 1925.

Roller, L. E. "Funeral Games for Historical Persons." *Stadion* 7 (1981): 1–18.

Rose, H. J. *Hygini Fabulae.* London: Sythoff, 1963.

Rose, V., ed. *Aristotle: Fragments.* Leipzig: Teubner, 1886.

Rosenmeyer, P. "Simonides' Danae Fragment Reconsidered." *Arethusa* 24 (1991): 5–29.

Rotroff, S. I. "The Artifacts from Well G5:3 and Some Conclusions concerning the Deposit." *American Journal of Archaeology* 103 (1999): 284–85.

Sartre, M. "Du fait divers à l'histoire des mentalités: À propos de quelques noyés et de trois petits cochons." *Syria* 70 (1993): 51–67.

Scanlon, T. F. *Eros and Greek Athletics.* New York: Oxford University Press, 2002.

Schmidt, M. "Medea und Herakles—zwei tragische Kindermörder." In *Studien zur Mythologie und Vasenmalerei: Konrad Schauenburg zum 65. Geburtstag am 16. April 1986.* Ed. E. Böhr and W. Martini. Mainz am Rhein: Zabern, 1986.

Scodel, R. "Hesiod redivivus." *Greek, Roman, and Byzantine Studies* 21 (1980): 301–20.

Scranton, R. L. *Corinth,* vol. 1, part 2: *Architecture.* Cambridge: Harvard University Press, 1941.

Scullard, H. H. *Festivals and Ceremonies of the Roman Republic.* London: Thames & Hudson, 1981.

Séchan, L. *Études sur la tragédie grecque dans ses rapports avec la céramique.* Paris: Champion, 1926.

Segal, C. *Pindar's Mythmaking: The Fourth Pythian Ode.* Princeton, N.J.: Princeton University Press, 1986.

Sergent, B. *Homosexuality in Greek Myth.* Boston: Beacon, 1986.

Severyns, A. *Bacchylide: Essai biographique.* Liège: Faculté de Philosophie et Lettres, 1933.

Shapiro, H. A. *Myth into Art: Poet and Painter in Classical Greece.* London: Routledge, 1994.

———. *Personifications in Greek Art: The Representation of Abstract Concepts, 600–400 B.C.* Zurich: Akanthus, 1993.

Simon, E. "Archemoros." *Archäologischer Anzeiger* (1979): 31–45.

———. "Die Typen der Medeadarstellung in der antiken Kunst." *Gymnasium* 61 (1954): 203–27.

Slater, W. J. "Pelops at Olympia." *Greek, Roman, and Byzantine Studies* 30 (1989): 485–501.

Slater, W. J., ed. *Aristophanis Byzantii fragmenta.* New York: de Gruyter, 1986.

Slatkin, L. *The Power of Thetis: Allusion and Interpretation in the Iliad.* Berkeley: University of California Press, 1991.

Snell, B. *Bacchylidis Carmina cum fragmentis.* Leipzig: Teubner, 1958.

Snell, B., and R. Kannicht. *Tragicorum graecorum fragmenta,* vol. 1. Rev. ed. Göttingen: Vandenhoeck & Ruprecht, 1986.

Snodgrass, A. "The Archaeology of the Hero." In *Oxford Readings in Greek Religion.* Ed. R. Buxton. Oxford: Oxford University Press, 2000.

———. "Les origines du culte des héros dans la Grèce antique." In *La mort: Les morts dans les sociétés anciennes.* Ed. G. Gnoli and J.-P. Vernant. Cambridge: Cambridge University Press/Paris: Maison des Sciences de l'Homme, 1982.

Sourvinou-Inwood, C. "Medea at a Shifting Distance: Images and Euripidean Tragedy." In *Medea: Essays on Medea in Myth, Literature, Philosophy, and Art.* Ed. J. Clauss and S. I. Johnston. Princeton, N.J.: Princeton University Press, 1997.

Stern, J. *Erotika Pathemata: The Love Stories of Parthenius.* New York: Garland, 1992.

Sweeney, R. D. *Lactantii Placidi in Statii Thebaida commentum*. Stuttgart: Teubner, 1997.

Taplin, O. *Comic Angels and Other Approaches to Greek Drama through Vase-Paintings*. Oxford: Clarendon, 1993.

Theodoridis, C., ed. *Photii patriarchae lexicon*, vol. 1. Berlin: de Gruyter, 1982.

Thummer, E. *Pindar: Die isthmischen Gedichte*. 2 vols. Heidelberg: Winter, 1968–69.

Trendall, A. D. "Medea at Eleusis on a Volute Krater by the Darius Painter." *Record of the Art Museum of Princeton University* 43.1 (1984): 5–17.

―――. *Paestan Pottery: A Study of the Red-Figured Vases of Paestum*. London: British School at Rome, 1936.

Trendall, A. D., and A. Cambitoglou. *The Red-Figured Vases of Apulia*, vol. 1: *Early and Middle Apulian;* vol. 2: *Late Apulian*. Oxford: Clarendon, 1978–82.

Trendall, A. D., and T. B. L. Webster. *Illustrations of Greek Drama*. London: Phaidon, 1971.

Uhsadel-Gülke, C. "Knochen und Kessel." *Beiträge zur klassischen Philologie* 43 (1972).

Usener, H. *Götternamen: Versuch einer Lehre von der religiösen Begriffsbildung*. Bonn: Cohen, 1896.

Vermeule, E. *Aspects of Death in Early Greek Art and Poetry*. Berkeley: University of California Press, 1979.

Vernant, J.-P. *Mortals and Immortals: Collected Essays*. Princeton, N.J.: Princeton University Press, 1991.

Vidal-Naquet, P. *The Black Hunter: Forms of Thought and Forms of Society in the Greek World*. Baltimore: Johns Hopkins University Press, 1986.

Visser, M. "Worship Your Enemy: Aspects of the Cult of Heroes in Ancient Greece." *Harvard Theological Review* 75 (1982): 403–28.

Waern, I. "Greek Lullabies." *Eranos* 58 (1960): 1–8.

Walbank, M. E. H. "Aspects of Corinthian Coinage in the Late First and Early Second Centuries A.C." In *Corinth: The Centenary*. Ed. C. K. Williams II and N. Bookidis. Corinth 20. Princeton, N.J.: American School of Classical Studies at Athens, 2002.

Wecklein, N. *Aeschyli fabulae*. Berlin: Calvary, 1893.

Wegner, M. *Das Musikleben der Griechen*. Berlin: de Gruyter, 1949.

West, M. L. *Ancient Greek Music*. Oxford: Clarendon, 1992.

―――. *The East Face of Helicon: West Asiatic Elements in Greek Poetry and Myth*. Oxford: Clarendon, 1997.

―――. *Hesiod: Works and Days*. Oxford: Clarendon, 1978.

Westermann, A., ed. *Mythographoi: Scriptores poeticae historiae graeci*. Brunswick: Georgius Westermann, 1843.

Whitley, J. "Early States and Hero Cults: A Re-appraisal." *Journal of Hellenic Studies* 108 (1988): 173–82.

Wilamowitz-Moellendorff, U. von. *Sappho und Simonides: Untersuchungen über griechische Lyriker*. Berlin: Weidmann, 1913.

Will, E. *Korinthiaka: Recherches sur l'histoire et la civilisation de Corinthe des origines aux guerres médiques*. Paris: Boccard, 1955.

Willetts, R. F. *Cretan Cults and Festivals*. London: Routledge & Kegan Paul, 1962.

Williams, C. K., II. "Pre-Roman Cults in the Area of the Forum of Ancient Corinth."
    Ph.D. dissertation, University of Pennsylvania, 1978.
Zeuner, F. E. "Dolphins on Coins of the Classical Period." *University of London Institute
    of Classical Studies* 10 (1963): 97–103.

Achilles: death of, 138; father of
Neoptolemos, 87; in the fire, 44;
funeral gifts for, 161; and Greek
athletics and heroism, 182; marries
Medea, 17; mourned in Panhellenic
rituals in honor of, 24–25, 115, 138;
Thetis and, 44, 79–80, 138; tomb of,
137, 176
Adrastos, 105–6, 112–13, 129
*adyton*, 152–54, 157, 169–70, 171–74,
209n57
Aegeus, 20, 21
Aelian, 24, 43, 47, 72
Aeschylus: *Athamas*, 140; *Lemniai*,
*Hypsipyle and Nemea*, 99, 117
Aetes: ghost of, 35, 39, 41
Agave and Pentheus, 56
age. *See* life stages
*agōn*, 94, 103, 144; catalyst for
instituting, 131; *epitaphioi*, 52; as
stylized revenge, 131
*ailinon*, 67
Ailios Aristeides, 76, 113, 135, 153–56, 158,
164, 176, 179–80
*aiora*, 187n19
Akrisios, 109
*alala*, 54
*alastôr*, 17
Alexiou, M., 139
Alkaios, 139
Alkeidai, 52
Alkeides, 57
Alkimenes, 18
Alkmene, 54, 57, 64; and Baby Herakles,
108–9
altar: of ancestral gods, 174; of Apollo,
64; on coins, 166–67; grave, 123, 125;

in *hērōon*, 114; in literary sources,
14–16, 21, 46; for Melikertes-
Palaimon, 152; on paintings, 61; on
vases, 8, 25, 28, 31–32, 37, 42, 46, 61,
118, 129. *See also* sacred space
ambrosia: anointing with, 74, 79; theft
of, 85
Amphiaraos, 98–103, 105, 112–13,
118–20, 123–29; fight with Lykourgos,
129–31, 203n68
Amphitrite: on painting, 163; on vases,
162–63
Amphitryon, 50, 53–54
*anaklaiein*, 69
Anakreon, 177
ancestors, 1, 3–4
Andromeda, 41
*anegerseis*, 108
*anēr*, 5
*anōros. See aōros*
*anthos*, 154
*anthrōpinos*, 88
*aōros*, 82, 89
*aōteein*, 99, 110
*aōteuein*, 99, 110
*apanthizestai*, 99
*aphradia*, 75
Aphrodite, 26; and Adonis, 86, 155, 177
*aphthitos*, 75
Apollo: and the children of Niobe, 62,
64; and Kyrene, 116; and Linos,
66–71; and Minos, 78; and Muses,
101; prophecy of, 112; temple in
Sikyon, 43–45; visit to Argos, 69
Apollodoros, 3, 6, 20–21, 52, 56–57, 62,
66, 75–76, 78, 86, 88–89, 93, 105,
147–48

Corinne Ondine Pache is an
assistant professor of classics
at Yale University.

The University of Illinois Press
is a founding member of the
Association of American University Presses.

---

Composed in 10/12.5 Adobe Minion
with Stone Sans display
by Bookcomp, Inc.
at the University of Illinois Press
Designed by Copenhaver Cumpston
Manufactured by Thomson-Shore, Inc.

UNIVERSITY OF ILLINOIS PRESS
1325 South Oak Street    Champaign, IL 61820-6903
www.press.uillinois.edu